SLACK
PACKING

SLACK
PACKING

A guide to South Africa's
top leisure trails

Fiona McIntosh

Edited by David Bristow

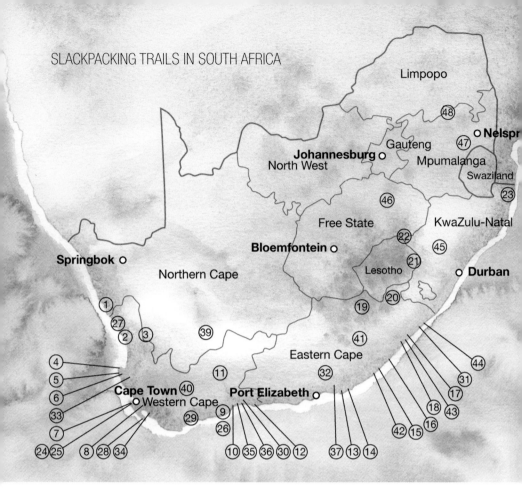

SLACKPACKING TRAILS IN SOUTH AFRICA

Key

1. Silver Sands Trail
2. West Coast Crayfish Trail
3. Cederberg Heritage Route
4. Five Bay Trail
5. Eve's Trail
6. Darling Stagger
7. Mountains in the Sea Trail
8. Green Mountain Trail
9. Oystercatcher Trail
10. Garden Route Trail
11. Donkey Trail
12. Dolphin Trail
13. Diaz Cross Trail
14. Three Sisters Trail
15. Wild Coast Amble
16. Wild Coast Meander
17. Wild Coast Hiking Tail –
    Port St Johns to Coffee Bay
18. Hole in the Wall Trail

19. Wartrail Skywalk
20. Mehloding Hiking Trail
21. Giant's Cup Hikeathon
22. Amphitheatre Heritage Hike
23. Kosi Bay Trail
24. Hoerikwaggo Tented Classic –
    Silvermine, Orange Kloof,
    Slangkop trails
25. Hoerikwaggo Table
    Mountain Trail
26. Hunter Gatherer Trail
27. Swart Tobie
28. Cape of Good Hope
    Hiking Trail
29. Whale Trail
30. Tsitsikamma Trail
31. Drifters Wild Coast
    Hiking Trail
32. Mosslands Two River Trail

33. Wellington Wine Walks
34. Walks for Wine
35. Garden Route Forest and
    Mountain Walks
36. Swartberg Slackpacking Trail
37. Eden to Addo – Great
    Corridor Hike
38. Elephant Gorge Trail
39. Karoo Erdvark Trail
40. Gamka Reserve to Bonniedale
    Wilderness Hike
41. Wolf River Trail
42. Cebe to Cintsa B&B Trail
43. Coffee Bay to Mbashe Trail
44. Wild Coast Pondo Walk
45. Swissland Cheese Saunter
46. Cannibal Trail
47. Queen Rose Trail
48. Num Num Trail

Contents

Key

Green Flag Accredited Hiking Trail

NC	Northern Cape	KZN	KwaZulu-Natal
WC	Western Cape	FS	Free State
EC	Eastern Cape	MP	Mpumalanga

Acknowledgements

When it comes to inspiring people to get out and do things, the photos in a book such as this are arguably just as important as the words, so I'm eternally grateful to Shaen Adey for all her efforts in lugging cameras up to the most scenic spots, and for allowing me to raid her extensive library of stock images. My thanks, too, to the trail developers who made their images freely available.

My wholehearted thanks go out to all the brains behind the trails: the guides, logistics staff, staff at the accommodation places and those involved in the marketing and the training of the guides. A number of people went the extra mile to welcome me and to show off their trail, to answer my barrage of questions and to ensure that my facts were correct. I'm particularly indebted to Professor Leon Hugo, the initiator of the Green Flag Accreditation scheme, who works tirelessly to ensure that the hiking

industry is well managed; that trail owners deliver a *value-for-money* product that is responsible towards the environment. In addition to spending hours discussing the nature of slackpacking, developing easy-to-understand symbols that summarise the key features of each trail and acting as a sounding block, Leon also wrote the Mehloding trail description.

I'm also grateful to my fellow hikers, particularly my husband Matthew Holt, who patiently indulged me as I quizzed the guides and wandered off on detours. I undertook many of these hikes when I was preparing for the Cape Epic cycle ride, so my heartfelt thanks go out to the long-suffering logistics managers who kindly added my bike to the overnight baggage, and to my companions on those trails who happily took care of any necessary admin while I got in some post-hike cycle training!

I came across slackpacking by chance when I prolapsed a disc and spent 3 months in traction in 2000. My orthopaedic surgeon advised against surgery but warned me I could no longer indulge in white-water kayaking and mountaineering, my true passions. I could swim and hike – provided my pack weighed no more than 1/10 of my body weight. So, for my first trail of the 21st century, the Wild Coast Hike from Port St Johns to Coffee Bay, I sought the aid of a porter. Port St Johns Tourism put me in touch with Jimmy Selani.

This young entrepreneur, for a modest fee, agreed not only to carry my pack but also to guide my group on the trail. He was our interpreter, chef and raconteur. Jimmy took us to shebeens, to meet sangomas and to local shops to buy supplies.

He took us to rock pools and helped us identify the marine life, to coastal forests where he pointed out the indigenous birds, and to deserted beaches and high cliffs where we soaked up the magnificence of the Wild Coast. That trail, the first of many when I would voluntarily relinquish my pack, was one of the most memorable hikes of my life. I walked free of a heavy load, and had to admit that I rather enjoyed the freedom. I am now smitten. These days if I don't have to carry my pack, why should I?

If you are a regular backpacker, I hope this book will encourage you to enjoy the same freedom. If you're someone who is in any way intimidated by the thought of multi-day trails, then I hope this will be the spur you need to get you out there, into the wilderness on a trail that is not just manageable but enjoyable. Researching this book has been fun. It has taken me to new places and introduced me to wonderful, like-minded hikers. I hope it will inspire you to shoulder your day pack and set out on the trail.

How to use this book

The whole point of this book is to make selecting a slackpacking trail as pain free as possible, so I have made the presentation here as simple and as user-friendly as I can. The trails are arranged in geographical order, starting in the Western Cape (with one in the Northern Cape), simply because the majority of the trails are in this province. In the introductory paragraphs to each trail I've also suggested the type of hiker to whom the trail might appeal – hardcore mountain lovers, twitchers or botanists, family groups, modern-day strandlopers or those who simply enjoy interacting with local communities along the way.

Each of the trails is also broken down into day sections, with each day described in detail, including the distance covered and average walking time. (I use the word 'average' loosely here, as one of the characteristics of slackpackers seems to be that there is no 'average'! Some groups dawdle, others stride out; some take the direct route, others tend to be sidetracked. What I quote is the walking time provided by the trail operator as a general guideline.)

Trail at a Glance boxes

- Distance
- Duration
- Difficulty
- Accommodation type
- Logistics
- Nature of trail, and
- Price category

All the trails and excursions listed in this book are graded for quick-and-easy reference, detailing the general nature of the trail – whether it's beach, bushveld, fynbos, forest or mountain, or a combination of these – distance and duration, the region in which it is located as well as the type of accommodation you will find.

The difficulty rating is given on a scale of 1–5 where 5 is the most strenuous trail in the book, the Tsistikamma Trail.

1 – easy
2 – moderate
3 – hard or long in places
4 – strenuous, might be long and hard in places
5 – tough, long and usually hard most of the time

Similarly, instead of giving the exact cost of each trail (which may vary according to the size of the group or choice of options as well as over time) trails are grouped into price categories based on the cost a person, a night for a group of 6.

R – less than R250
RR – R250–R499
RRR – R500–R999
RRRR – R1000–R1499
RRRRR – more than R1500

Familiarise yourself with the 'Trail at a Glance' categories and you'll find it easy to navigate your way through this book.

Green Flag Accreditation

The principle behind the Green Flag accreditation is not to distinguish subjectively between 'good' and 'bad' trails, but to give recognition (and a marketing edge) to trail owners who adhere to the concept of responsible management: delivering a product that is both *value for money* and which is responsible towards the environment.

Imagine having to lug your pack over those Tsitsikamma mountains! Thank goodness for slackpacking.

The Green Flag Accreditation System (GFT) is run under the auspices of the Hiking Organisation of Southern Africa (HOSA) and overseen by the SA Hiking Trail Owners' Association (SAHTOA). The Green Flag system is being implemented by many major trail owners in South Africa, including SANParks, Cape Nature, Komatiland Forest, MTO (Mountain to Ocean) Forestry, KZN Wildlife, regional and provincial authorities and some of the larger municipalities such as Johannesburg and Tshwane. This is the only national (and international) accreditation system for hiking trails, much akin to the international Blue Flag beach grading system.

If you would like to find out more on the green-flag accreditation system see www.trailinfo.co.za or contact its local founding champion

Leon Hugo, cell 082-578-3023 or e-mail leonhugo@vodamail.co.za.

In a nutshell

In an effort to be as thorough as possible, I also provide other critical information that will help potential slackpackers decide on a particular trail. This information is summarised in the 'In a nutshell' fact panel at the end of each trail description, and details the minimum and maximum group size that can be accommodated, as well as when best to do the trail, what to take and who to contact.

Also included are quick-and-easy references that will help you evaluate individual routes at a glance. **Up to it?** gives you an idea of whether the trail is easy or challenging. Use this with the **difficulty rating** at the start of each trail.

The **survival notes** that round off each panel also allow you to quickly assess the key features of the trail.

Introduction

Most simply, slackpacking is backpacking without the schlep. Slackpacking trails are a relatively new genre of multi-day hiking trails, which allow you to travel light, carrying only your water, lunch, camera and waterproofs in a day pack while someone else takes care of transporting all your overnight stuff.

So what's all the fuss about?

Have you listened to the tales of valiant but exhausted trailists who've survived 5 days of rock hopping with 20 kg packs on their backs on the Otter Trail? Or those who've endured 4 days in the same dirty kit and with no washing facilities in the Cederberg Wilderness Area. Or those who spent sleepless nights in wind-beaten tents on rocky beds during long weekends in the Drakensberg? While they rave about the experience, the scenery and the quaint overnight spots, you know – or you certainly imagine – that it's also a celebration of pain and discomfort: lugging around camping pots and soggy clothing, sleeping in smelly, communal huts and enduring a diet of tasteless rice crackers and no beer. So, if you're not a regular backpacker, you've probably thought 'Aah, what losers – they can keep the discomfort. Backpacking sucks.'

But overnight hiking need not be a pain in the back. With a minimum of planning

Bontebok are often seen by hikers on the Cape of Good Hope Trail, Whale Trail and Two River Trail.

you can organise – for example – to link a series of day hikes even in remote places, leaving vehicles at the trailheads and descending each day for a bath, a bottle of fine wine, a juicy steak and a soft, warm bed. Surely that's a little more tempting? Think laterally and you'll realise there is another option: letting someone else take care of the logistics. That's slackpacking.

Slackpacking is well established in the popular backpacking destinations of the USA, New Zealand and Europe, yet has been slow to catch on in South Africa. In a way, that's surprising. Multi-day hiking trails – of which South Africa has many – are a fabulous way of destressing, of getting out and enjoying the wonderful scenery and wildlife of this spectacular country. But many run through wilderness or sparsely populated areas where the only accommodation is in basic huts and refuelling is not an option. Everything you need for the trail you carry on your back, and that requires not only a strong back and a good level of fitness, but also careful planning.

The magnificent 5-day Tsitsikamma Trail, as an example, is going to test your endurance. The trail winds up steep hills and down deep valleys. The huts are high in the mountains and sparse, so it gets cold at night and a good sleeping bag and warm clothing are essential. Even if you're going light you need cutlery and crockery, a first-aid kit, a torch, camera, binoculars, towel, perhaps a tree guide and notebook. And then, of course, there's the food – but there's

Picnics above the vineyards of the Elgin-Grabouw valley are one of the spoils on the Green Mountain Trail.

not much space in the pack so it's going to have to be compact and light.

Unless you're experienced in the art of backpacking cuisine or have masses of time to plan tasty meals, I bet you'll go for the easy, obvious option. Mmm … 5 packets of dehydrated pasta, some rusks, cheese and crackers and biltong to keep the wolf from the door – some holiday this is going to be!

Now I like my creature comforts: a pillow, good food and a little tipple. I've lugged bottles of wine on the Otter Trail, taken all the fresh ingredients for a Thai green curry for the second night's meal on the Drakensberg escarpment, and even surprised our hiking group by serving up crayfish tails on a desert hike when the majority were looking bleakly at their 2-minute noodles. So you can imagine how quickly I converted to the idea that you don't need to rough it on long-distance trails. If you can organise for your bags and cooler boxes to be transported from hut to hut you can really hike in style.

But having your bag transported to each overnight spot is only part of the attraction of many of the slackpacking trails included in this book. At least half of them take the concept to higher levels of luxury and comfort by accommodating hikers in luxury hotels or guesthouses and providing gourmet meals. These luxury hiking trails are a genre in themselves, but they're only one end (obviously, the more expensive end) of the slackpacking spectrum.

Learning from the locals

Many slackpacking trails are also guided. This has many advantages: the hiker benefits from local knowledge and actually learns about the natural and cultural environment he or she is travelling through, has greater security in remote areas or on trails that are not well marked and, at the same time, creates job opportunities and gives something back to local communities passed along the way.

What this adds up to is making long-distance hiking more accessible – particularly to tourists, the active over-50s who see no reason to take on unnecessary burdens, groups of women who would otherwise feel insecure, family groups and those whose busy lives mean they'd rather have

Crossing the bridge over to the island at Mazeppa Bay on the Wild Coast Meander.

never see the logistics staff so you can hike alone, or with a partner, without risk of intrusion but still find your bag and food waiting at the end of each day.

Backpacking is no longer the realm of only the fit and fanatical. Gone are the days when you had to brave smelly socks, a bulging rucksack, struggle up the mountains and arrive tired and sore at your rustic camp. Slackpacking allows you to enjoy the challenge of a tough hike by day – but to enjoy the luxuries wrought by some 10 millennia of civilisation: a hot shower, soft bed, change of clothes, chilled G&T and a real meal afterwards.

So go on, treat yourself – if just once. Slackpacking is not just about lessening the load and saving your shoulders. If you carry a light pack you cover the ground faster, so you have more time to go off and explore, to swim, laze in the sun, slow down to smell the flowers and enjoy the other good things in life. Unless you're in training, or just enjoy suffering, I'll bet you'll never look back.

Finding your trail

This book is a collection of the best slackpacking trails available in South Africa – the product of 10 years of hiking along some of the most spectacular mountain ranges and stretches of our coastline. I have deliberately excluded the guided bush walks offered in the Kruger National Park and in other public and private game reserves. They are fine and wonderful if you're looking for a game experience on foot, but they cater to a different type – bush lovers – and, well, it's just not real hiking by my book.

The degree of logistical support varies, and is usually directly proportional to the cost of the trail. What is refreshing is that taking the schlep out of backpacking need not be expensive. The trails featured

someone else organise the logistics. People who would never have done a trail if they'd had to carry a pack are now enjoying a new-found adventure. Those who are looking for a meaningful experience and greater understanding of an area and its people are enthralled by the knowledge imparted by the guides. And, of course, walking with a guide and in a group means that personal safety is no longer a concern.

Now, don't get me wrong, 'pampered' guided and catered hikes are not for everyone (or certainly not for everyone all of the time) – but there are also self-guided and self-catered trails to choose from. So, if your penchant for skinny-dipping or your food fetishes dissuade you from joining an organised group, fear not. Skip Part 1 – the guided, catered hikes – and go straight to Part 2, the section on unguided/guided, self-catered trails.

At least some of the slackpacking options should appeal to most hikers. There are trails where you're guided and mollycoddled the whole way; others where you here range from self-guided hikes, staying in very comfortable overnight accommodation complete with hot showers and refrigeration facilities for only R150 a person a day, right up to the ultra-luxurious, all-inclusive options that are closer to the R2 000 mark a day.

I have grouped the trails according to the type of trail – guided or unguided, whether accommodation is in luxury private accommodation or utilising existing hikers' huts or community resources, and whether it's catered or self-catered. In most instances bags are driven around between the overnight spots, but occasionally porters are employed to carry the packs.

Wherever possible a full trail description is given, as well as recommendations for the best maps and further reading; all the unguided hikes being well marked. However, many of the luxury, guided hikes do not follow a set route or formula; the route is tailored to the weather conditions, fitness levels, interests and accommodation preferences of the group.

Slackpackers' bags are not always driven around; these are the beasts of burden on the Donkey Trail.

'Other slacker trails'

The final section of the book contains short descriptions of other trails I researched for this book. Some have only recently come online or are launching soon, so I was not able to hike them for inclusion in this edition (hopefully next time). Others were in my original line-up as individual chapters, but as the book evolved I decided they did not merit a major feature because, for one reason or other, they don't quite fit the mould. In some, you're based in one place doing a network of day walks rather than having the option to follow a 'trail' and overnighting along the way; on others you have to carry your bag for part of the way or, you can have your bags ferried between huts if you ask (sometimes for a fee, other times not); while others, such as the wine walks, are special interest trails, where you spend a good portion of the day wine tasting and enjoying leisurely lunches and on which the walking is a way of making you feel better about over-indulgence rather than serious hiking!

What to pack

The range and diversity of the various trails featured in this guide means a 'what to pack' list cannot be exhaustive. Clearly, if you're going into the mountains on the unguided Tsitsikamma Trail, or on the guided Hoerikwaggo trail, serious all-weather gear and sturdy boots are required. But even these have bad-weather 'escape routes' so the normal self-sufficiency required on some wilderness trails may not be necessary. On the coastal trails you are never far from civilisation so you certainly won't have to be carrying much in the way of emergency gear or heavy-duty weather gear.

Slackpacking trails are aimed to be accessible to less-experienced hikers: they are guided or clearly marked, almost all have cellphone coverage for most of the way and there is back-up in the form of the logistical support crew if you do get into difficulties. So enjoy the freedom that this brings. Pack light during the day and spoil yourself by including changes of clothes, reference books, your favourite tipple, braai meat and whatever else you need to make a perfect holiday in your overnight pack or cooler box. If you like your creature comforts, make a plan to ensure they're met.

Each operator will provide a detailed list of what to bring, and all are extremely enthusiastic about their trails, so if you need more detailed information, just ask – but the following guidelines might help....

During the day

Your bags are transported between evening stops, so all you need carry during the day is a small day pack. A small to medium-sized day pack (25–35 *l*) is ideal. Waist and sternum straps make these more comfortable, and pockets on the waistband mean you can easily access your camera and other items you may need at hand. An integrated hydration bladder (typically holding up to 2 *l* of fluid) means you can drink as you walk.

In your pack you'll need:
- A full water bottle or hydration bladder (as above)
- Waterproofs
- Binoculars
- Camera
- Sunscreen and lip salve
- Swimming costume
- Kikoi
- Snacks
- Insect repellent

What to wear

What you wear depends on the trail and the weather for the time of year, but it's also a matter of personal choice (particularly when it comes to the choice between long and short pants!).

I'd recommend the following:
- Comfortable walking shoes or training shoes. Hiking boots are rarely required, except on the mountain walks if you're expecting rain, or if you prefer the ankle support and added protection of high-cut boots. For the beach walks a pair of lightweight shoes or sandals will probably suffice.
- Change of socks for each day. If you're wearing training shoes, lightweight trail or running socks are perfectly adequate.
- Sun hat, preferably with a wide rim, and sunglasses.
- Wicking T-shirt and shorts or long pants (zip-offs are ideal).
- Lightweight, quick-drying, warm mid-layer (lightweight fleece-type fabric).
- Lightweight waterproof jacket – and, if you're in the mountains, waterproof pants or poncho.

One of the great advantages of not carrying a heavy pack is that you can move faster, and enjoy other activities on the trail ...

... such as birdwatching. The vlei at the end of the Silver Sands Trail is a great spot for twitchers.

- Lycra cycling shorts to wear under your normal shorts or trousers to prevent chafing.

Other useful items:
- A waterproof pack liner or cover (a black plastic rubbish bag does the job if necessary).
- Trekking pole or walking stick.
- Waterproof bag for keeping electronic equipment (like cameras) dry when it rains, during river crossings or on boat/canoe trips. Ziplock bags are a less-than-ideal alternative – they will protect your gear against showers but if your camera takes a swim, don't expect them to be watertight!
- Mask and snorkel – a luxury, I know, but when you see some of the rock pools you'll wish you had one.
- Plasters and antiseptic cream in case of scratches and blisters. If you're prone to blisters, take a clean pair of socks for every day, some Vaseline to prevent blistering – wearing a thin 'pop sock'

is another tried-and-tested method of reducing friction – and some Compeed or Second Skin dressings. There is nothing worse than hobbling along with sore feet, so if you feel a 'hotspot' developing stop and deal with it straight away.
- Merthiolate, for when a severe blister has developed: lance with a clean, sharp blade, spray 'muti' into the blister (it burns like the devil for a short, sharp while) and apply a plaster.
- Money for snacks or additional supplies along the way.
- Ziplock bags … Yes, I know I said they are not a substitute for true waterproof bags, but they're great for keeping sarmies and other gear 'almost' dry.

In your overnight bag:
- Change(s) of clothing.
- Toiletries (including a travel hair dryer if you're on a luxury trail where there will be electricity).
- Spare batteries for electronic equipment and an adapter plug for charging.

- Head torch or small penlight, and, for the hutted and community-run trails, some candles.
- Insect repellent spray or cream.
- Bird, tree, flower, mammal and other relevant field guides. You're out to have fun here and you're unlikely to remember everything the guides point out. So it's great to be able to look things up later.
- Notebook and pen, and a novel to read in the evenings.
- Sleeping bag and pillow (for all but the luxury trails).

Trail menus for the self-catered trails

You have the opportunity to eat pretty much what you want, but on certain trails – such as the Whale Trail – you pay for each box/cooler bag transported, while on the Hoerikwaggo Tented Classic fridge space is limited. So it pays to be canny. If you're really on the ball, make friends with the logistics staff so your wine and beers are in the fridge on your arrival. And plan interesting meals that don't require a lot of effort at the end of the day.

Many of the trails featured traverse the Cape Floristic Region Protected Area World Heritage Site.

Useful tips for preserving or whipping up tasty meals include:

- Vacuum pack meat so that it stays fresh.
- Bring low volume foods such as hard cheeses (like parmesan) and nuts or dried foods such as biltong and dried fruit.
- Carry salt and pepper, and a small sealable plastic bottle of quality olive oil – great for cooking, salads or instead of butter on bread.
- Pack fresh herbs and spices – some sprigs of rosemary, basil or coriander as well as garlic and chili can liven up even the dullest food.
- Include a small coffee percolator for your group and plenty of fresh coffee – you want to make friends, not enemies, so be ready to share. A bread or pancake mix has a similar aromatic effect on most hikers after a few days.
- And, finally, pack in your favourite tipple – many of these trails are in remote areas where you have to make do with the choice from the honesty bar. So bring your own booze if you're going to be fussy about what you drink.

Wild Cards

The Wild Card is a joint initiative by SAN-Parks, Ezemvelo KZN Wildlife, Msinsi KZN (dams) Resorts and Reserves, CapeNature and Big Game Parks of Swaziland that gives you free entry to their parks and reserves for 1 year (i.e. you don't have to pay the entry and conservation fees) as well as a CashBack rewards incentive. And at the same time you are supporting conservation. Wild loyalty cards are available for individuals, couples and families and can be purchased for all the national parks and reserves of these organisations, or for regional parks and reserves, known as clusters, at CapeNature and SAN-Parks offices or through www.wildcard.co.za, 086-123-4002.

Silver Sands Trail

Northern Cape

DISTANCE 55 km • **DURATION** 5 days (plus extra day travelling home) • **DIFFICULTY** 3
TRAIL TYPE Beach (southwards) • **LOGISTICS** Bags driven around • **COST** RRR
ACCOMMODATION TYPE Luxury tents • **AREA** Namaqualand

This guided, fully catered hike along the west coast luxury trail leads along the coast of a newly proclaimed national park – an extension of the Namaqualand National Park – between Spoegrivier and Groenrivier. While the big draw-card of Namaqualand is obviously the spectacular wild flowers that explode into a kaleidoscope of colour from August through until late October, the wilderness trail has many other highlights, including magnificent coastal scenery, sightings of whales and dolphins, exquisite rock pools full of colourful marine life, extremely comfortable, mobile overnight camps and wonderful food.

This trail in the Northern Cape is a wonderful way to see what is otherwise an extremely inhospitable, remote section of South Africa. The sand roads are accessible only by 4×4 vehicles, there is no water along the coast, no cellphone reception, no development or facilities of any kind. The Silver Sands Trail has opened up this exquisite area to hikers seeking a luxurious journey down the pristine coastline of the country's premier Namaqualand flower-viewing area.

▶ DAY 1 Spoegrivier caves to Spoegrivier camp

2 KM ◆ 1 HR

We met the rest of our group and our hosts Anzanne and Ernst at Diemerskraal, at Ernst's family's guest farm, in the Wellington wine region some 70 km northeast of Cape Town. After a hearty brunch and a briefing, we hopped aboard the 20-seater Samil that was to take us up the coast to the start of the trail. It was a 400 km drive that took most of the day but we sat back and relaxed, slept and watched an introductory

The famous 'dog stone' of Hondeklipbaai is just up the road from Speogrivier caves, the start of the Silver Sands Trail.

video on the trail so the time past quickly – it was a relief not to be driving! We passed Bitterfontein, famous for an extremely rare green form of marble found nowhere else in the world. The town's name originates from a nearby spring that supplies the town's drinking water, but only after it has been desalinated! At Garies, our next brief stop, Anzanne quickly filled us in on one of the town's main attractions. 'Letterklip', the huge granite boulder koppie at the back of the town, bears the names of early travellers who, it is claimed, used it as a post office. Also, during the Anglo-Boer War British forces garrisoned in the local blockhouse also apparently inscribed their names and dates into the granite rocks.

After a brief stop at Hondeklipbaai, where we clambered up the famous 'dog stone' after which the bay takes it's name, we visited Spitfire Rock, and watched with awe as the surf crashed over the dramatic rock formation, before continuing south to explore the wreckage of the *Aristea*, a World War II minesweeper. From there it was only a short drive to the trail head at Spoegrivier. Anzanne pointed out the obvious sheep's skull formation and we wandered around the caves and overhangs admiring the rock formations and the history of the place – an old Khoisan dwelling that is believed to have been utilised some 2 000 years ago. Our first camp was only a couple of kilometres along a sandy road, but we were glad of the exercise after the long drive. A swim off the sandy bay of Spoegrivier looked enticing but we were warned that the water of the Atlantic Ocean was icy, so we headed to the rocks with a beer to enjoy the sunset.

Our mobile camp can only be described as extraordinary. In this arid land the trail organisers had set up a flush toilet, a hot-water shower and a large inflatable communal tent in which we enjoyed our meals. There was a

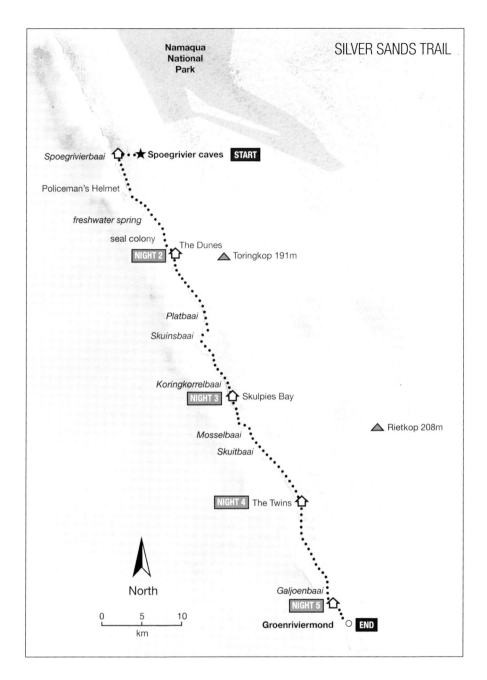

SILVER SANDS TRAIL

Namaqua
National
Park

Spoegrivierbaai — ★ Spoegrivier caves START

Policeman's Helmet

freshwater spring

seal colony   The Dunes
NIGHT 2   ▲ Toringkop 191m

Platbaai

Skuinsbaai

Koringkorrelbaai
NIGHT 3   Skulpies Bay

▲ Rietkop 208m

Mosselbaai

Skuitbaai

NIGHT 4   The Twins

North

Galjoenbaai
NIGHT 5

0   5   10
     km

Groenriviermond   ○ END

generator for lighting and to charge camera batteries, a donkey boiler for hot water and a full dining table and chairs. We relaxed and enjoyed the solitude of this beautiful spot, aided by the 5 glasses of wine a night that are included in the trail fee. Dinner was an absolute feast – a mussel pot, crayfish, snoek and Hottentot fish on the braai with sweet potatoes, spicy rice and home-made bread. After admiring the starlit sky we headed to our 2-person tents where the sound of the waves lulled us to sleep.

▶ DAY 2 Spoegrivier mouth to The Dunes

15 KM • 7 HR

After breakfast we stuffed our lunch into our day packs and set off along the coast following sandy jeep tracks through the veld and descending to the beach when we fancied a swim or when we spotted something of interest. We scanned the ocean for marine mammals, regularly sighting dolphins surfing the back line or whales blowing out at sea, and stopped often to admire the various flowers for which Namaqualand is so famous. Anzanne pointed out the familiar Namaqua and African daisies, which cover the plains in a blaze of colour in spring, but we also sought out the lesser-known beauties.

Particularly prolific is the yellow shrub locally known as *perdibos*, a protea that is common all the way north from Piketberg to southern Namibia. At one point she had us in stitches when she insisted that the petals of a pretty little purple flower looked like drumsticks. I couldn't see the resem-

Magnificent granite boulders make for fun scrambling on day 2 – the less energetic can follow the jeep track.

blance but it gradually dawned on me that I understood 'drumsticks' to be the long thin pieces of wood used by musicians, rather than the chicken drumstick shapes that I now recognised in the flower head of the *Zaluzianskya villosa*. There was so much to see that we covered less than a kilometre in the first hour so, reluctantly, Anzanne forced us to keep walking. Pretty as the blooms were, we were going to have to pick up the pace a bit if we were going to get into camp at a decent hour in time to enjoy our 5 glasses!

It was only a short meander through the dunes until we came to the first of the 'features' on the trail, the great granite mound of the Policeman's Helmet which we scrambled up to admire the view. At roughly the halfway point we stopped for lunch on some rocks set high above Boggeralbaai and looked around, amazed that there was no sign of habitation anywhere.

We were really out in the wilderness here; we had come across a rough campsite that morning, but otherwise nothing – no sight nor sound of other human beings. It was wonderful to be alone in such a beautiful and unspoiled place.

A short detour took us to a small natural spring at Strandfontein, a watering hole for the sheep and goats that grazed here many moons ago, then we followed the coastal sand road again until Anzanne indicated that we should follow her down to the rocks. She put her finger to her lips – we were clearly stalking something. Sure enough, as we scrambled over the rocks we heard the distinctive barking of seals and peered over to see a large colony that was clearly disturbed by our presence. As quietly as we could we moved to a good vantage point then watched as the great bulls and the tiny pups flopped clumsily over the rocks. Once in the water, however, they were clearly in

Long empty beaches flanked by dunes on one side and the icy sea on the other are a highlight of day 3.

their element and were transformed into graceful, sleek water babes.

We continued along the coastline following the rocky paths and stopping often to admire the sea birds until we spotted our camp on a grassy terrace among the rocks. It was still early in the afternoon, so after a cup of tea we grabbed our masks and snorkels and checked out the marine life in the gullies. There were definitely crayfish to be had here, so if you hike the trail in season bring a permit! After a hot shower, thanks to a clever pump system that raises water to the showerhead from a hot-water bucket to the shower-head, it was time to enjoy yet another amazing meal, before retiring to bed exhausted from our exertions and the invigorating coastal air.

▶ **DAY 3** The Dunes to Skulpies Bay

15.5 KM • 7 HR

We woke to find a thick sea mist had enveloped the coast. 'We're in the Nama Suc-culent biosphere,' explained Anzanne. 'It's this mist off the cold Atlantic Ocean that feeds the profusion of flowers in the otherwise dry Namib Desert.' Ernst announced we were going on a trip, so we all got on to the Samil for a drive through the dunes up to Toringkop. On this rocky outcrop is a beacon that was erected by Sir Thomas Maclear (the astronomer royal who also constructed the beacon on Table Mountain that bears his name) and then it was back to camp.

Again much of the day was spent admiring the flowers – we could now recognise the dominant species and had begun to spot less conspicuous specimens such as the beautiful yellow blooms of the tiny oxalis and patches of pretty pink hongerblom (*Sencio arenarius*). We stopped to admire the birds, to swim and have lunch at Bitterrivier, then followed the coastal path for a while enjoying the smell of the sea and the flocks of cormorants and gulls. Comely pairs of African black oystercatchers would take off as we approached only to land a few hundred metres up the beach, repeating the process each time we neared them before finally flying back to where we first spotted them. The highlight of the day was an amazing long stretch of beach backed by dunes which we could not resist exploring. The great mountains of coastal sand dunes were covered with wonderful wind-sculpted ripples, which had us stop for the superb photo opportunities.

Back on the beach again we enjoyed the tiny little strandlopers (sanderlings) that left delicate footprints in the sand and our eyes were drawn to the striking geology of this stretch – great outcrops of white quartzite and dramatic pink intrusions that snaked through the granite boulders. Our camp that night was near Koringkorrelbaai and as we sat around the fire Ernst revealed more secret stories of this coast. 'It was here, in 1941, that the Nazi-trained Sidney Robey Leibrand landed on a covert mission to create a revolution that would overthrow General Jan Smuts's government and to create a revolution in order to install a Nazi puppet regime.' Operation Weissdorn failed and the Fourth Reich stayed an illu-

Just look at all those mussels!

The combined result of the southerly winds and the earth's rotational movement along this coastline results in up-welling along this coastline. Icy cold but nutrient-rich 'bottom water' is forced to the surface. This creates a fertile environment, which ensures the prolific supply of phytoplankton. Small fish as well as other marine life including black mussels live on this plankton. Blooms of phytoplankton and the extensive kelp beds support a food supply for seals and sea birds.

sory dream, but the story had us debating long into the night. The harsh coastline of Namaqualand clearly has a shady past but it only added to the intrigue of this magnificent wilderness.

▶ DAY 4 Skulpies Bay to The Twins

16 KM ◆ 8 HR

Anzanne led us out of camp and onto the beach where the wide shelves of black mussel shells made the going quite tough; but we were fit and getting into the swing of things now. Again the geology was fascinating: there were great outcrops of white quartzite, wriggling snakes of bright pink running through ancient granite and great folds of rock that told of tectonic upheavals in the distant past. More recent forces of nature, the crashing of waves and blasting of the wind, have produced dramatic coastal landforms:, intriguing caves, sea arches and deep gullies alive with limpets, mussels and red bait.

It was a relief when we were able to hike along the firmer sand. The next stretch,

It's hard to resist climbing the rippled dunes then sprinting back down to the beach.

along to Kwas se Baai (Paradise Bay), a popular fishing spot where we stopped for lunch, was glorious. The coast was less rugged and there were no cliffs backing the beach so we were able to enjoy the sea and the veld simultaneously. A pair of ostriches bounded away and a little further on, close to another fresh-water spring, we spotted a little duiker. 'There are also gemsbok, red hartebeest and steenbok in the park,' Anzanne informed us.

▶ DAY 5 The Twins to Groenriviermond

This is a pristine stretch of coast where you're unlikely to encounter another soul.

8 KM ◆ 4 HR

Our route on the final day of the hike again led along glorious empty beaches to the mouth of the Groenrivier. This area is a famous breeding ground for oystercatchers. So, after a a hearty brunch and a late start, we set of to explore some black oystercatcher nests among the kelp on the beach. Out to sea we saw the dramatic breakers known, as The Twins, which form when waves pass over big off-shore reef. Then we spotted signs of habitation in the distance – shacks on the far side of the Groenrivier mouth. A sand bar blocked the river mouth, creating a shallow vlei alive with birds, so we sat on the dunes with our binoculars and

enjoyed the late afternoon sun. We easily identified grey and giant herons, greater flamingos, Egyptian geese, coots and cormorants, while Anzanne pointed out the smaller inhabitants – black-necked grebes, Cape dabchicks, plovers and terns.

Relaxed and happy, we headed back along the beach to the overnight camp perched on a sandy ledge that we hadn't even noticed when we hiked past earlier in the day. After a swim we climbed the dunes behind the camp and, with some sense of loss, looked back along the trail. It was a magnificent sight and we felt a sense of regret that we

Long train running

Sishen Mine was established in 1953 by the Iron and Steel Corporation (ISCOR) and it soon grew to become one of the largest open-cast mines in the world. It is situated in the Northern Cape, approximately 280 km northwest of Kimberley. It is, supposedly, one of the 7th largest open-cast mines in the world with a

pit approximately 11 km long, 1.5 km wide and almost 400 m deep. The ore is usually transported to Saldanha by trains 2.3 km long, comprising 210 wagons each carrying 85 tonnes of ore – a total of 17 850 tonnes a train. In August 1989 a train with 660 wagons set a world record for the longest train (7.3 km) and heaviest load (68 640 tonnes of ore). Most of the ore is destined for Japan.

were going to have to leave this glorious wilderness the following day and head back to the world of traffic and e-mail.

▶ **DAY 6** Travelling home

After a final swim in the sea we departed for Diemerskraal, stopping for lunch at the Lutzville Cellars for lunch and a wine tasting, a fitting end to a luxury trail. The small town of Lutzville is also on the route of the Sishen train, which carries iron ore from ISCOR's Sishen mine in the Northern Cape interior to Saldanha Bay. On our way back to Vredendal we passed under the towering pillars of the Sishen–Saldanha railway bridge, a handsome feat of engineering that gave Ernst the opportunity to share more of the interesting facts about the region with us and remind us once again that this trail was much more than just a hike; it had been a truly memorable safari.

In a nutshell · Silver Sands Trail

BOOKINGS Jacana Marketing & Reservations, 0861-JACANA (086-152-2262) or 011-656-0606, bookings@jacanacollection.co.za, www.jacanacollection.co.za.

START/FINISH Diemerskraal guest farm, near Malmesbury, 70 km northeast of Cape Town.

HIGHLIGHTS The wild flowers; the sense of wilderness; the incredible geology of the coastline; the indigenous bird life and marine mammals; the very luxurious overnight camps; super food.

LONGEST DAY 16 km.

SHORTEST DAY 2 km.

GROUP SIZE Minimum 6, maximum 20.

UP TO IT? This is a hike for those who want to stop and smell the flowers and enjoy being out in a beautiful wilderness, so it's ideal for novice hikers and family groups. Daily distances are moderate, though walking on sand is quite tiring.

DON'T FORGET! Swimming costume, mask and snorkel, camera, mosquito repellent and binoculars. Crocs or sandals are ideal footwear.

STYLE A guided and fully catered trail staying in 2-person tents in safari-style mobile camps complete with shower and flush toilet.

WHEN TO GO The trail is closed during July. Spring (August–October) is wonderful as whales are usually seen in abundance and the flowers are at their best. Autumn (March–May) is also a good time. Summers (November to February) are often very windy.

LOOK IT UP No doubt there will be maps once the park is proclaimed, but until then Google Earth and Tracks for Africa are good sources of info.

Survival Notes

- Hikers have to carry all their own drinking water as none is available on the hike.
- Fully catered, guided hike staying in tented accommodation.
- Self-catering option also available.

2

West Coast Crayfish Trail

Western Cape

DISTANCE 55 km ◆ **DURATION** 4 days ◆ **DIFFICULTY** 3 ◆ **TRAIL TYPE** Beach and coastal cliffs (northwards) ◆ **LOGISTICS** Bags driven around ◆ **COST** RR ◆ **ACCOMMODATION TYPE** Community guesthouses, B&B ◆ **AREA** Cape west coast

The west coast has a special charm, largely because development is limited to a few fishing villages and holiday towns. Snoek and crayfishing have been the mainstays of the local economy for years, but the decline in the fishing industry has seen a number of tourism initiatives offered as alternatives. The West Coast Crayfish Trail is one of these, initially funded by Eco-Africa and operated by the communities along the route. Accommodation is in comfortable, if at times rustic, community guesthouses and one private B&B. This is not quite a luxury trail, but what it lacks in sophistication it makes up for in the cultural experience and in the warmth of the local people.

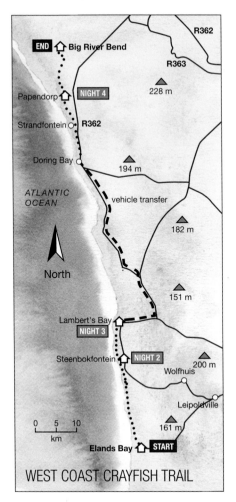

WEST COAST CRAYFISH TRAIL

off the rocks or dig white mussels from the sand or fossick for food in the intertidal zone. It's a fascinating trail from both a cultural and a geological perspective, which will delight hikers, birders and those wishing to gain a deeper insight into the west coast region.

▶ NIGHT 1 Settling in

The drive from Cape Town had been glorious – we opted for the route from Piketberg down past Verlorevlei, arriving at the guesthouse just outside Eland's Bay to find 2 large bullocks blocking our entrance. A herd boy rustled them up and we sat down under the starlit sky to a meal of snoek, salad and potatoes prepared by Maria, the jolly chef. The lights were still twinkling across the vlei water as we retired, so come dawn we were refreshed and raring to go.

▶ DAY 1 Elands Bay to Steenbokfontein

18 KM • 5–6 HR

We awoke to the sounds of birds and staggered out onto the stoep of the Vleihuis stone cottage. Pelicans and flamingos coloured the shallow but wide estuary, while spoonbills and a number of small waders flitted in and out of view. We'd arrived too late to explore Elands Bay the night before and wanted a quick look around, so when our guide arrived we jumped into the car and headed to the rock-art site, Bobbejaansberg, where excavations have revealed evidence of human habitation as much as 15 000 years ago. The cave was covered with ochre hand prints; we could make out images of a large fat-tailed sheep and an eland and the guide explained the background to the paintings and the various attempts at their interpretation.

The trail starts at the surfing el dorado of Elands Bay, famous for its fabulous point break as much as for the famous archaeological cave site. It then heads along white beaches, past old fishing villages, wetlands and rivers to a farm on the Olifants River near the old C17 mission station at Ebenhaezer. It traverses varied west coast environments – hills, rivers and wetlands, endless beaches and multicoloured dunes where, for the first couple of days, you can tie your shoes to your backpack and wander the long beaches and snow-white dunes barefoot, stopping to chat to the wizened local folk as they gather limpets

It was a perfect day – there was not a breath of wind and the sea was flat. I guess the surfers wouldn't have called it 'perfect'; it is hard to believe that when they're working, the waves here are probably the best left-hand breaks in the country.

We left the car safely parked outside the police station until our return and strolled to the beach: it was the last time we were to wear shoes for the next 2 days. A rumbling in the distance announced the imminent arrival of the freight train that shuttles iron ore between the iron-ore mines of Sishen and Saldanha Bay, so we scaled the dunes and waited for the snaking monster to pass.

A group of figures huddled in the shallows a couple of kilometres along the beach – women with their skirts held up out of the waves. Kids played in the sand around a number of colourful net bags filled with shells. When we went over to investigate we discovered that the 'shells' were in fact white mussels, collected as bait at low tide. The gatherers had staked their claims, planted their permit numbers and were hard at work in the water or looking for telltale signs in the dry sand. Fortunately, we'd also brought our mussel permits so we quickly joined in, the cold water a shock to our city-softened feet.

You'll come across local people collecting white mussels for bait – bring a permit and you can gather your own for hors d'ouevres.

Dinner at the end of the first day is a hearty meal at Die Plaaskombuis – the farm kitchen.

It wasn't long before I felt a hard shell beneath my foot. I waited for the wave to recede, then bent down and dug my hand a few centimetres into the sand. The mussel was filtering and fully opened so there was initially quite a resistance, but soon I had it out of the water and was triumphantly displaying my catch to the rest of the group! It became competitive as we all twisted our feet into the sand, often stumbling on a rich seam and pulling out 3 or 4 in quick succession. The toothless old woman who'd showed us the technique grinned at our delight and, once we'd gathered a handful to cook later, we handed over the surplus. At 20 cents a mollusc we weren't going to make her rich.

You could easily live off this coastline. Vast black mussel beds cover the rocks and the tidal pools are a mass of colourful anemones and limpets. It was slow going as we stopped to admire the resource-rich gullies and to cool off with a swim in the waves. Time passed quickly and soon after Kreefbaai (crayfish bay) we saw a clump of

The 'take home only memories, leave nothing but footprints' hiking ethic in practice on the west coast.

to hear, was just shy of 80 years old) but she patted me on the shoulder as she removed my empty plate – clearly delighted by my appetite. The coffee was dark and strong; '*moer koffie*,' laughed our hostess. 'The shopkeeper knows that if I ever pay a visit and find none in stock, I'll *moer* (beat) him!' Our new guide arrived and we waddled back to the beach, startling the cormorants, juvenile kelp gulls and plovers, which took flight as we approached.

The guide pointed out to sea. The diving birds suggested a school of fish moving through – and, sure enough, we were soon witnessing a feeding frenzy. We'd seen dolphins playing in the back line on the first day, but this was amazing. A large pod of dolphins swam a couple of hundred metres out, leaping out of the water and riding the surf, but as we drew nearer we saw that it wasn't just dolphins – the wave was also full of playful seals.

We had our first close encounter with a seal later on – a frightening reminder of the destructive influence of humankind on the coast. A young pup had become trapped in a net, the nylon cord acting as a noose that cut deep into its neck. We tried to catch it to see if we could cut it free, but to no avail – and we were fearful of its bite.

It was almost low tide when we came across some interesting characters who

trees. This was Steenbokfontein, our home for the night, and Tannie Burger welcomed us with tea and cakes and then showed us our rooms in Dollika, her B&B. She helped us fry up our catch with butter and garlic, a tasty appetiser to the main event – a magnificent spread of mussel soup, chicken pie, vegetables and salad finished off with koeksisters at the adjacent Plaaskombuis (farm kitchen).

▶ DAY 2 Steenbokfontein to Lambert's Bay

9 KM ◆ 2–3 HR

The people of the west coast clearly pride themselves on feeding you up, so don't expect to lose any weight on this trail! I don't think I've ever had such a mammoth breakfast as the one Tannie Burger served before we hit the trail. Stewed fruit, yoghurts and cereals were followed by the biggest omelette I've ever seen. Those of a weaker constitution failed to make an impact on our sprightly hostess (who, we were astounded

Fishing boats bob on the waters of Lambert's Bay.

sat, smoking a roll-up, on the rocks. They demonstrated how to remove the juicy flesh from the shell of the limpets they'd just harvested. The guide elaborated on their recipes: once boiled and cleaned, the limpet flesh is often minced to make curry with potatoes or cooked on the braai with garlic and butter.

Another stretch of glorious, empty beach and we were on the outskirts of Lambert's Bay. Apparently the spring flowers here are amazing, but we had to content ourselves with the odd bloom before heading off to Bird Island. It is acknowledged as a key Cape gannet breeding site and home to around 25 000 gannets (as well as numerous cormorants and a few African penguins), comprising some 15 per cent of the total population of these threatened sea birds.

We took a stroll along the walkway from the town's harbour to the new visitors' centre and a big hide on the island, from where

Where have all the gannets gone?

When the gannets that inhabit Lambert's Bay's Bird Island took flight in 2005, custodians CapeNature and the local tourism bodies also took fright. The birds began leaving in December 2005 following attacks by Cape fur seals, which many believe were after the fish in the birds' stomachs. Within a matter of weeks, Bird Island was deserted and there was no breeding season in 2006. In the months that followed, the town saw its tourism revenue drop by as much as 65 per cent. A number of measures were put in place to deter rogue seals from attacking sea birds on the island, but local experts were at a loss as to how to entice the gannets back to their breeding spot.

Then a visiting birder came up with a bright idea. Why not use decoys, – in much the same way that hunters of waterfowl have used carved replicas of birds for centuries? Local artist Gerrit Burger, who'd lived among gannets all his life, was called in and, with the help of a fibreglass model cast from a dead bird, created 50 surprisingly life-like model gannets in plaster of Paris.

These, were then painted by hand and arranged in small groups around the breeding site. Within a few weeks the gannets began to return. Burger recalls his joy at seeing how the real birds reacted to his creations: 'When the first returnees were scared, they ran back and hid in among the decoys,' he told iafrica.com, which reported the story.

Whether the return of the birds is due to the decoys or to the genetic rhythms that dictate that they should mate for life and return to the same spot every year to breed is hard to say, but for Lambert's Bay the return is a major relief. For more information on Bird Island, visit www.capenature.org.za.

North of Doring Bay the flat terrain changes and the trail leads along the top of precipitous cliffs.

we were able to watch the gannets jostling for position. Their constant squawking and landing manoeuvres had us in stitches – after a couple of over-flights to warn their partners and neighbours that they were coming in (and create a bit of space), the big, clumsy birds lowered their undercarriages and approached the improvised runway, then throttled back on landing. It was not unlike watching large cargo planes touching down.

In the hide we learnt about the background to the colony and the elaborate

Top Tip

Take time to explore the rock pools and to talk to the local people. You rarely need shoes – a pair of light shoes or slops tucked into your pack will be ideal. Beer and wine are for sale at Plaaskombuis and at Isabella's at Lambert's Bay, but not anywhere else so bring your own tipple.

mating dances and other social behaviour of the birds. Earlier that year the gannets had moved off, apparently as a result of seal predation, and had been cleverly lured back by decoys.

After a trip to the town museum and a hearty lunch of fish, fish cakes and other local treats we retired to our home for the night, the Eureka flats on the waterfront.

► **DAY 3** Doring Bay to Papendorp

15 KM ♦ 5 HR

After breakfast we were transferred by vehicle from Lamberts Bay to Doring Bay where we began the third day of the trail. The scenery north of Doring Bay was quite unlike that which we'd experienced on the first half of the hike. The trail followed the a line of coastal cliffs, past old diamond workings that were abandoned – without any attempt at restoration – once they were no longer viable. The scenery is more like that of the Tsitsikamma coast – precipitous, wind-sculpted cliffs with deep gullies and tidal pools at their base ... but no forests in this arid landscape.

We hiked through the Strandveld fynbos as our new Doring Bay-based guide pointed out the attempts that had been made at recent dune rehabilitation and some, still current, small-scale mineral extraction points. A new guide took over at Strandfontein, a rather strange holiday town that seemed centred on a very well laid-out campsite. Then it was back to the beach again – and one of the most interesting sections of the trail. Initially, the golden sands were stained with black ore, then littered with smooth, round pink-and-orange pebbles, often showing the marbled effect of a quartz layer. The guide directed us behind a yellowish rock and bid us touch a hidden band of soft, pliable clay, then took us to a natural gallery where, in a cliff face, were what appeared to be rock paintings – shades of orange, red, pink and white decorating the rock wall.

But these were natural colourations, mineral intrusions that formed spectacular patterns visible from afar. And just when we thought we'd seen it all we came upon high red dunes of fine sand such as you find in the Kalahari. It was as if some geologist had come along and mixed everything together – a 5 km stretch of bizarre and magnificent formations.

Where 'Kalahari sands' gave way to golden dunes, we left the beach and headed inland to Papendorp on the Olifants River. The villagers have rights to extract salt from the pan that dries up in summer and we passed deep pits encrusted with sodium-nitrate crystals. The deck of the guesthouse overlooked the river and herons and egrets nested in the tree that shaded it so we had our binoculars at the ready as we ate out, watching a line of sacred ibises fly home.

Golden dunes flank the beach for much of the trail.

Life in Africa doesn't get much better than this, we toasted.

▶ DAY 4 Papendorp to Big River Bend

18 KM ◆ 5–6 HR

A heron was feeding its chicks as we enjoyed our morning coffee – and through our binos we could see the distinctive 'punk-rocker' style hairdo of the greedy young birds as they pecked at their provider. The vlei was a mass of activity as we shouldered our packs and set off for the river. Our last day was very different yet again – along the floodplain of the Olifants River, where our guide pointed out the various water birds.

We had an interesting crossing on a log spanning a small riverstream and stopped for lunch on the one rocky promontory that afforded a view of the river valley. The wine bottles were uncorked and we celebrated the end of an excellent walk. All that remained was the short transfer back to our cars the following day, back to the relative bustle of the Elands Bay. The 4 days had gone quickly, yet we felt we had been in another world – it had been quite a journey.

Other options

A self-catered, tented trail option is available, in which hikers supply their own tents, bedding and cooking equipment, for example, but have the use of cooking and ablution facilities at the overnight spots.

Cyclists with their own mountain bikes also have the option to cycle along a gravel road next to the sea from Elands Bay to Lambert's Bay on Day 2 and, on Day 3, to cycle along a gravel road through the inland strandveld to Doring Bay.

In a nutshell · West Coast Crayfish Trail

BOOKINGS Coreen Coetzee 027-432-2875, 073-370-0782, coreenc@lantic.net, www.south-north.co.za.

START/FINISH Elands Bay / Big River Bend.

TRANSFERS Transfers back to the start are included in the cost of the trail.

HIGHLIGHTS Beautiful, empty beaches; the gannets; the Olifants River and its birds; coastal vegetation, sea birds and, in season, wild flowers, whales and dolphins; Tannie Burger's breakfast; the coast north of Doring Bay, with its ocean views; West Coast crayfish and snoek; wines from the Olifants River Valley; sunsets over the Atlantic and the opportunity to meet locals along the way.

LONGEST DAY 18 km.

SHORTEST DAY 9 km.

GROUP SIZE Minimum 6, maximum 10.

UP TO IT? The trail is flat and distances are modest so it's a good trail for novice and averagely fit hikers.

DON'T FORGET! Binoculars, warm and waterproof clothing and personal gear.

If you want to shuffle for white mussels you'll need a permit to gather molluscs (available from any post office; there's one in Elands Bay at the start of the trail).

LOOK IT UP The West Coast Crayfish Trail brochure, available at the start, has a useful map.

STYLE Guided and fully catered hike, staying in community-run guesthouses and 1 private B&B.

WHEN TO GO The trail can be walked year-round. Spring (August–October), when the wild flowers are at their best and when whales are often spotted from the coast, and autumn (March–May) are ideal times. Winters are cool and sometimes wet – though the morning fogs certainly add atmosphere – while it can be windy in summer.

BEFORE AND AFTER The Vleihuises in Elands Bay can be rented out independently of the trail (as can the other accommodation) and there are numerous other places to stay in the area.

Survival Notes

- Although the duration is 4 days and 5 nights, many hikers prefer to visit the cave on their day of arrival and make this a 5-day trail.
- No water is available on the trail so hikers need to carry sufficient daily.

3

Cederberg Heritage Route, Klein Krakadouw Trail

Western Cape

DISTANCE 55 km, 12 km optional ◆ **DURATION** 2½ days ◆ **DIFFICULTY** 4 ◆ **TRAIL TYPE**
Mountains, craggy ◆ **LOGISTICS** Guided and catered, bags driven around ◆ **COST** RRR
ACCOMMODATION TYPE Community guesthouses, B&Bs ◆ **AREA** Cederberg mountains

With its spectacular scenery and incredible rock art, it's hardly surprising the
Cederberg Wilderness Area is one of the showpieces of the Cape Floristic Region
World Heritage Site. Until recently the lack of tourist infrastructure meant most
of the remote wilderness was the preserve of hardy backpackers and hikers. The
community-run Cederberg Heritage Route (CHR) has changed all that. Now visitors
can enjoy guided 3- to 5-day hiking trails, overnighting in mission villages and
taking in a range of cultural visits, rock-art tours and the unique Cederberg flora
along the way.

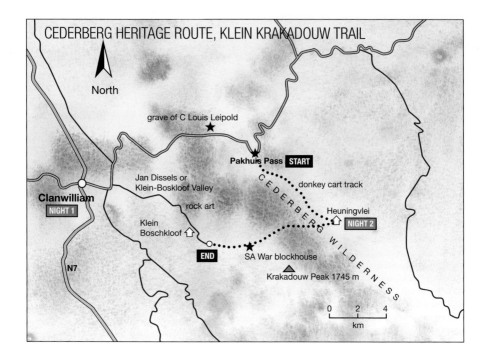

The Cederberg Heritage Route comprises 4 guided, catered and portaged hiking trails through one of South Africa's most spectacular wilderness areas: the 3-night Klein Krakadouw and Pakhuis trails and the 4-night Groot Krakadouw and Wuppertal trails. All start and end in Clanwilliam, one of South Africa's older towns. Hikers enjoy some of the most impressive rock-art sites in southern Africa and traverse some of the most beautiful and botanically diverse sections of the Cape Floristic Region.

The Klein Krakadouw Trail, the most popular of the routes, is described below but various elements, such as visits to rock art sites and the (optional) ride in the donkey cart, are common to all, so the route you choose will depend largely on your fitness and the time you have. Although certainly not a walk in the park, most of the hiking is of only moderate difficulty and, though the paths are often rocky and uneven, you can take it slowly so the trails are suited to those of average fitness and family groups.

The key to enjoying the CHR is to go with realistic expectations. Although accommodation at the beginning and end of the trail is in comfortable guesthouses with en-suite bathrooms, it is not a luxury trail. The community guesthouses are basic (shared rooms and bathrooms and no heating in the winter, for example,) but clean and adequate. Similarly, hikes are led not by accredited guides but by members of the community who have lived in the mountains all their lives and delight in sharing the secrets of the beautiful landscape. It's a fabulous walk, and if you're patient and inquiring you'll gain a wonderful insight into life in these remote Moravian mission-based communities.

▶ DAY 1 Settling in

Clanwilliam, the starting point of the CHR, is a 3-hour drive from Cape Town, and what a beautiful journey it is. Once over the Piekenierskloof Pass the Cederberg mountains were revealed in all their glory – great jagged peaks and deeply eroded gorges that provide a magnificent backdrop to the fields of vines and citrus orchards of the Citrusdal valley that flank the road. Although the mountains are most impressive in golden late afternoon light, we'd decided to arrive in Clanwilliam ahead of the 17h00 'meet and greet' session in order to explore.

Clanwilliam was settled in around 1820 by immigrants mainly from Ireland and is now the centre of a thriving agricultural community as well as a budding tourism centre. We spent a pleasant afternoon wandering between quaint cafés, craft shops and historic buildings. At 17h00 we returned to the Clanwilliam Living Landscape Project premises (where we would leave the car for the duration of the trail) and, after a warm welcome and briefing at which we were handed our permits, we hopped in the vehicle for the short transfer to Klein Boschkloof in the Boskloof valley. (Alternative accommodation is in a very well appointed, 1820s settlers' house in Clanwilliam, The Long House).

▶ DAY 2 Circular rock-art tour

3 KM ◆ 3 HR
(Plus optional hike from Pakhuis Pass to Heuningvlei – 12 KM ◆ 3 HR)

After a hearty breakfast, which included all sorts of local fruits and delicacies, we spent a delightful morning exploring the rock-art sites of the Boskloof valley with a local guide trained up as part of Clanwilliam's Living Landscape Project. The guides have been mentored by some of South Africa's top rock-art specialists such as John Parkington and so are extremely knowledgeable and enthusiastic about the paintings. Our guide bounded from site to site, squatting down to show us ochre-coloured eland, tiny outlines

The Cederberg is one of the best areas in the world to view rock art. Evidence suggests these shelters were inhabited by San people 4 000 years ago.

of fat-tailed sheep and the distinctive depictions of shamans, all the while explaining trance scenes and pressure points.

It was an enchanting, leisurely walk and by the time we'd retraced our steps and driven the short distance to the lunch stop on the Pakhuis Pass at the grave of a famous local doctor and poet, C Louis Leipoldt, we had shaken off the stresses of the city and were enjoying the pace of life in the mountains. We looked around the overhang as we munched our wholesome sandwiches. Leipoldt (1880–1947) trained as a doctor and, after specialising in pediatrics, went on

Sederville Slinger

If you have time to spare, sign up for a short, guided tour of the historical town. The Sederville Slinger is an hour-long walking tour of the major attractions – the Old Gaol Museum, rooibos tea factory, craft shop at the Living Landscape Project and the shoe factory where the famous Strassberger's veldskoens are made.

San (Bushmen) rock art

The Cederberg is one of the best areas in southern Africa to see rock art, with around 2 000 discovered sites, many of which are very well preserved. Evidence from rock-art shelters suggests the San inhabited the Cederberg area from around 4 000 years ago and that Khoi herders introduced domestic stock around 1 800 years ago.

to become the first lecturer in the diseases of children at the University of Cape Town. A highly accomplished man, he was also a passionate botanist and cook, but is perhaps best known for his writing. Leipoldt became a leading poet of the Second Afrikaans Language Movement, writing poetry, drama, travel books, detective stories and books on Cape cookery. He loved the mountains and the 3 peaks at the top of the pass, Faith, Hope and Charity visible from his grave were named by him.

After lunch we were driven to the top of Pakhuis Pass and from there walked a short way down the jeep track to find the donkey carts by the side of the track. The drivers were trying to round up some obstreperous donkeys. Once the beasts had been harnessed our bags were strapped onto the back (and we understood the importance of the instruction in the pre-trip notes to keep weight low and pack everything in soft bags rather than suitcases) and we clambered aboard the old carts. It was clearly going to be a bumpy ride, so we braced ourselves as the driver cracked his whip and set off along the track.

To our right were the spectacular sandstone cliffs of Rocklands, a renowned rock-climbing area where climbers from all over the world come to hone their bouldering skills (climbing on low boulders without ropes). Telltale chalk marks on the craggy boulders suggested recent activity, but we all agreed the routes looked impossible! Once we reached the top of the hill the track levelled out so we took a break to enjoy the magnificent views over towards the Brandwyn River valley, an area, according to the guides, rich in rock-art sites. (We discovered later that the Sevilla Rock Art Trail along the Brandwyn River is the final day's hike on the longer Wuppertal variant of the CHR.) The flower fundi in our midst kindly identified the prolific fynbos species we could see around us, then it was all aboard again.

The remainder of the journey can only be described as exhilarating. The donkey cart is still one of the main forms of transport in the area and the donkeys clearly know the ropes, straining up the hills then chafing at the bit on the descents. We clung on, knuckles white as we bounced up and down on the cushions covering the hard wooden benches, hoping the animals could canter faster than the cart's gathering momentum. At the bottom of each hill the pace would slacken, allowing our thumping hearts to calm down before the next charge. After a couple of hours of this we were exhausted, so it was a relief when we spotted a cluster of white cottages in the distance. 'Heuningvlei', the driver informed us as we raced down the final hill and were met by a gaggle of village kids who had come out to run alongside the carts as we drove into 'town'.

The old mission village of Heuningvlei, nestled under the towering Krakadouw peak, was the end of the road so our luggage was unloaded and Anna Ockhuis welcomed us into her home, one of the community guesthouses that has opened its doors to hikers. Although new to the game, and by no means fluent in English, the villagers have embraced this new venture and what they lack in sophistication they more than make up for in warm hospitality.

There are several very basic, old wood-cutters' huts in the Cederberg Wilderness Area that can be used by hikers, but until the trail was developed there was nothing more comfortable. Now, as we were experiencing, you can hike all day and arrive at a village to find a cup of tea, a wholesome meal and a soft bed. There was plenty of room for our group of 6 in Anna's home, though access to the single bathroom was through one of the bedrooms. But it was of little inconvenience and we were grateful for the warm fire in the kitchen and a hot shower.

Among the principles of the trail is to involve as many local people as possible, so our chefs were other villagers who popped in shortly after our arrival to find out what time we'd like to eat. Dinner was a whole-some affair with meatballs, roast chicken, boerewors, potatoes, macaroni cheese for the vegetarians, vegetables and fresh salad followed by a bread-and-butter pudding. We ate heartily, joking that it would be easy to gain weight on this trail. The very thorough pre-trip notes had warned that there was no alcohol to be had in the mission villages, so we'd secreted some whisky (and a couple

The journey from the top of Pakhuis Pass to Heuningvlei is by donkey cart, still a major form of transport in this remote area.

of wine boxes) in our bags. The liquor was certainly shaken not stirred and we appreci-ated why we'd been urged to decant it into plastic bottles! Before we retired our guide for the following day came by to discuss the programme, then we admired the starlit sky before collapsing into bed.

The hardy hiker

There are no specified (i.e. named or marked) trails within the 75 000 ha Cederberg Wilderness Area but the extensive network of unmarked, but well-preserved, footpaths (largely old woodcutters' paths) make the wilderness a wonderful playground for well-prepared, self-sufficient backpackers. Krakadouw peak – where you can sleep out among the bizarre rock formations and enjoy unbelievably spectacular sunsets – is a wonderful overnight hike, while the challenging but very rewarding traverse from Pakhuis Pass to Tafelberg will take about a week. Permits are available from CapeNature. Apart from a few basic huts there is no accommodation other than that at Algeria, the main campsite (where you can purchase hiking permits) and at the privately owned campsites/chalets at Driehoek, Sanddrif and Cederberg Tourist Park.

▶ DAY 3 Heuningvlei to Boskloof

13 KM ◆ 6 HR

Our chefs duly arrived with the sun, bearing another enormous spread of breads, sausages, eggs, cheese and jams to set us up for the day. After saying fond farewells to Anna we headed up the trail behind the village towards Krakadouw nek. Strong hikers who've signed up for the longer trail have the option of climbing Krakadouw peak. It's a hike I'd thoroughly recommend to peak baggers but it's a tough, full-day climb with some scrambles near the top so we were more than content to skirt the mountain's flanks. We climbed slowly, admiring the views back over Heuningvlei, until we reached a rock shelter with some poorly preserved paintings; apparently it had been inhabited for many years by a local man while he was working on the jeep track to the Pakhuis Pass (the one we'd come down in the donkey carts). Shortly we arrived at the stone hikers' hut at the base of the peak. It was basic to say the least so we were very grateful that we'd chosen the 'slackpacking' approach to Cederberg hiking.

Refreshed by our short break, we filled our water bottles in the stream and headed on up. The path steepened, but was in surprisingly good condition with stone steps and rainwater channels. These paths were constructed some 200 years ago by the woodcutters for their timber-laden donkeys and require very little upkeep. The great walls of the imposing buttress rose above us, punctuating the deep blue sky. At the saddle the exposed, weathered sandstone rocks were a burnt orange – a stunning backdrop to the clusters of purple and pink everlastings. We unpacked our sandwiches and sat on the eroded boulders of the watershed admiring the views in both directions. Not a bad lunch spot, we agreed.

The trail leads past a stone blockhouse that was built during the Anglo-Boer War.

Once over the pass the scenery changed dramatically. We dropped down sharply into a green, vegetated kloof and enjoyed the shade provided by stands of yellowwoods. The contrast was amazing. Half an hour earlier we had been exposed to the baking sun as we hiked over dry, stony ground. Now we were on a muddy path in a moist forest. Our guide cautioned us to watch out for low branches and slippery sections and held out some small plants for us to taste – 'yum yums' he called them – a sweet, refreshing clover. After a couple of hours the gradient eased off and a round fort came into view on the ridge above us.

'The blockhouse was built by the Brits to help defend Clanwilliam from encroaching Boer commandos, when, during the Anglo-Boer War, nearby Calvinia was briefly held by the Boers,' our guide informed us. We'd had no idea the conflict had penetrated so far into this mountainous terrain.

Below us we could see the Boskloof cottages and the end of the trail. We sauntered along a stream, enjoying the sunshine and the yellow daisies. Although we'd climbed about 300 metres then descended some 900 metres to the valley floor, the pace and terrain of the hiking section had not caused our averagely fit group any problems. Our celebratory braai that night, in Klein Boschkloof, a delightful guesthouse on a citrus farm, was under a star-studded sky. It was a perfect end to a magnificent trail.

Other Cape Heritage Route options

Both the 4-night **Wuppertal Trail** and **Groot Krakadouw Trail** also start with a rock-art trail and donkey-cart ride as above. Hikers on the Wuppertal Trail spend 2 nights at Heuningvlei and have the option to summit Krakadouw peak or enjoy a more leisurely hike in the area taking in some rock art, enjoying the floral and geological splendour, and swimming in rock pools before continuing the hike (with an overnight stay in Brugkraal) down to Wuppertal for the final night.

This quaint mission village, the largest in the area, was founded in the early 19th century and is still largely untouched by

Top Tip

Take note of the advice in the pre-trip notes and go 'with an attitude of acceptance'. Remember that revenue from your walking trail is directly helping the local community. The village guest cottages are well kept, but they may not have the bathroom facilities or perhaps the level of comfort that you may be used to on other slackpacking trails.

the 21st century. You'll have time to visit the old attractive Moravian church, the museum and the veldskoen shoe factory before finishing off with the short, but highly informative, Sevilla Rock Art Trail, on the way back to Clanwilliam.

Hikers on the **Groot Krakadouw Trail** complete the rock-art trail in the Boskloof valley on their day of arrival. Then, on the morning of the second day, they take the donkey-cart trip down to Heuningvlei where they have lunch before continuing for a further 8 km on a donkey-cart trail via Witwater village to Brugkraal for their

The Clanwilliam cedar

The Cederberg is incredibly biodiverse, hosting 97 plant families, 409 genera and 1 778 known species including numerous endemics, such the as the famous Clanwilliam cedar, *Widdringtonia cedarbergensis*, from which the Cederberg takes name. You'll see several cedars growing against cliffs and overhangs on the higher reaches of the trail. The Clanwilliam cedar is one of 630 cedar species worldwide, of which only 3 occur in South Africa. It's listed in the South African Red Data Book as 'vulnerable' and has also been shortlisted by the IUCN as a species worthy of protection.

The Clanwilliam cedar was once prolific in these mountains but intensive harvesting for timber, grazing by domestic livestock and changes to the fire regime have led to its decline. The durable and fragrant wood of the tree was used for furniture, coffins, fence and telephone poles – the telephone line from Piketberg to Calvinia for example used around 7 000 cedar poles. No wonder it's in need of protection.

second night. They then hike back up via Grasvlei and the Boontjieskloof Hut to Heuningvlei. There they overnight before completing the section over the Krakadouw Nek and down the Krakadouw Pass to the guesthouse in the Boskloof valley for the final night, the same as for the final day on the Klein Krakadouw Trail.

The 3-night **Pakhuis Trail** is almost the Klein Krakadouw trail in reverse – but with some extra hiking thrown in! Hikers have lunch at the Yellow Aloe Nursery on the day of arrival followed by a tour of the Ou Tronk (old jail) Museum and the rock-art sites of the Boskloof valley before overnighting in Clanwilliam. Day 2 consists of a 17 km, largely contouring or downhill, hike from the top of the Pakhuis Pass to Krakadouw Cottages while day 3 is a hike over Krakadouw Pass and down to Heuningvlei. On the final day you have the option of taking the donkey cart or hiking up from Heuningvlei to the top of the Pakhuis Pass.

In a nutshell · Cederberg Heritage Route

BOOKINGS Cedarberg African Travel, 027-482-2444, info@cedarberg.co.za, www.cedheroute.co.za.

START/FINISH Clanwilliam.

TRANSFERS Transfers from Cape Town can be organised on request.

HIGHLIGHTS The sense of wilderness; spectacular rock formations; some of the best preserved San rock paintings to be found; magnificent displays of spring flowers; the opportunity to stay with, and learn about, the hospitable local communities.

LONGEST DAY 13 km.

SHORTEST DAY 3 km.

GROUP SIZE Minimum 2, maximum 12.

UP TO IT? This is a very straightforward mountain trail, but the paths on the top of the mountain are uneven. The path down is steep in places and can be slippery after rain so good footwear is important.

DON'T FORGET! Waterproof hiking gear, day pack, camera, bird/plant guides, binoculars, your favourite tipple, snacks.

STYLE Well-guided, amply catered hike, staying in comfortable B&Bs and basic community guesthouses with linen provided.

WHEN TO GO The trail can be hiked year round but spring (August–November) is wonderful as the weather is at its most predictable and the flowers are at their best. Autumn (April/May) is also a good time. Summers are hot and dry.

The Cape experiences winter rainfall so it can be very wet during June and July, but if you're prepared to take the risk, these months are cool and pleasant for hiking.

BEFORE AND AFTER For options on where to stay and what to do before and after the trail, contact Cedarberg African Travel or Clanwilliam Tourism Info, 027-482-2024, cederberg@lando.co.za, www.clanwilliam.info. Try to factor in a couple of extra days to visit 2 of the most spectacular rock formations in the Cederberg (both close to Sanddrif) the Wolfberg Arch and Maltese Cross.

LOOK IT UP Peter Slingsby's 'the map' of the Cederberg.

4

Five Bay Trail

Western Cape

DISTANCE 32 km ◆ **DURATION** 2½ days ◆ **DIFFICULTY** 3 ◆ **TRAIL TYPE** Beach, dunes and fynbos
LOGISTICS Guided and catered ◆ **ACCOMMODATION TYPE** Luxury guesthouses
COST RRRR ◆ **AREA** West coast

This trail is a leisurely saunter along the coast between Paternoster and Saldanha bays. The area is known for its spectacular wild flowers, crayfish and fossils, with the central focus being the history and heritage of fishing and seafood gathering through the ages. Hikers will see artefacts left by San hunter-gatherers, later Khoi herders and modern-day fishing communities along the way and within the Cape Columbine Nature Reserve: stone tools, bones, shells and pottery tell of successive waves of hunter-gatherers and then pastoralists who used the coast to gather seafood. If you're a beach lover with a sense of history this trail is a winner.

The, guided, fully catered, 2½ day trail takes hikers southwards along one of the most scenic sections of the west coast from the traditional fishing village of Paternoster south to Jacobsbaai just north of Saldanha. The guides are drawn from these communities so it's very much a journey through time on which hikers learn about the ancient as well as the contemporary local fishing culture while enjoying outstanding accommodation and cuisine in Paternoster each night.

▶ **DAY 1** Tweemosselbank to Paternoster

4 KM ♦ 1.5 HR

This trail is ideally suited to busy people needing a 'power break': we arrived late on a Friday afternoon and, after a welcome at our luxury guesthouse in Paternoster, hopped into our guide's off-road vehicle (an old Landy used for trek fishing) and set off along the back of the dunes to Tweemosselbank for a sunset walk on Paternoster beach. It was great to stretch our legs and smell the sea air and we soon shook off the worries of the working week and slipped into holiday mode – there is something invigorating about walking barefoot on a long sandy beach and we soon understood why recreational aficionados escape to the west coast when they are in need of space and silence.

As we walked our guide, a local fisherman who had grown up in Paternoster and had fished these waters all his life, entertained us with fishing lore and local stories. We learnt about the relationship he had with the ocean, how reliant his community is on the sea for both income and food and got a sense of the skill it requires to reap a good shoal using the old trek-netting technique. Just off the beach were vast mussel banks and we walked past some pipes sticking out of the sea that fed the oyster farm just over the dunes – a land of plenty if you knew its secrets.

After a brief stop at a big outcrop of granite boulders to take in the scene, we meandered back. The quaint whitewashed buildings of Paternoster lit up as evening approached and we entered the village, washed clean of city dwelling and ready to experience an amazing 3-course meal of

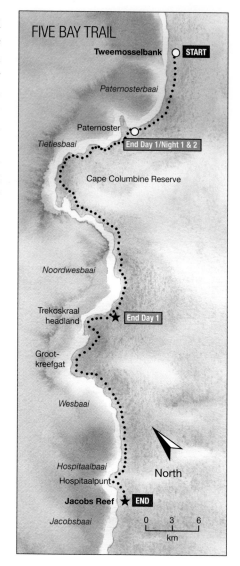

FIVE BAY TRAIL

Tweemosselbank ○ START
Paternosterbaai
Paternoster ○
Tietiesbaai End Day 1/Night 1 & 2
Cape Columbine Reserve
Noordwesbaai
Trekoskraal headland ★ End Day 1
Groot-kreefgat
Wesbaai
North
Hospitaalbaai
Hospitaalpunt
Jacobs Reef ★ END
Jacobsbaai

0 3 6
km

Great granite boulders, long empty beaches and solitude are a highlight of the Five Bay Trail.

local cuisine washed down with some fine wines from the nearby Darling area.

► DAY 2 Paternoster to Trekoskraal

15 KM ◆ 5 HR

We had chosen to start our day with a stroll rather than breakfast at the guesthouse, so picked up our packed meals before setting off along the beach again past the beachfront houses and the charming Voorstrand Restaurant. Paternoster has a wonderfully laid-back feel and the uniform white-washed fishermen's cottages retain the charm of yesteryear here. One of the highlights of this trail is the varying coastal topography and the changing natural vegetation you encounter on the granitic, limestone, sand and clay soils. Granite outcrops dominated the landscape and the crystals in the massive boulders glistened in the sunlight.

The sky was blue and the sea so calm we joked that it felt like we were in Seychelles and not in the 'stormy' Cape. But the colourful local fishing boats pulled up on the

sand and the crayfish factory reminded us that we were indeed on the west coast. Before long we were in the Cape Columbine reserve, one of South Africa's little-known gems, following a sandy path past vast towering boulders covered with lichens, great littoral gullies full of kelp and mussels and along little bays where it was tempting to stop and swim.

A wooden head perched on top of a high boulder caught my eye – and soon a rustic camp came into view. The Beach Camp, where we stopped to say hello to owner Sonya and her team, enjoys an idyllic setting opposite a vegetated outcrop of land that is an island at high tide and offers a range of activities, including sea kayaking and guided floral tours and is a very popular backpacker destination.

The coast gets very rugged from this point on and the campsites are separated by deep steep-walled gullies and densely vegetated patches. If you feel like scrambling and bundu bashing you can stay close to the coast, otherwise it's easier to follow

Sadly, as fishing has declined, many of the buildings in the remoter areas of the coast have become derelict.

the dirt road slightly inland. We opted for the latter, so after breakfast on the rocks strolled slowly through the magnificent reserve checking out birds such as herons and sacred ibises, tortoises, wonderful vygies and other wild flowers, and spying fishing boats out at sea.

Our guide pointed out various shell middens en route. They are the domestic waste dumps of people who lived in the area in prehistoric times where, over many years, a phenomenal amount of shell fish was eaten. They are important achaeological sites and when excavated reveal bones, stone

The west coast is famous for its beautiful wild flowers.

tools, shells and pottery that tell of successive waves of hunter-gatherer strandlopers and then pastoralists who came to the west coast to gather seafood.

Soon we came to the main beach in the reserve, the beautiful golden crescent of Tietiesbaai – look at the granite mounds and you can easily guess the origin of the name! In the holiday season this beach is packed with tents but in the week, and out of season, it's a peaceful place to chill out and swim.

Cape Columbine lighthouse dominates the granite outcrop known as Castle Rock, behind the beach. The last manned lighthouse on the South African coast, and usually the first South African lighthouse seen by ships coming from Europe and South America, its design – a tapered, square-based tower with heavy buttresses on the 4 corners – differs markedly from the conventional round tower of most lighthouses. Cape Columbine, commissioned in 1936 and named after the *Columbine*, which was wrecked about 1.5 km to the north in

1829, was the first lighthouse to receive all 3 navigational safety features, i.e. a light, a fog signal and a radio beacon. The optical apparatus, supplied by Messrs Chance Brothers, was the first lens system designed for use with a 4 kW incandescent electric lamp on the South African coast. All prior installations had been designed for wick or petroleum vapour burners.

The boundary of the Cape Columbine reserve is not far beyond the beach, but the coastal footpath continues through the strandveld fynbos onto private land, past more gullies and little beaches covered with mussel shells. A big gully with enticing swells proved irresistible and we jumped into the water halfway along and rode the surge of the incoming tide past the streaming kelp, before drying off and tucking into our sandwiches.

Thereafter we passed Varswaterbaai, the source of fresh water for Paternoster in days gone by, then strolled along the beach (the alternative option is to explore the tranquil tracks behind the vegetated dunes) stopping to swim at bay number 2, Noordwesbaai. Just as we were tiring from walking along the sand we arrived at a simple shelter at Trekoskraal where, after a welcome cool drink, we jumped into the vehicle for the short journey back to Paternoster. After freshening up, we sat around the braai enjoying local delicacies and learning more about this fascinating and surprisingly isolated stretch of coast.

▶ DAY 3 Trekoskraal to Jacobsbaai

13 KM ◆ 4 HR

After morning coffee, we grabbed our day packs and were transferred back to Trekoskraal. The pre-breakfast stroll took us around the Trekoskraal headland, past rustic beach shelters, Groot Kreefgat (big

The trail ends at Jacobsbaai, where you can celebrate with a drink at the beachside hotel.

crayfish hole) and granite boulders surrounded by delicate flowers. Our guide stressed the importance of this habitat – apparently only a tiny fraction of South Africa's granite and limestone fynbos is conserved, so we enjoyed learning about some of the main plant species: the botterboom, an indicator species of healthy granite sandplain fynbos, and the endemic orange bokborri vygie. As we walked he pointed out other common plants such as the dune pumpkin, which sports tiny silver hairs on the leaves, dune spinach which, we learned, is closely related to the New Zealand spinach, soutslaai (salt salad) and brown sage, which the local people use to flavour fish. At his bidding we tasted sea lettuce (*Sarcoconia* sp) which I recognised as a delicacy I'd once enjoyed while holidaying on the south coast of England.

After an hour and a half we stopped for breakfast then explored the cliffs, dunes and wave-scoured beaches of Wesbaai, bay number 3. Amazingly, we spotted turtle tracks in the sand as we wandered up to inspect the clay conglomerates and limestone cliffs, which were riddled with nesting holes.

From here we were offered a choice of route: along the beach or the coastal path on the top of the cliffs. We opted for the latter, enjoying the high vantage and the fynbos. Just before we reached the attractive holiday homes of Swartriet we descended again and traversed our fourth bay, the tiny Hospitaal-baai where, in the mid- to late 1800s, ships stopped to drop off the sick to be quarantined before they reached Cape Town. Once past the little island-like rocky outcrop of Jacob's Reef – which had been our 'end of trail' marker for the day – it was only a short walk to our final bay, Jacobsbaai, where we enjoyed a picnic on the shore. The trail had seemed much longer than just 2½ days – in that short time we had learnt so much about the culture of the west coast.

In a nutshell · Five Bay Trail

BOOKINGS Cape West Coast Biosphere Reserve 022-492-2750 (weekday office hours), info@capebiosphere. co.za, http://cwcbr-trails.blogspot.com.
START/FINISH Paternoster/Jacobsbaai.
TRANSFERS Transfers from the end of the trail back to the start are included in the package. Transfers to and from Cape Town can be organised on request.
HIGHLIGHTS The unique and diverse habitats of Cape Columbine and the west coast; the charming village of Paternoster and its excellent range of accommodation and gourmet options; the fascinating culture of the west coast.
LONGEST DAY 15 km.
SHORTEST DAY 4 km.
GROUP SIZE Minimum 2, maximum 8.
UP TO IT? Although flat, the trail is largely along the beach, jeep tracks or sandy paths, which can be quite tiring. But you stop often to explore the rocks and the tidal pools, to swim and to enjoy the flowers and the fishing lore so it's suitable for hikers of all ages and fitness levels.
DON'T FORGET! Waterproof hiking gear, swimming costume and kikoi, day pack, camera and binoculars. Light shoes or sandals are ideal footwear.
WHEN TO GO The trail can be hiked year round but spring (August–November) is wonderful as the weather is at its most predictable and the flowers are at their best. Autumn (April/May) is also a good time but winters can be a bit chilly – particularly for swimming.
BEFORE AND AFTER Paternoster has lots of accommodation to suit all budgets.
LOOK IT UP A map of the trail is available from the organisers.

Survival Notes

- Drinking water not available on the trail, except at Tietiesbaai (day 2).
- Wine is included with the meals.

5

Eve's Trail

Western Cape

DISTANCE 30 km ◆ **DURATION** 2 ½ days ◆ **DIFFICULTY** 3 ◆ **TRAIL TYPE** Beach, dunes and fynbos
LOGISTICS Bags driven around ◆ **ACCOMMODATION TYPE** Luxury manor house and chalets
COST RRRR ◆ **AREA** West coast

The Western Cape coast should be as famous for its fossils as it is for its spring flowers: it is the unique paleoanthropology of the West Coast National Park and the surrounding area that is the focus of Eve's Trail – though of course the landscape that you walk through is spectacular. This easy trail starts on the dunes of Elandsfontein Private Nature Reserve and ends at a viewpoint overlooking the Langebaan Lagoon in the West Coast National Park.

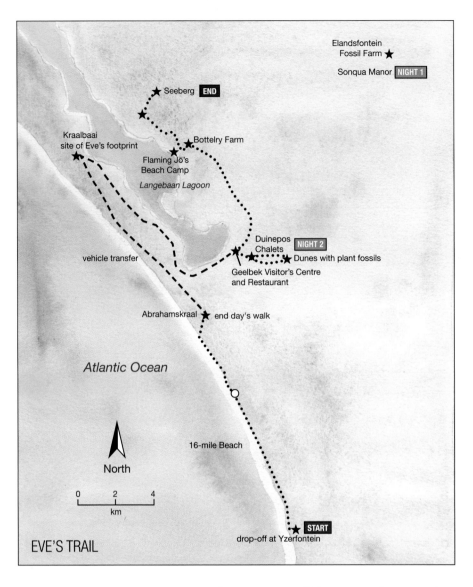

Elandsfontein
Fossil Farm ★

Sonqua Manor **NIGHT 1**

★ Seeberg **END**

★

Kraalbaai
site of Eve's footprint
★   ★ Bottelry Farm
Flaming Jo's ★
Beach Camp
Langebaan Lagoon

Duinepos
Chalets **NIGHT 2**
vehicle transfer   ★ ★••••••★ Dunes with plant fossils
Geelbek Visitor's Centre
and Restaurant

Abrahamskraal ★ end day's walk

Atlantic Ocean

North

0   2   4
km

16-mile Beach

★ **START**
drop-off at Yzerfontein

EVE'S TRAIL

After exploring the fossils on the magnificent dune fields of a private nature reserve you walk from Yzerfontein into the rarely visited southern section of the national park, through a stretch of pristine strandveld, onto rolling dunes and along the shores of the Langebaan Lagoon before ending on a high, quite literally, at a magnificent viewpoint on a granite mound. Along the way you have plenty of opportunities to swim in the Atlantic Ocean and in the

lagoon, you'll learn about the unique flora and the medicinal uses of common plants, likely see tortoises, ostriches and various types of antelope, view the migrant wader species, herons and other water birds that the lagoon supports and enjoy west coast hospitality at its best.

If you are someone who enjoys beautiful scenery, good food, fine wine and a truly fascinating interpretive experience, this is the trail for you.

This easy 2½-day, 30 km trail starts on the dunes of Elandsfontein Private Nature Reserve and ends at a viewpoint overlooking the Langebaan Lagoon in the West Coast National Park. Although guided by the local community members, it is very much a luxury trail. The first night is spent in the 5-star Sonqua Manor on the reserve and the second in cute, very comfortable 3-star chalets in the national park. Trailists follow in the footsteps of 'Eve' (from who some scientists suggest that all human life has descended), learning about the plants, animals and people that once inhabited this stretch of coast.

▶ DAY 1 Quad bike tour and game drive on Elandsfontein Private Nature Reserve

3 HR

The transfer from our secure parking to Sonqua Manor on the Elandsfontein Private Nature Reserve was enlivened by sightings of antelope, some wonderful agama lizards and rare flowers. The members of staff were all outside clapping and singing a welcome as we drove up to the lodge, by far the larniest accommodation available on any of the slackpacking trails featured in this book.

After settling in and enjoying a dip in the magnificent pool, it was time for high tea – a sumptuous spread that was a mere small taste of things to come (be warned, this trail is not for those on diet) before we jumped back into the vehicle again for a game drive. After half an hour or so, which included a stop to enjoy a large herd of eland (the 6 000 ha estate is well stocked with plains game, including zebra, kudu, African buffalo, duiker and gemsbok) we transferred onto eco-friendly quad bikes, and, after a short lesson and a strict eco-briefing to stay on the tracks, headed into

the sand dunes stopping at different sites to explore some of the fossils that have been uncovered by the wind.

'The fossils are still being studied by UCT scientists,' explained our guide, 'so we don't know a huge amount about them yet – but they have identified the fossilised remains of some extinct mammals such as the 3-toed horse and short-necked giraffe that are millions of years old.' While we hunted around discovering bits of bone and stone tools on the golden dunes, he explained the process of fossilisation and the way the landscape constantly changes as the wind scours and covers the sites. It was a wonderfully orchestrated tour, combining both the adrenalin of the quad bike adventure and a fascinating introduction to the extensive fossil record of the west coast. The game drive continued, with sundowners en route, until we arrived back at the lodge to be welcomed (again) with cold towels.

Sonqua Manor is simply divine. Built as a private family retreat, it is ultra-exclusive

Fossilised bones are often exposed by the wind in the dunes at Elandsfontein Private Nature Reserve.

yet manages to achieve a wonderful home-from-home feel where you can really relax and unwind. The 3 bedrooms and the honeymoon suite all have far-reaching extensive views over the fynbos. They're exquisitely decorated and equipped with all mod cons and the attention to detail shows in everything from the top-class toiletries to the little pot of honey that rested, with a bead-wrapped bed-time snack, on the pillow at night. But what really makes this place is the ever-smiling, passionate and professional staff, nothing is too much trouble and they anticipate your every need, making you feel like a king or queen.

By the time we emerged from our rooms for pre-dinner drinks a big fire was burning outside, so we toasted a great day with local wines and some tasty snacks before moving to the dinner table. Papa Wemba, appropriately decked out in his chef's uniform and hat, presented the menu, a magnificent 3-course meal that would have impressed any gourmand, before we retired to our rooms, enjoyed the twinkling stars from the deck then slept with the doors ajar.

▶ DAY 2 Yzerfontein to Abrahamskraal

16 KM ◆ 5–6 HR

We woke to the sound of birdsong and were soon out on the terrace enjoying the peace and the incredible views over the fynbos. The 'light breakfast' indicated on our itinerary turned out to be another 3-course affair – stewed apple and muesli, eggs Benedict and orange crêpes for 'dessert' so we were feeling replete and very sorry to leave this idyllic place when we were transferred to Yzerfontein for the start of the day's hike.

We had our binoculars out as we approached the trail head, having spotted flamingoes and other waders in the lagoon behind the beach. Our local guide Eddie met us at the parking area behind the open-air seafood restaurant and led us over the dunes onto 16-mile Beach. We kicked off our shoes and followed him, noting the disturbing amount of litter washed up on the beach. 'Coast Care does its best to clean up the beaches, but so much gets washed up that removing the waste is an on-going battle. And it can kill the wildlife,' the guide informed us, pointing out pellets of raw plastics, which the sea birds often eat.

Soon we were within the boundary of the West Coast National Park, hiking over big banks of black mussel shells. 'You find lots of white mussels too,' he said. 'They move in and out with the tide to collect the nutrients.' Some sections of sand looked as if they were covered with molehills and by way of explanation the guide dug into the sand and extracted a sea louse, a *tolbos*, from its burrow. Judging by the amount of disturbance there were great colonies of lice down there.

We continued along the beach looking at the shells, crabs and some weird, worm-infested kelp, stopping occasionally to swim in the cold water. A sea gull entertained by repeatedly swooping up high and dropping a shell, which it was clearly trying to smash, and we identified 3 types of cormorant and,

You're thoroughly spoilt on Eve's Trail – the accommodation at Sonqua Manor is 5-star.

bizarrely, an ibis. After a couple of hours we stopped for lunch – a tasty, wholesome meal of home-made bread sandwiches, flapjacks and fresh fruit all beautifully wrapped and tied up with the Elandsfontein trademark beads, then headed up the dunes. The view from the top is magnificent. To the south is the quaint village of Yzerfontein, while to the north we could see the wreck of the *Pantelis A Lemos* and beyond that the granite hills of Postberg. The trail now followed a sandy track along the dune ridge and back of the dune, with great views over fynbos, the coastal plains and the exposed golden sand dunes deep within the park.

We stopped often to learn about the strandveld vegetation: the melkellie – the fruit of which looks like a fig when cut open; the pyjama bush with its silver-green leaves and trumpet-shaped flowers; wild rosemary; and the hiker's nightmare; the wild asparagus; or *wag-'n-bietjie*, the spines of which inflict wicked scratches and can tear your clothing. Apparently the young shoots can be eaten, like commercially grown asparagus, with butter, lemon juice, salt and pepper, while the red berries are used to treat lung conditions such as TB, and bladder and kidney ailments. After another half hour we came across some interpretive boards indicating that we were now out of the remote, unmarked section of the park and on the Strandveld Hiking Trail.

The tortoise bush or *skilpadbessie* is a 'veld snack' the board suggested. And, sure enough, the red berries were quite tasty. A tangled, gnarled and prickly euphorbia, Medusa's head, sprawled along the path contrasting with the beautiful flowers of the *eland vye* (sour fig). We learnt about the other common species such as the bitou, which is also laden with edible berries in early spring, brown sage, which is apparently used to treat asthma, pig's ear, which

Lunch on day 2 of the trail is on the beach, then you head up the dunes and into the strandveld.

can be ground into a poultice to put on corns, and the 'toilet paper bush', *brandbos*. The early inhabitants of these areas certainly knew how to live off the land and yet again we appreciated the journey through time that we were experiencing.

We were met at Abrahamskraal, a picturesque self-catering cottage next to a waterhole, and after refreshing drinks and a snack we were driven the short distance to Kraalbaai, enjoying sightings of ostrich and kudu en route. The West Coast National Park is well stocked with plain game so eland, bontebok and zebra are also often sighted from the road. The drive was incredibly scenic: to our left were fynbos-covered plains and the Atlantic Ocean, while on our right we could see across the lagoon to the great granite mound of Seeberg where we would end our trail. Soon the magnificent crescent of Kraalbaai came into view. I've seen this view countless times but the granite backdrop of the Postberg mountain, the houseboats and the clear blue water of the Langebaan Lagoon always takes my breath away.

From the car park we could see the white homestead of Geelbek, the salt marshes and the bird hides across the la-

Disappointingly, the site where Eve's footprints were discovered in Kraalbaai is simply an uninspiring cement block. But the natural scenery of the bay is impressive.

goon. 'The park has 32 per cent of South Africa's salt marshes,' explained the guide. 'They're incredibly fragile so are completely off limits; if you were to walk in them your footprint would still be visible 2 years later.' We walked down steps to the beach and along the white sands to a big free-standing rock slab of consolidated sand. On the far side of it is a big cement block indicating the inauspicious site where, in 1995, Dr Dave Roberts of the Council for Geoscience discovered the fossilised human footprints of 'Eve'.

Evidence from Kraalbaai suggests that sea levels were 2 metres higher than at present so, using a dating technique called luminescence, Roberts surmised that 'Eve's footprints' (as they were termed) were made during a warm period some 120 000 years old. The footprints themselves were removed from the site to ensure their preservation and are now in the Iziko SA Museum in Cape Town. Walking in the footsteps of Eve, we were reminded of what life must have been like for this early hominid as she gathered food near the Langebaan Lagoon.

The fragile dunes near Duinepos contain exposed plant fossils so can only be explored with a guide.

The warm, shallow water of the lagoon was a pleasant change from the icy Atlantic, so we enjoyed a final swim before the transfer to Duinepos Chalets, our home for the night. The lovely, community-run guesthouse consists of 11 2-bedroomed, fully equipped chalets clustered around a

What's so exciting about some footprints?

Best current theory suggests that all modern human life – marking the emergence of *Homo sapiens* – is descended from 1 common female ancestor, known as Genetic Eve. We do not know absolutely whether the prints are hers (the chances of that are incalculably small), but experts say they were made at the right time and place to fit her profile.

Rick Gore, the senior assistant editor of *National Geographic*, who first wrote up the story of the finding of these footprints, ended the article with the following words:

'We cover the prints with sand and head back down the beach. I turn and conjure a parting image of that lone figure standing atop the dune, hair blowing in the breeze, dark skin aglow in the sunset. In my mind she will forever be Eve. I know that's romantic, but I'm a modern human, and I need my symbols and stories to make sense of this world. I imagine her taking that first step down the dune. It's a small and tentative step, latent with curiosity and 117 000 years later we still don't know where it will ultimately lead.'

Geelbek restaurant is housed in a magnificent Old Cape building that dates back to the 18th century.

central swimming pool and braai area. After a swim and a shower, we were treated to a traditional fish braai of snoek, prepared by Eddie Papier, one of the park rangers, and accompanied by salads, sweet potato and local wines.

A good place to just sit

Langebaan is the most important stretch of water (although it's commonly called a lagoon, it is really a very long and narrow sea inlet) in southern Africa in terms of the population of migratory wading birds from the northern hemisphere that congregates to feed there in our southern summer. Consequently it is the best place to sit with your binoculars in one of the hides admiring colourful flamingoes, pelicans and numerous migrant birds – most numerous by far of which are the curlew sandpipers.

▶ DAY 3 Duinepos to Seeberg

14 KM ◆ 4–5 HR

After a cup of coffee we set off on a pre-breakfast walk up the Dawid Bester Trail – another interpretive trail with fascinating boards about the vegetation – to the dunes behind Duinepos. This fragile site, with its exposed plant fossils from an ancient marsh, can be explored only with a guide and we felt very privileged to be wandering among such treasures high up on the golden dunes in the beautiful morning light.

It was hard to tear ourselves away – we could have spent hours exploring the extensive dune field and enjoying the views, but breakfast waited so we hiked down to Geelbek Visitors' Centre and Restaurant. The restaurant, housed in a fabulous Old Cape building dating back to 1744, has an extensive breakfast and lunch menu, which includes hearty portions of freshly made, traditional west coast food (as well as a great selection of local wines which we didn't have time to sample!).

After breakfast we wandered across to the adjacent information centre where a replica of Eve's footprints is on view, along with some informative displays about the ecology of this very understated park. We then set out on the road to the salt marsh. 'Eland were grazing around Geelbek last night,' our guide pointed out, as he noticed the spoor in the soft sand. 'We often see them late in the evening or in the early morning.' A flurry of activity overhead drew our attention, and we soon spotted herons nesting high in some blue gums beside the road.

We followed the sandy track, once the road from Cape Town to Langebaan and Saldanha, past the salt marsh and the old Bottlery farmstead before stopping for a welcome swim at in the lagoon at Flaming Jo's Beach Camp. The lagoon is home to the largest oyster fossil cemetery in the world, we were informed, so we kept searching the rocks for fossilised oyster shells and remains exposed by the outgoing tide, then followed the beach around a rocky head-

The trail ends on the granite mound of Seeberg, a wonderful vantage point.

land before heading up the granite mound of Seeberg, the highest point in the park.

The view from the top over the park and the Langebaan Lagoon was incredible

Cape West Coast Biosphere Reserve

Biosphere reserves are regions with beautiful landscapes, an abundance of fauna and flora and unique cultures where a balance between development and the natural surroundings are recognised and promoted.

All biosphere reserves have 3 basic functions: to conserve the natural resources, biodiversity and landscapes of the local culture; to protect social and economic progress without damaging or depleting the natural resources; and to promote education, investigation and permanent observation related to environmental and natural resource conservation.

There are currently 6 proclaimed and designated biosphere reserves in South Africa namely the Cape West Coast – Kogelberg, Vhembe, Waterberg and the Kruger to Canyons Biosphere Reserve – of 507 biosphere reserves worldwide. The Cape West Coast Biosphere Reserve (one of the few in the world that was driven by the local communities living within the region rather than a state driven initiative) was designated under UNESCO's Man and the Biosphere Programme in 2001. It stretches northward from the Diep River to the Berg River, covering approximately 378 000 hectares of coastal lowlands and marine environments.

and a surprise waited. The historic and usually empty cottage on the summit had been swept clean and lit with candles, the sparkling wine was on ice and a sumptuous picnic lunch was laid out on a white cloth. There was even a basin in which to freshen up and a mirror to check that we'd be looking good for our final feast.

All that remained was the transfer back to Elandsfontein to fetch our cars, and again we were sad to leave. Though refreshed and invigorated by the trail, we were only beginning to understand the importance of this little corner of the Cape West Coast Biosphere Reserve and could have lingered longer in this unique place.

In a nutshell · Eve's Trail

BOOKINGS Cape West Coast Biosphere Reserve 022-492-2750 (weekday office hours), info@capebiosphere.co.za, http://cwcbr-trails.blogspot.com.

START/FINISH Elandsfontein Private Nature Reserve / West Coast National Park.

TRANSFERS Transfers from the end of the trail back to the start are included in the package. Transfers to and from Cape Town can be organised on request.

HIGHLIGHTS The unique and diverse habitats of the Langebaan Lagoon and West Coast National Park; swimming in the warm waters of the lagoon; exceptional hospitality and guiding; topnotch accommodation and gourmet food; incredible birding.

LONGEST DAY 16 km.

SHORTEST DAY 14 km.

GROUP SIZE Minimum 2, maximum 8.

UP TO IT? This is a very flat, straightforward trail, largely along the beach, jeep tracks or sandy paths so it's suitable for hikers of all ages and fitness levels.

DON'T FORGET! Waterproof hiking gear, swimming costume and kikoi, day pack, camera, binoculars, bird book. Crocs or sandals are the ideal footwear.

WHEN TO GO The trail can be hiked year round but spring (August–November) is wonderful as the weather is at its most predictable and the flowers are at their best. Autumn (April/May) is also a good time.

BEFORE AND AFTER Hikers wishing to extend their stay can book into Sonqua Manor (www.elandsfontein.co.za), Duinepos Chalets (www.duinepos.co.za) and the other accommodation in the national park (the self-catering Abrahamskraal cottage, Jo-Anne's Beach Cottage and the 2 houseboats at Kraalbaai) www.sanparks.org and there are a few upmarket cottages to rent www.perfecthideaways.co.za.

LOOK IT UP A map of the trail is available from the organisers.

Survival Notes

- Drinking water not available on the trail.
- Wine is included with the meals.

6

Darling Stagger

Western Cape

DISTANCE 30 km ◆ **DURATION** 2½ days ◆ **DIFFICULTY** 3 ◆ **TRAIL TYPE** Farmland, gravel and sandy tracks ◆ **LOGISTICS** Guided and catered ◆ **ACCOMMODATION TYPE** Luxury lodge and rustic cottages ◆ **COST** RRRR ◆ **AREA** Swartland

This new trail starts in Darling, known for its annual wild flower show and as the home of Pieter-Dirk Uys's Evita se Peron. It's a beautiful walk over rolling hills and through the olive groves, vineyards and fynbos of the coastal plain north of Cape Town. It is led by one of the guides from the !Kwha ttu San Cultural and Educational Centre, so it's also a cultural experience. The hospitality and guiding are superb, with specialist guides from the various farms enlightening you about the olive and wine industries as you traverse their properties, so by the time you reach the end you have a real feeling for the biodiversity and rich heritage of the region.

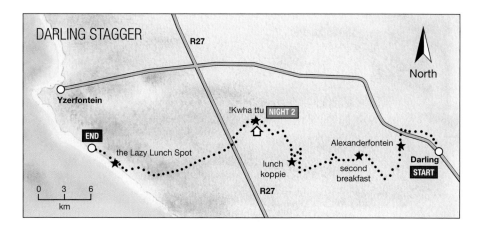

This 2½ day, 25 km guided trail begins with a wine tasting and overnight stay in the sleepy town of Darling, tucked away between hills of vineyards and golden wheat fields of the Cape West Coast Biosphere Reserve and ends at the coast in Yzerfontein. Along the way you taste olives, sample the fruits of the vine, meander through renosterveld and fynbos full of game and birds, as well as flowers most of the year. At the San Cultural Centre at !Khwa ttu overnight spot you learn about the San people and the opportunities and challenges that they face. The finer details of the trail were still being finalised when this book went to print so there may be minor changes to the itinerary, but the overall experience will be much

The overnight accommodation at the San Cultural Centre at !Kwha ttu is in rustic cottages.

the same. As the name suggests, this is not intended as an endurance event: you take it slowly, stopping to smell the flowers and to enjoy good food and fine wine.

▶ NIGHT 1 Settling in

We arrived in Darling mid-afternoon and installed ourselves in Darling Lodge – a tranquil guesthouse with carefully decorated rooms complete with big, old-fashioned en-suite bathrooms, a swimming pool and lush garden – before going for a wander around town. The old quarter of Darling is quaint and we spent time photographing the church and checking out the local architecture, art and the book shop before returning to the lodge to freshen up before dinner in a local restaurant. There was no show at Darling Station, the 'Peron', on the night we were there; when there is, hikers are offered the chance to dine there as they enjoy the evening performance.

▶ DAY 1 Darling to !Kwha ttu

15 KM ◆ 6 HR

After strong coffee and a light breakfast of fresh fruit and homemade muffins, we wandered up through the vineyards of Ormonde estate to Alexanderfontein for

A highlight of the trail is a visit to a reconstruction of a San village where the guides explain the traditions of San and Khoi societies.

tasting sessions. And what a tasting it was. Despite the early hour, once we heard how special the wines were (there are only 1 000 bottles of white and the same number of reds produced each year exclusively for cellar sales) we couldn't resist sampling them as we learnt about the wine and olive growing on the farm (a dry-land farm where there is no irrigation) and tried the various olives, pastes, jams and even olive chocolate.

Accompanied by our guide from !Khwa ttu and Willem Rheeder, the farm manager, we set of across the hilly land. It was a privilege to walk across such a beautiful, well-managed farm. In keeping with the Biodiversity and Wine Initiative to which Alexanderfontein subscribes, chemical use is kept to an absolute minimum. A nostalgic touch is that horses are still used to round up the sheep and cattle!

From the top of the highest hill we could see how the soil changed from the sandy soil of the lower slopes to a deep red Hutton soil that Willem explained was perfect for dryland farming. Around us was a patchwork

of different vineyard blocks and we learnt that the redder vines were Merlot, Chardonnay grapes produced the dark green fields, while the lighter greens were Sauvignon Blanc. The excellent terroir ensures the production of high quality wine grapes, which Willem proudly announced are sold to the top winemakers at selected farms such as Graham Beck. Our guide, a trained tracker, added another dimension, pointing out and explaining the spoor of tortoise, small antelope, caracal and various birds.

We staggered on up hill and down dale enjoying the beautiful views of Table Mountain, Dassen Island and the Atlantic Ocean and gleaning more information about the olive and local farming industry before stopping for lunch on a granite outcrop. It was a magnificent feast of farm products: fresh bread, olive pastes, Lubneh Makbus cheese and ham, which we wolfed down as Willem explained the on-going conflict between agricultural and biodiversity needs. 'The dominant vegetation type is Swartland granite renosterveld, which is unique to this Cape Floral Region,' he told us. 'But only 0.02 per cent of the ecosystem is conserved as these soils are incredibly rich in nutrients so are ideal for agriculture. The national government is supposed to conserve 10 per cent of each ecosystem, so creating biodiversity corridors along the ridges of the hills is a conservation priority. The Cape West Coast Biosphere Reserve is working with the farmers to create these corridors and buffer zones in order to ensure the survival of the rare flora and fauna. If the predictions of future climate change are realised, they will be driven to the higher altitudes if they are to survive. So we are trying to reconcile these goals with our commercial needs.'

We stopped to pick up porcupine quills and peer down burrows; to watch raptors and a grey heron; to learn about the medicinal uses of the various plants; to smell the buchu and to nibble small red berries that tasted like tomatoes. From there we contoured around Rheebokskloof farm to !Kwha ttu, a rehabilitated farm that is now home of a San Cultural Centre. As we approached the cottage that was our home

The traditional heritage and the challenges that have faced the San are depicted in a series of murals at the !Kwha ttu museum.

for the night we saw springbok, zebra and eland grazing peacefully and when our guide explained how the early San people would have lived off this land, we felt a strong sense of timelessness.

Our rooms were comfortable but simple, with shared bathrooms, kitchen and great views but we were eager to learn more about the centre. So, after a short break we wandered over to the photographic museum and took a short tour of the medicinal garden, then sat watching the sunset from the boma before a traditional braai and story-telling around the fire.

▶ **DAY 2** !Kwha ttu to Yzerfontein

10 KM ◆ 4 HR

In the morning we were up early and set out on a short hunter-gatherer trail on which we learnt more about the centre, the history and language of San and Khoi peoples and how they track game and use the fruits of the veld. We stopped at a reconstruction of a traditional village and one of the female guides explained the different roles of the men and women in traditional San society and entertained us with a Cupid story. Apparently the men would hide as the women went out to collect water: if a man fancied one of the girls he would sneak up and shoot a miniature arrow at her buttocks or leg, which she could then take back to the village in order to identify her would-be suitor!

The sun glinted off the distant Atlantic Ocean and we could see far-off Yzerfontein, our destination for the day, so we set off down the gravel road towards the coast. Once over the R27 coastal road, we hiked through pristine west coast strandveld vegetation to the farm of Tygerfontein and followed a farm track running parallel to the sea, trundling over the dunes with coastal vegetation. The strandveld was a

The descent from the dunes to the beach at Yzerfontein bay is a fittingly dramatic note on which to commence the final section of the Darling Stagger.

kaleidoscope of colours and we stopped to admire the delicate paper flowers and to enjoy views of the beach and dolphins playing in the waves from occasional high points.

'Now we're moving into limestone fynbos,' our guide advised and pointed out the change in vegetation as we went. Sure enough the restios (reeds) had disappeared and we noticed more succulents, including brightly coloured vygies. Large white chunks of limestone littered the path and our eagle-eyed tracker spotted distant ostrich and steenbok and pointed out bontebok droppings and black-backed jackal prints. He had us enthralled as he studied the changing sky; interpreting the clouds and yet again taking us back to the days when instinct and experience of the natural environment were the tools humans lived by.

We breached the horizon and an empty beach and rolling sea stretched as far as we could see, so we raced down to the water for a bracing swim. By the time we returned a magnificent seafood picnic was spread out – a fitting end to a fascinating coastal journey. All we still had to do was stagger a couple more kilometres to the road where a vehicle awaited to whisk up back to our cars, and, sadly, to the 21st century.

In a nutshell · Darling Stagger

BOOKINGS Cape West Coast Biosphere Reserve 022-492-2750 (weekday office hours), info@capebiosphere. co.za, http://cwcbr-trails.blogspot.com.
START/FINISH Darling / Yzerfontein.
TRANSFERS Transfers from the end of the trail back to the start are included in the package. Transfers to and from Cape Town can be organised on request.
HIGHLIGHTS Superb guiding; fine food and wine; the pristine fynbos, vineyards and olive orchards; the San Cultural Centre.
LONGEST DAY 15 km.
SHORTEST DAY 10 km.
GROUP SIZE Minimum 2, maximum 8.
UP TO IT? The distances are short and the pace is slow, so even novice hikers should take it in their stride. This is a trail for those who know how to experience the good things in life.
DON'T FORGET! Waterproof hiking gear, day pack, camera, binoculars and a hunter-gatherer's appetite.
WHEN TO GO The trail can be hiked year round but spring (August–November) is wonderful as the weather is at its most predictable, the flowers are at their best and you'll often see whales off the coast. Autumn (April/May) is also a good time weather-wise.
BEFORE AND AFTER There are several charming guesthouses in Darling as well as a tented camp and self-catering cottages at !Kwha ttu.
LOOK IT UP A map of the trail is available from the trail organisers.

Survival Notes

• Drinking water is not available on the trail.

7

Mountains in the Sea Trail

Western Cape

DISTANCE 73 km • **DURATION** 5 days; 2–4 day options available • **DIFFICULTY** 4
TRAIL TYPE Mountain, fynbos • **LOGISTICS** Luxury B&B, bags driven around • **COST** RRRRR
ACCOMMODATION TYPE Luxury guesthouses or hotels • **AREA** Cape Peninsula

The Mountains in the Sea (an approximation of the Khoi name for the place) Trail starts at the foot of Table Mountain, literally minutes from the centre of Cape Town and, after a steep climb up to the top of the famous peak, follows the spine of the Peninsula all the way to Cape Point.

The hike, through the heart of one of the Cape Floristic Region Protected Area World Heritage Site sections (there are 7), leads through pristine fynbos with a celebration of wild flowers and magnificent views over the Atlantic and False Bay coasts. Whales are often seen in the bays, sunbirds and sugarbirds flit between flower heads, and along the way you'll see lizards and hyraxes scuttling about the rocks, tortoises, small antelope and, if you're fortunate, endangered species such as Cape mountain zebra. Much of the trail, which links 2 of South Africa's most spectacular icons, is little known even to most Capetonians and, since it is run from Monday to Friday, you rarely meet another soul up there. Yet it's one of the finest walks in the world.

This guided trail starts by going up Platteklip Gorge, one of the most straightforward, albeit steepest, trails up onto Table Mountain. Once on the summit of the main table, it follows the mountainous spine of the Cape Peninsula to Cape Point. It's a wonderful outing that demands a good level of fitness but on which hikers are thoroughly spoilt with excellent guiding, extremely comfortable guesthouses and the opportunity to sample top-class cuisine and fine wines in local restaurants. Except

Hiking with a flora fundi means that you have plenty of time to smell, and learn about, the flowers.

at the beginning and the end of each day, when there are inevitable encounters with other people and occasional shuttles to overnight spots, the hike is through pristine wilderness, giving hikers the opportunity to appreciate the magnificence of Cape Town's great green lung – Table Mountain National Park.

▶ DAY 1 Platteklip Gorge to Constantia Nek

16 KM ◆ 6 HR

We met Steve Bolnick, the trail developer and our guide, on Tafelberg Road at the foot of one of the most popular hikes up Table Mountain, the daunting-looking Platteklip Gorge. After a short briefing Steve set the scene, explaining a little about the history of the Cape and introducing us to the uniqueness of the Cape Floral Kingdom. We had only gone a few steps when he paused to look at the flowers:

'You're all familiar with the dominant vegetation in these parts, the fynbos, or fine-bush, I'm sure,' he said while explaining the various ways in which the proteas, ericas and restios are adapted to the shallow, acidic soils and warm dry summers of the Cape. 'The fynbos is incredible, there are some 2 285 species on the Peninsula, and that is just a tiny part of the Cape Floral Kingdom, which stretches in a narrow ribbon from around Niewoudtville up in Namaqualand to a bit beyond Port Elizabeth. It's the smallest but most diverse floral kingdom in the world. So ask me questions when you like, but I hope you won't expect me to identify everything … at least not until I've consulted a flower book!'

It was a tough start as the path is steep and sustained, with big step-ups, but we took it gently, enjoying the views back over the city and of the neighbouring Devil's

Peak and Lion's Head. After 10 minutes or so we had a brief reprieve as we joined the level Contour Path, but all too soon we were climbing again as the path zigzagged up to the obvious fault line in the mountain's sheer upper cliffs. As we climbed Steve stopped often, ostensibly to show us the sights – but we suspected it was as much to let us catch our breaths. Pointing out the location of various landmarks, he sketched the history of the city from pre-colonial times, through the days of the first Portuguese explorers, Dutch, French and British settlers and its development during and since the apartheid era.

According to the history books we were following the route taken by the first white man to step foot on Table Mountain. Antonio de Saldanha, commander of a Portuguese fleet sailing around the Cape of Storms en route to India in 1503, became separated from the rest of the fleet and took refuge in an unknown bay sheltered by a high, flat-topped mountain. Anxious to orientate himself, Saldanha struggled up the gorge that split the front of the mountain to the summit plateau. From the top he could see that, as he feared, the fearful Cape of Storms had still to be rounded before he reached the safety of False Bay. Nevertheless the trip was a fruitful one for water cascaded down the gorge through which he climbed. Thereafter Table Bay, known as Aguada de Saldanha (the watering

Did you know?

Although the French occupied the Cape for only 3 years (while supporting Dutch rule from 1781–84), they had such a great impact on Cape Town it became known as Little Paris for a time.

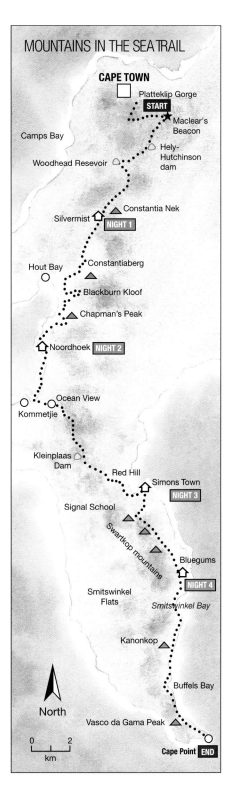

MOUNTAINS IN THE SEA TRAIL

CAPE TOWN
Platteklip Gorge
START
Maclear's Beacon
Camps Bay
Hely-Hutchinson dam
Woodhead Resevoir
Constantia Nek
Silvermist
NIGHT 1
Hout Bay
Constantiaberg
Blackburn Kloof
Chapman's Peak
Noordhoek NIGHT 2
Ocean View
Kommetjie
Kleinplaas Dam
Red Hill
Simons Town
NIGHT 3
Signal School
Swartkop mountains
Bluegums
NIGHT 4
Smitswinkel Flats
Smitswinkel Bay
Kanonkop
Buffels Bay
North
Vasco da Gama Peak
0   2
km
Cape Point END

A Mountain in the Sky

In the mid-18th century, while living in Cape Town, Abbé Nicolas-Louis de la Caille observed a constellation of more than 10 000 stars, which he named Mons Mensa (Latin for Table Mountain). This faint constellation near the Southern Cross overlaps the Large Magellanic Cloud (a neighbouring galaxy), which, if you use your imagination, looks like the Table Mountain tablecloth. It's the only constellation in our night sky named after a geographical feature on earth.

place of de Saldanha) became a regular stopover for the Portuguese fleets.

In 1652 Jan van Riebeeck sailed into Table Bay with 3 ships to set up a way station for Dutch ships sailing around the Cape. Under his governorship Cape Town grew into an important, almost self-sufficient outpost of the Dutch East India Company. Shortly after his arrival he began work on a fort, close to the site of the existing Castle of Good Hope (completed in 1679) which we could see below, and encouraged settlers to grow crops. Soon the slopes of the mountain were being cultivated, the first Cape vineyards were planted and a European settlement was firmly established in the Cape. 'You'll see some of the Constantia vineyards later today,' Steve added as we moved on upwards towards the table top.

We stopped again as the path steepened near the top. We'd been walking over great gabion steps of rock designed to stabilise the path and prevent erosion. The construction and maintenance of the paths that crisscross Table Mountain is part of an excellent public works programme whereby, thanks to funding from the Department of Environmental Affairs and Tourism (DEAT), previously disadvantaged people from the local communities have been employed in Table Mountain National Park, creating jobs and empowering them with skills. Below us to the right was District Six and of course we could see Robben Island in the centre of the bay, which prompted a discussion on the influence of apartheid, and of course the ongoing issues, and hopes, of the post-apartheid era.

We could see both Signal Hill and Lion's Head and again Steve had a fascinating tit-bit for us. He quoted from a journal entry by the governor of the Cape Colony, on 12 September, 1659: '... the clothing, skull and bones of the soldier given up for lost on the 30th of last month were found at the extremity of the Lion Mountain, about 300 roods (7 metres) from the beach. The cranium was half bitten off, so it is presumed that he was devoured by a lion.'

History also records that when, in 1679, a certain Nicolaus de Graaff decided to sleep out on the mountain, his companions voiced their concern that lions, bears, tigers and other wild beasts that dwelt amongst the crags would devour him. Fortunately De Graaff encountered only a few 'roebuck' and survived, but it's hard to imagine that wild predators once roamed the now very civilised and cosmopolitan Cape.

Finally we reached the junction of the paths at the top and headed towards Maclear's Beacon. It had been quite a slog, but the story of the first white woman known to have climbed to the top of Table Mountain put our achievement in perspective. In July 1797, the wife of the deputy colonial secretary, the formidable Lady Anne Barnard, her maid, 3 gentlemen and several slaves carrying provisions made the ascent of Platteklip Gorge in around 3 hours. In keeping with the times they celebrated with a summit banquet consisting of a selection of cold meats washed down with wine and port. A toast to the king and a joyful refrain preceded their descent, which Lady Anne accomplished by sliding down the more difficult sections on the seat of her long pants (which her husband had kindly lent her for the occasion).

Lady Anne concluded that 'we reached home, not more tired than I expected and more than ever convinced that there are few things impossible where there is in women a decided wish of attainment.' (From: *South Africa a Century Ago: Letters and Journals, 1797–1801*, Lady Anne Barnard, Maskew Miller). Oh, they did things in style in those days!

We followed the well-trodden trail across the flat table top towards the obvious high point, again commenting on the work that had been done to protect the fragile environment and the utilisation of raised wooden footpaths in the boggier sections.

Soon we arrived at Maclear's Beacon where we stopped for lunch. The 3-metre-high cairn, topped with a beacon, marks the highest point on Table Mountain, 1 086 m, (3,564 ft) and was constructed in 1844 by the then astronomer royal at the Cape, Sir Thomas Maclear, as part of his efforts to measure the arc of the meridian of the earth. Steve pointed out Hout Bay and the route of our hike all the way down the mountain range to Cape Point. It looked a long way away. To our left, beyond the Cape Flats, were the rugged peaks of the Hottentots Holland mountains while False Bay shimmered in the bright sunlight.

From the beacon we headed down the Smuts' Track to the back table, noting the famous Newlands cricket and rugby stadiums off to our left, then followed a fairly even path along the mountain's eastern edge

As you climb up Chapman's Peak the views over Hout Bay to the Sentinel just get better and better.

as Steve pointed out some wonderful king proteas (*Protea cynaroides*), the national flower, among the fynbos.

The large Hely-Hutchinson dam, still a source of water for the city, was to our right, while below us were the beautifully laid out Kirstenbosch National Botanical Gardens that cover the lower flanks of the eastern side of the mountain. Steve stopped again to point out some yellowwoods (*Podocarpus latifolius*), just beyond the top of Nursery Ravine. 'This is the national tree,' he reminded us. Moments later he led us to a spot where beautiful red disas (*Disa uniflora*) were flowering. 'And how's this, the provincial flower too!' Just beyond the Overseer's Cottage (the very comfortable overnight stop on the Hoerikwaggo Table Mountain Trail, see page 205) we headed down, initially on the jeep track, Clayton's Road, then onto the steep footpath that led eventually through the trees to Constantia Nek. Once across the tarred road it was only a short walk to Silvermist Mountain Lodge, our home for the night.

Dinner there is not included in the trail package, so trailists can choose to eat anywhere in the city bowl, Hout Bay or Constantia. It was a hard decision, but when we were showered and rested we took a taxi to the Chapman's Peak Hotel and sat out on the terrace enjoying the evening sun – an excellent choice. (Smaller groups are often transferred to a B&B near to Constantia Village, within easy walking distance from several good restaurants.)

▶ DAY 2 Constantia Nek to Noordhoek Beach

16 KM ◆ 9½ HR

After breakfast at Silvermist Mountain Lodge we headed from the lodge up the Vlakkenberg Trail, a slightly more gentle start than the previous day's. Unfortunately this is a rather unsightly, scraggy section of the route, which has been cleared of alien trees (wattle and hakea) and not yet rehabilitated, but the views north across to the dense indigenous forest of Orange Kloof and down to Hout Bay were superb. Again Steve was a fount of information – this time on the development of Hout Bay which, as it's name suggests, was a source of wood for ships sailing around the Cape. Once out of the cleared area we continued traversing Vlakkenberg in pristine fynbos

Mountains of flowers and ore

Manganese was discovered in the Constantiaberg in 1873 and was mined in Hout Bay between 1909 and 1911. If you look down into the bay you'll see the ruins of the manganese ore jetty, where the ore was loaded after being sent down from the mine on a chute.

rich in pincushions (*Leucospermum conocarodendron*) and tree pagodas (*Mimetes fimbrifolius*). Steve took the opportunity to discuss the importance of fire in fynbos regeneration. The path continued past old manganese mines on the lower flanks of Constantiaberg, descending towards the snaking tarmac strip of the scenic Chapman's Peak Drive before climbing again into the shaded Blackburn Ravine.

We stopped to watch a whale blowing in the bay and then traversed along the cliffs of Constantiaberg and Noordhoek Peak as a pair of Verreauxs' (black) eagles soared overhead. Ahead loomed Chapman's Peak, while to our right we could see the sheer cliffs of the Sentinel across the glistening blue of Hout Bay. The gradient increased as the path wound around Lower Chapman's Peak and up to the summit of Chapman's Peak, but the scenery more than compensated for the effort. A quick scramble up the final rocky section and we had a 360-degree view to die for. Ahead of us stretched the vast empty sands of Noordhoek Beach. The water was an incredible blue and we could see surfers trying to catch waves, horse riders and dog walkers on the beach and, in the distance, the unmistakable tower of the Slangkop lighthouse. Once we'd taken it all in we started down, first on a steep path and then more gently until we reached the road from where it was only a short walk to the upmarket De Noordhoek Hotel (or the alternate accommodation, the House at Pooh Corner).

▶ DAY 3 Noordhoek Beach to Simon's Town

12 KM ◆ 5 HR

After the exertions of the previous day we were relieved to learn that day 3 was a relatively easy stroll. From the hotel we walked

On a fine day from the top of the Swartkop mountains you can see right across False Bay to Hangklip.

down to the empty sands of Long Beach and kicked off our shoes. It was a wonderful beach walk. At the Noordhoek end there are great granite boulders and relatively sheltered spots where you can swim if you're brave enough to face the freezing Atlantic waters. We stopped at the wreck of the *Kakapo*, a rusty skeleton of a ship high and dry on the sand. In 1900 she ran aground soon after leaving Cape Town for Sydney. Apparently the skipper mistook Chapman's Peak for Cape Point and turned left too soon. Oops.

Once past the meagre remains of the *Kakapo* we crossed the stream formed by the outlet of Wildevoëlvlei (wild bird wetland). Not surprisingly the birdlife is prolific here and we soon identified African black oystercatchers, grey heron, red-knobbed coot, dabchick, little egret and a cute pied kingfisher.

From Wildevoëlvlei we walked up to Imhoff's Gift where we stopped for a cuppa at the farm stall. 'Apparently a certain Christina Diemer was farming very successfully at Noordhoek and, since there was a great need for more produce to supply the ships calling at Simon's Town Harbour, the then governor, Baron Gustav Wilhelm von Imhoff, gave her a gift of the land now called Imhoff's Gift. Bearing in mind that in those days it was a long ride from Cape Town to the south Peninsula and Christina Diemer was a lonely widow, I wonder whether the gift of the land had nothing to do with farm productivity but was rather a gift to his paramour,' laughed Steve as he led us across the road and through Ocean View, a coloured settlement which, he explained, grew up as a result of the Group Areas Act evictions of coloured folk from Simon's

The *Kakapo*, which was wrecked on Long Beach in 1900, is a good excuse for a breather.

Simon's Town has many excellent pubs and restaurants within walking distance of your chosen overnight spot.

Town, Fish Hoek and Noordhoek in the 1960s and 1970s.

We kept going up the small hill behind Ocean View admiring the views back over Noordhoek Beach, Slangkop lighthouse and the quaint village of Kommetjie and debating issues such as the challenges facing the country, particularly in balancing housing provision with environmental concerns. Soon we had left the Atlantic coast and all trace of habitation behind and were deep in the mountains again, following the undulating path through exquisite fynbos to the Kleinplaas dam. Steve identified some delicate little flowers and yet again emphasised the extraordinary level of endemism in the Cape Floristic Region. Fish eagles are regular inhabitants of the dam so, if you're lucky, you might be treated to the distinctive 'call of Africa'.

We were now walking towards the eastern side of the Peninsula and could see all the way across False Bay to the small harbour of Gordon's Bay. This, Steve explained, is the start of another extremely scenic coastal road, the narrow, winding Clarence Drive, which rivals Chapman's Peak Drive for

its mountain and sea views and is another popular whale-watching spot. Below us was the historic town and naval base of Simon's Town where we would be spending the night, so we headed down an old mule trail. We passed a simple granite headstone marking the grave of one of Simon's Town's most famous sons, Able Seaman Just Nuisance.

Just Nuisance, a Great Dane, was the only dog ever to be officially enlisted in the Royal Navy. During World War II he served at HMS *Afrikander*, a Royal Navy shore establishment in Simon's Town. When he died in 1944 his body was draped with a Royal Naval White Ensign and was buried with full naval honours, including a gun salute and the playing of the *Last Post*. We resolved to seek out his statue in Simon's Town's Jubilee Square later in the day.

The mule track brought us out above Simon's Town station from which it was only a sort walk to the Quayside Hotel. It was early afternoon so we spent the rest of the day exploring the historic sites and wandering along to Boulder's Beach to see the penguins before splashing out on a superb seafood meal at Bertha's right on the waterfront. Again we were spoilt for choice – a number of good restaurants are within

The trail on day 4 climbs from Simon's Town to the mountain ridge behind Boulder's Beach.

Make time to wander along from Simon's Town to check out the penguin colony at Boulder's Beach.

walking distance, and there's also option of the informal Salty Dog Fish & Chips or a pub meal at 'two & sixpence'.

▶ DAY 4: Simon's Town to Smitswinkel Bay

12 KM • 6 HR

Rested after our leisurely afternoon, we set off up the trail behind Simon's Town with a spring in our step. It was a steep climb but as the path zigzagged through the fynbos we were constantly distracted by the changing views. Halfway up Steve stopped and bid us look around. It was an unusually clear day and we could see all the way to Cape Hangklip, False Bay's most easterly point. Devil's Peak and the top of Table Mountain were clearly outlined and – with a little help – we traced the route that we'd followed over the past 3 days. Below us were the wonderful cove beaches of the False Bay coast, the clear blue water sparkling beneath towering granite boulders. We recognised Boulder's Beach and could see divers in the water a little further south. Despite the known presence of great white sharks in the area –

particularly around Seal Island, which we could see clearly in the bay – this is a popular area for scuba divers.

The path led past a stone blockhouse, built during the 19th-century British occupation, which made another excellent

The extraordinary Cape Floral Kingdom

South Africa is the only country in the world to have an entire floral kingdom – the Cape Floral Kingdom – within its borders. Although tiny in area, the kingdom is a global epicentre of biodiversity with nearly 9 000 plans, ⅔ of which are endemic (found nowhere else). Table Mountain has around 1 500 species, roughly the number of plants found in the whole of the British Isles. The Cape Peninsula, roughly the size of the City of London, has an incredible 2 285 plant species! (*Fynbos*, Richard Cowling & Dave Richardson, Fernwood Press, 1995)

The final descent to Smits Forest Station is steep but affords magnificent views of the Cape of Good Hope Reserve.

viewpoint, particularly over Simon's Town. We could pick out the old mule track that we'd come down the previous day as well as the naval base, Simon's Town's Martello Tower and many of the historic buildings that we'd wandered around. We kept climbing through Blockhouse Gap until we could see clearly into the Klawer Valley. I'd never seen the valley before and was surprised by the extent of the naval installations – there was a veritable village hidden in the hills. We'd heard some gunfire earlier so were not surprised to see a large firing range, but fortunately the intrusion into our tranquil walk was short-lived.

The proteas on this stretch are a highlight, particularly in July and August when the cone bushes (*Leucadendron* sp) light up the hillside with their bright yellow leaves. Steve pointed out beautiful little pink Cape fellwort (Penaeaceae) and other rare species that are easy to walk past. As we scrambled up a slightly steeper section, then detoured slightly to a wonderful lookout point on a rocky plateau just east of the path, we brushed against the shrubs and caught the citrus aroma of buchu – such an evocative

fynbos scent. Another short scramble and we stood atop the ridge admiring the old stone-built beacons that dotted the horizon – so much grander than the modern white survey beacons.

'The Scots are very proud of their heathers – or ericas,' said Steve, 'but they have only 4 species – while there are at least 660 endemic species of erica in South Africa. I'm Scottish,' I reminded him. 'We have every right to be proud of our glorious heather. Even if it is only 4 species the sight of a Scottish glen clothed in purple and pink is quite magnificent!' Finally we gained our first peak of the day, Swartkop, at 678 m, the third highest peak of the Peninsula range.

The good news was that we could clearly see half a dozen southern right whales just off the coast below: the bad news was that the path led down to the valley between Swartkop and the next ridge on the Swartberg plateau. And what goes down has to go up again. 'It's not as bad as it looks,' Steve assured us.

'Mmm,' I thought as we shouldered our packs and headed down the trail. Sure enough we'd gained the ridge in another half hour and enjoyed the views over the Cape of Good Hope Reserve, to Cape Point, over the marshy plains to the west and back along the route that we'd come as we tucked into lunch. It was a fabulous ridge walk, airy and with ever-changing flowers and views.

Then came the crux, the long, rocky descent down to Smits Forest Station on the main road. The knife-edge ridge seemed to drop off into Smitswinkel Bay and looked quite intimidating, but the path proved easier than it looked. Again we took it very gently, with Steve helping us down the scrambles and offering a rope – which we declined. When there are only 2 hikers on the trail they are accommodated a little way back along the road to Simon's Town, in the delightfully secluded, quaint Cape Point cottage. However, since we were a big group we were transferred back to the Quayside Hotel for another night in Simon's Town.

▶ DAY 5 Smitswinkel Bay to Cape Point

13 KM • 7 HR

Steve was even perkier than usual and we could tell we were in for a treat. Sure enough, the hike along the eastern edge of the Cape of Good Hope section of the park proved a fitting end to a truly spectacular hike. From the entrance gate to the reserve we followed the route of the Cape of Good Hope Trail (see page 227), first above the high cliffs overlooking the picturesque Smitswinkel Bay. We passed Judas Peak, then Paulsberg, the highest peak in the reserve, and rested at the old signal cannon at Kanonkop before heading down a winding path with wonderful views and plenty of sunbirds, emerging at the sea at Booi se Skerm.

Flocks of gulls and terns took flight as we followed the coast round to Bordjiesrif and the tidal Venus Pools. Tempting as it was to stop and bathe we continued a few minutes further to Buffels Bay, where we enjoyed lunch on the beach and a refreshing swim in the turquoise waters. An easy stroll along the white sands brought us to a shower where we rinsed off the salt before continuing along the rocky shores, with surf crashing to our left and mountains on our right.

Our super-guide pointed out tracks and resting places of the shy Cape clawless otters that frequent this area and hyraxes dashed off the path to seek refuge in the rocks. After a short, steep and spectacular ascent up the cliffs of Rooikrans the trail follows the cliff path – a wonderful stretch. On numerous occasions we saw whales

blowing out to sea and at times we could see both the False Bay and Atlantic coastlines. Steve was bubbling with enthusiasm about the flowers – this section of the trail was particularly rich and diverse – and the twitchers were in their element; now they had the chance to see fynbos dwellers such as striking orange-breasted sunbirds and sugarbirds, as well as a variety of gulls, terns, cormorants and other sea birds. We spotted ostriches at a distance and a few small antelope darting off onto the rocks as we approached, but the large mammals that inhabit the park, the Cape mountain zebra, red hartebeest, bontebok and eland eluded us. After a short scramble we headed inland past the overnight cottages and over Vasco da Gama Peak to the car park at Cape Point.

The park's most troublesome animals, chacma baboons, were up to their usual tricks and this again provoked lively discussion. Sadly the baboons have become habituated and are unafraid of human visitors so, despite the attentions of special baboon minders, they are destructive and totally opportunist, jumping into cars to steal food the second the occupants are not paying attention, ripping off windscreen wiper blades and generally being a menace.

You appreciate not having to carry a heavy pack as you scramble down the knife-edge ridge above Smitswinkel Bay.

From the car park we eschewed the funicular railway and hiked up to the original lighthouse, erected in 1857. Steve explained: 'Unfortunately, at 211 m above sea level, sea mists frequently rendered it redundant so it was replaced in 1911.' Its position on top of steep cliffs and crashing waves gives it a sense of drama. After the compulsory photo stop we followed the well-marked trail to a viewpoint above it's replacement, a lower lighthouse, which, at 71 m above sea level, is much more easily visible to ships at sea.

We retraced our steps back to the car park where our transfers awaited. I was so invigorated by the natural abundance of the Pensinsula that I felt I could go on walking forever.

In a nutshell · Mountains in the Sea Trail

BOOKINGS Walk In Africa 021-785-2264, reservations@walkinafrica.com, www.walkinafrica.com.

START/FINISH Bottom of Platteklip Gorge (Tafelberg Road) / Cape Point.

TRANSFERS From Cape Point back to the start are included in the price.

HIGHLIGHTS Outstanding guiding; spectacular scenery; pristine fynbos; indigenous birds and wildlife; seasonal whale sightings; historical features; opportunity to choose from local restaurants each evening.

LONGEST DAY 16 km.

SHORTEST DAY 12 km.

GROUP SIZE Minimum 2, maximum 16.

UP TO IT? This is a strenuous trail and the paths on the mountain are uneven. Some days are long and some of the ascents and descents are steep and sustained. You'll be scrambling at times, so good footwear is important.

DON'T FORGET! Hiking gear, hat, sunscreen, sunglasses; daypack, water bottles, fleece and windbreaker or rain gear (depending on the season); trekking poles (if you use them) or walking stick, camera and spare batteries/charger, bird and/or plant guides as well as binoculars.

LOGISTICS Guided hike staying in extremely comfortable hotels and lodges with breakfast and lunch included. Dinner is not included, rather hikers are given the opportunity to eat out in local restaurants.

WHEN TO GO Spring (September–November) is wonderful as the weather is at its most predictable and the flowers are at their best. Autumn (March–May) is also fantastic. Summers are hot and dry, and often very windy. The Cape experiences winter rainfall so it can sometimes be very wet and cold in winter, particularly in July, but if you're prepared to take the risk these months are cool and pleasant for hiking and the air is clear, offering fabulous views.

BEFORE AND AFTER For options on where to stay and what to do before and after the trail, contact Walk in Africa or Cape Town Tourism, 021-487-6800, www.capetown.travel.

LOOK IT UP The best maps are those of Peter Slingsby's 5-map series of Table Mountain National Park, which is widely available.

8

Green Mountain Trail

Western Cape

DISTANCE 60 km ◆ **DURATION** 4 days ◆ **DIFFICULTY** 4 ◆ **TRAIL TYPE** Mountain, fynbos and vineyards ◆ **LOGISTICS** Bags driven around, luxury, catered ◆ **COST** RRRR
ACCOMMODATION TYPE Luxury guesthouses ◆ **AREA** Elgin Valley and Overberg

The Green Mountain Trail, a luxury trail up and around Groenlandberg (green land mountain) and through the vineyards and fruit farms of the Elgin, Vyeboom and Bot River area, is as much a gourmet experience as it is a beautiful hike. The guiding is superb, the fynbos is exquisite and you are spoilt at every turn. And since Green Mountain is only an hour from Cape Town, it's a quick and easy escape from the stresses of city life.

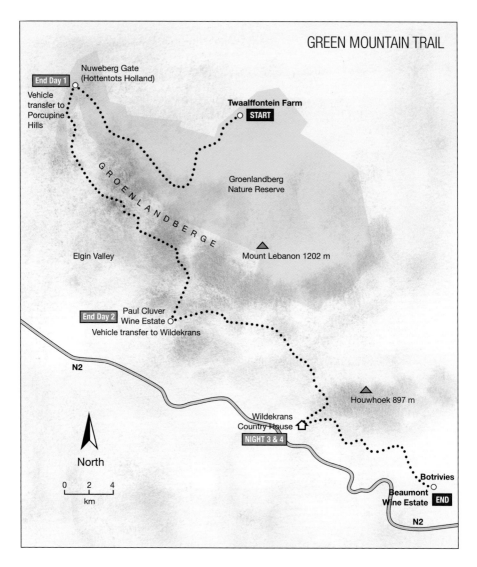

GREEN MOUNTAIN TRAIL

Nuweberg Gate
(Hottentots Holland)
End Day 1

Vehicle
transfer to
Porcupine
Hills

Twaalffontein Farm
START

GROENLANDBERGE

Groenlandberg
Nature Reserve

Elgin Valley

Mount Lebanon 1202 m

End Day 2
Paul Cluver
Wine Estate
Vehicle transfer to Wildekrans

N2

Houwhoek 897 m

Wildekrans
Country House
NIGHT 3 & 4

North

0   2   4
km

Botrivies
Beaumont
Wine Estate   END

N2

The guided and fully catered trail is the brainchild of Dr Paul Cluver, Alison Green and Murray Weiner – members of the Green Mountain Eco Route (a Biodiversity and Wine Initiative that promotes conservation and sustainability) centred around Houwhoek and Groenlandberg. The route is more than a stroll in the hills: the first day, for example, takes hikers over the top of the daunting Groenlandberg – but it is slackpacking at its finest. Knowledgeable guides and hosts place the em-phasis on appreciating the amazing fynbos as well as wine, olive and fruit farms that dominate the area.

The trail is linear, but hikers spend 2 nights at each of the 4-star graded guest-houses, Porcupine Hills and Wildekrans Country Estate, both of which offer superb cuisine, magnificent settings, mountain views and pre-dinner wine tastings. And if that isn't enough of a spoil, the lunches that are laid out in the mountains have to be seen to be believed. The trail follows jeep tracks for about half the way and though the views are fantastic, they are largely over farmlands and the local towns of Grabouw and Botrivier so it's certainly not a wilderness experience. But with its pristine fynbos, wonderful birding and plains game viewing (on Paul Cluver's private game farm) the Green Mountain Trail will appeal to nature lovers who appreciate a stiff walk by day but a soft bed, good food and fine wine at night.

▶ NIGHT 1 Settling in

The drive to Porcupine Hills Guest Farm, on a dirt back-road (part of the old Van der Stel Pass) to Bot River, was simply beautiful in the late afternoon. The folded rocks behind the farm were bathed in golden light. Murray Weiner, our highly entertaining host, showed us to our cottage. There is a choice of accommodation (depending on the number of people on the trail) in the farmhouse, the main cottage and 3 chalets on the Kloof River at the back of the reserve: all are luxurious with underfloor heating and ceiling fans, top-of-the-range bed linen, big fluffy bath towels and wonderful bathroom amenities. And the pride and attention to detail that the owners have is evident in the little touches – fresh flowers in the rooms and fridges stocked with cold drinks, beer and wine – which really make you feel special.

Our first port of call after we'd settled in was the bar. Green Mountain is an emerging premier wine-growing area so we were keen to sample the wines of the nearby Witklip and Oak Valley wineries, which were accompanied by Murray's famous chilli-cured home-grown olives and freshly baked bruschetta with red pepper pesto and artichoke hearts. The 4-course dinner of roasted tomato and butternut soup with thyme, baby garden greens with beetroot, chevre, roasted walnuts, and crispy leeks followed by chicken *paillard* with roasted vegetables and *salsa verde* and rounded off with pear frangipane with caramel sauce and home-made vanilla ice cream was simply amazing and set the tone of the trail. Murray is a chef of note who cooks on demand for his guests and local gourmands and the dishes and classy table setting scored top marks for presentation. Chez Murray would rival any chic city joint.

▶ DAY 1 Twaalffontein Farm to Hottentots Holland Nuweberg gate

18 KM ◆ 5 HR

The trail starts with a jolt. Literally. After breakfast and a short transfer to Twaalffontein Farm, we were bundled into fruit bins on the back of a tractor. The 10-minute ride was quite enough in this unusual carriage and we were glad to dismount at the top of the farm. The mountain fynbos was

A world first

The Green Mountain Eco Route, the world's first biodiversity wine and eco-route, is centred around the Groenlandberg in the heart of the Cape Floral Kingdom. The route offers visitors a range of experiences, including wine tastings and wine tours, diverse accommodation, gourmet dinners and organic food stalls, flower tours and outdoor adventures such as marked and graded mountain biking routes, 4×4 and quad bike trails, abseiling and bass fishing with the aim of creating employment and developing a new ecotourism angle for South African wine tourism.

The climb up Groenlandberg is steep, but the fynbos is so wonderful that you barely notice the exertion.

magnificent. Dominic Chadbon, our guide, pointed out the last vestiges of the lower level renosterveld – just about the most endangered natural veld type in the country.

'Fynbos sits on well-drained and nutrient-poor sandstone where not much else grows; so that's why so much of it remains in these areas,' he explained. 'Renosterveld is unlucky in that it likes fertile clay and granite soils, most of which have long been cultivated as orchards and wheat fields so not much of it has survived.'

We hiked up through dense thickets of bearded proteas, stopping often to admire interesting-looking plants. Dominic reminded us of the characteristic fynbos species – identifying wonderful lime-green leucadendrons, weird-looking spider-head and sceptre proteas. He identified several species of erica, but in the spirit of a keen birder, admitted that others were LPJs – 'little pink jobs' – to him.

'With 650 or so ericas in the Cape Floral Kingdom, I have to leave correct identification to the chaps with PhD after their names,' he joked. The more we looked, the more we saw – so distracted were we that we barely realised we were gaining height – and the 6 km climb up the shoulder of the Groenlandberg was painless. There was a wonderful stand of bright red pincushions right next to the path, which we snapped away at with our cameras, and the slopes were covered with bright pink watsonias and yellow butterfly lilies.

'These are *impepho* (helichrysums), which are traditionally burnt to get rid of the shack-dwelling *tokoloshe* or to treat chest complaints. And these button bushes (berzelias) indicate water courses and seeps,' continued Dominic. Being in the presence of a fynbos fundi with such sharp eyes and humour made the trail fascinating and Dominic's excitement at finding plants that he hadn't seen before was infectious.

Back at Porcupine Hills that night our guide poured over his guide books and identified a beautiful pink geranium with maple-like leaves as a crane's bill, and some delicate purple flowers as roellas, part of the bell-flower family. The upper slopes were covered with restios and, feeling frivolous, we threw ourselves into huge tufts of orgy grass before the final climb to the telecommunication towers on the summit. Leopards had clearly roamed here recently – spoor was evident in places along the path.

A surprise awaited. Murray suddenly appeared from the rocks close to the summit where he'd spread out a feast of Nicoise, coleslaw and pasta salads and home-made mini-doughnuts. We tucked in happily and enjoyed the glorious views all the way to Hermanus and Cape Point to the south, and across Theewaterskloof Dam to the Franschhoek mountains and Villiersdorp to the north. The views were even more spectacular from the towers themselves, particularly the view of False Bay across Steenbras Dam. From this high vantage it looked as if the dam was part of the ocean, so it took me some time to orientate myself and to work out that the land to the eastern side of the dam was not a peninsula. We had plenty of time to enjoy being on top of the world before following the jeep track down through a recently burnt area to the Nuweberg gate of the Hottentots Holland Nature Reserve, near the top of

Dining at Porcupine Hills is an absolute treat as host Murray Weiner is a chef of note.

Viljoen's Pass. The slopes on this side of the mountain support a different community of plants and we stopped often to inspect bright yellow cone-bushes, delicate blue lobelias and wonderful clusters of white and cerise everlastings (helichrysums).

We arrived at our pick-up point exactly on schedule, a trifle weary, but thrilled to have learnt so much on the hike. A bespoke minibus taxi ferried us back to Porcupine Hills where we freshened up before regrouping in the bar to sample yet more of the local wines and another gourmet feast.

▶ DAY 2 Hottentots Holland Nuweberg gate to Paul Cluver Estate

15 KM • 5 HR

Yet again Murray surpassed expectations, providing such a magnificent breakfast we couldn't help thinking it was going to be difficult to keep up these incredible standards of catering. We were transferred to the trail head just beyond the Nuweberg gate where we had finished off on day 1.

The first section of the trail took us along a jeep track through a forest, then past a rather scraggy area of cleared trees and a stand of tall blue gums before we emerged into pristine fynbos. This was the original Viljoen's Hoop Pass that Charles Darwin, accompanied by a Khoisan guide and a couple of donkeys, crossed in order to go exploring inland when HMS *Beagle* docked in Cape Town for a couple of months on its momentous voyage in 1836.

Again the pace was slow as Dominic stopped often to point out interesting plants, explaining their various methods of pollination and survival and their medicinal uses. Yet again he spotted several species he had not seen before, including a variety of roellas, which on some plants sported only blue flowers, on others white, sometimes of the mountains and just why the Cape Floristic Region has been declared a World Heritage Site.

The hike then took us through the Molteno farm with its cultivated fields of button bushes and proteas, then along a track cut specially for the Green Mountain Trail which runs parallel with an irrigation ditch, a very pretty section of trail which contoured around the cliffs of the Groenlandberg and the masts where we had lunched the day before.

The landscape changed all the time and with it came different plant species: the amazing variety of micro-habitats is one of the reasons – if not the main one – for the great diversity of the fynbos. We spotted numerous yellow daisies, the gorgeous red and silver flower heads of the *Mimetes cucullatus* and 2 species of carnivorous sundews. 'They're called *snot rossies* in Afrikaans, while mimetes are *rooi stompies*. Afrikaans is a language that has a simple grammar but a knack for the vernacular,' observed Dominic.

with a blue or black marking around the stamen and sometimes without. 'I'm not sure of the reasons for this,' he confessed. 'To start with, I thought they might be 2 different species, but I see on that specimen there are both blue and white flowers and different hues in between, so that theory goes out the window. It's possible that the petals change colour with age.'

He drew our attention to *Serruia altiscapa*, a protea found only in this immediate stretch of mountains. The purple-flowered *rooi wortels* (blood roots, or *Dilatris corymbosa* the red produced by haemoglobin) were in full bloom but their cousins, the Cape edelweiss, were a bit behind. He pointed out various penaeaceae, a weird-flowered family found only in the fynbos; medicinal plants such as slangbos (a daisy, *Stoebe*, used for snake bite venom) and lobestemons, members of the forget-me-not family. 'In Afrikaans, this is called the 8-day healing bush,' he laughed. 'It supposedly cures all within 8 days, but that's a little disingenuous as after 8 days one is generally either better anyway, or dead!' We stumbled on a beautiful yellow flowering star grass – a solitary individual that we didn't see again on the trail – and began to appreciate the extraordinary diversity

Energetic hikers can take the steep trail to the eroded outcrop of Hanging Rock.

We gained a rise and there, above the vineyards of Oak Valley, we beheld an incredible sight: in the shade of big umbrellas a sit-down lunch had been set up that would have impressed Lady Anne Barnard, let alone some sweaty hikers. The table was covered with a linen cloth, bowls of homemade muffins and freshly picked strawberries, drinks were cooling in a big silver bowl and a selection of the estate's wines stood to attention.

We were each handed an individual picnic hamper full of skewers of melon and ham produced on the farm, local chicken and marinated vegetables, while winemaker Pieter Visser answered questions about the wines and the immaculately maintained hiking and mountain biking trails on the farm. One of the most interesting aspects of the trail and the Green Mountain Eco Route is the constantly changing fynbos that we saw as we walked.

Visser explained how the same diversity of micro-climate and habitat that accounts for the amazing diversity of the fynbos, what wine people refer to as terroir, accounted also for the great differences in wines. Here this is true not only of neighbouring estates, but from vineyard to vineyard. In fact each wine tasting around the mountain is testimony to the rich biodiversity of the area. Lethargic after our indulgence we had to drag ourselves back onto the trail, initially a beautiful stretch of path with prominent rocks at both sides, then onto Paul Cluver's land along a track that was somewhat less well defined!

The trail split, giving the option of a high, gentle countour path or a more adventurous, steep and – at times – slippery route leading down to Hanging Rock: we decided to follow the latter. A little Cape grysbok scuttled away, then we entered a forested kloof where rooiels trees (*Cunonia*

Lunch on day 2 is an elaborate, sit-down picnic of locally produced meats and fruits supplied by Oak Valley.

capensis, identified by its 'butter spoons'), yellowwoods, Cape beech (*Rapanea melanophloes*) and one of the few trees that grows in the open fynbos, the mountain cypress (*Widdringtonia nodiflora*), dug deep into the clay soil.

A dark brown pool in front of a tumbling waterfall offered welcome respite from the heat, but we were soon warm again from the steep climb out to join the jeep track that led down to Paul Cluver Estate. A final flourish of ericas, keurbooms (*Virgilia oroboides*) and Cape sweet peas and we were strolling through rows of vines.

Yet more spoils came as we entered the elegant buildings of the apple brandy still, where we were greeted with cool flannels, fresh apple juice and tea and scones. Refreshed, we cleaned ourselves up a bit (the bathroom is worth a visit to admire the view!) then moved to the wine tasting room to sample some of the award winning Cluver wines before being transferred to our base for the next couple days.

At Wildekrans Country House, Alison Green welcomed us and showed us around her lovely home. With its awesome views of the mountains, its beautiful gardens, four-poster beds and the feel of the kind of home you'd love to have, Wildekrans has a real charm; in fact it's somewhere where I could happily retire to. Alison's husband Barry is a wine maker and bottles of his easy drinking red wine were on sale along with olives and preserves produced on the farm. We had plenty of time to explore before dinner so, with the aid of a basic map, wandered around the property, admiring the artworks, which included a very realistic herd of peacefully grazing sheep – that was a piece by Wilma Cruise inspired by the slaughtering of the Boer's sheep during the Anglo-Boer War. And, not to be outdone by Murray, Alison produced an absolute feast which she served in up the barn that doubles as the wine cellar.

► DAY 3 Paul Cluver Estate to Wildekrans Country House

15 KM ♦ 4 HR

Our reliable taxi dropped us back at the private De Rust Nature Reserve on the Paul Cluver Estate where eland, zebra, springbok and bontebok eyed us as we walked towards the big blue gums surrounding the amphitheatre. 'The lower-level land is fertile clay soil and covered in grasses – this

The opportunity to sample, and buy, wines from the wine farms you traverse is a highlight of the trail.

The sleeper plantation

Although the gums, or eucalyptus trees, of the Elgin area are considered ugly aliens by many people now, they were planted for a very good reason. The rapidly growing trees were grown in the Elgin bluegum plantation for use as sleepers when the first main-line railway lines were constructed in 1900. Although fast growing, the wood is extremely dense and hard – and they grow in just about any conditions.

was where herds of game would have been found 300 years ago,' Dominic said. After an hour or so of wandering through agricultural land and patches of dreaded alien trees, we broke out onto pristine fynbos.

'This is the most dazzling mix of protea I have ever seen,' enthused our guide. 'All the major genera are represented here: protea, leucadendron, leucospermum, serruria, paranomus ... Awesome!'

He pointed out some delicate cerise-coloured paper daisies, which contrasted with the yellows and greens of the fynbos, and some pincushions he hadn't seen before. After a couple of gentle climbs and some contouring around Houwhoek mountain, we could see Wildekrans farm below. There were quills on the path – porcupines had been digging up watsonia bulbs, just as the Khoi did centuries ago. The path doubled back and we headed down to the blue gums above the farm and up through the beautifully tended gardens to our rooms. It had been a spectacular end to the trail, but there was more to come. After tea, a shower and a short rest we moved over to the barn for a tasting of Wildekrans wines, followed by yet another 3-course, gourmet feast.

Spend time exploring the gardens at Wildekrans Country House – artworks are tucked away in the greenery.

▶ DAY 4 Wildekrans to Beaumont Wine Estate

11 KM ◆ 4 HR

Our guide for this section was Gerald McCann, previously a forester and, in the 1970s, head conservator of the Kogelberg Biosphere Reserve. Gerald is a colourful character, a true fynbos fundi who usually guides both this and day 3 of the trail. After introducing himself – he's also an author, artist, photographer and minister – he led us down to the start of the trail. 'This was the old road that the first wagoneers would have taken after they crossed the Mountains of Africa from Cape Town via the Hotten-tots Holland Pass, north of the present-day Sir Lowry's Pass,' was our first taste of things to come.

'That flat area of land there, known as Koffiekraal, is where they outspanned to water the oxen and enjoy coffee before tackling the formidable Houwhoek moun-tain crossing. A succinct mention in the annuls of the Cape's history tells us that "in 1669 Olaf Bergh crossed the Houwhoek Mountains with 2 wagons (to reach the Promised Land of the Overberg)".'

As we hiked he enthralled us with the incredible journey that those early pioneers had undertaken in their ox-wagons. He pointed out the distinctive and widespread waboom (wagon tree, *Protea nitida*), which was used to make the brake blocks for the wagons. 'People often think that the wood was used to make the wagons themselves but you can see that the trunk and branches are much too short.' The soft protea would wear out and not the harder wheels, and brake blocks were easy to replace.

Soon we left the jeep track and cut down to the river on one of the trails Gerald has cut. 'Now that I'm retired I build trails as a hobby,' he explained. 'I've developed quite a few on the Beaumont estate and the slopes of the Houwhoek mountain. Until a few years ago the place we crossed the river was a popular local recreation spot for the people of Botrivier, known as Stone Beach. But now they're too lazy to hike up here.'

As we climbed out of the river valley we spotted a number of ticks on our clothing. Again Gerald was a fount of information: though when he described the antics of the 'acrobat-ticks' with a straight face we realised we were being gently teased! He

There's little about the fynbos that floral fundi Gerald McCann, your guide on days 3 and 4, doesn't know.

stopped to inspect a nondescript scrubby bush. 'This is *gonna*, it looks like an erica but has a strong, sinewy bark that can be peeled off and twined to make rope. Worth remembering for essential hiker repairs!' As we walked he pointed out and explained the medicinal and other uses of many of the other species: the erica that resembled the *gonna*, the pod-bearing butterfly bush, wild sage and wild rosemary.

We stopped for a break at a viewpoint above Bot River and, after pointing out some tracks on the opposite slope, Gerald told us more about the old wagon routes. The wagons were very top-heavy, so contouring on steep side-slopes was difficult. When it was unavoidable, such as on the route we were looking at, all the men would haul on ropes attached round the wagon to prevent it toppling – they would '*houw op die hoek*' (hold on the bend), from which the Houwhoek pass and area takes its name.

While history was obviously a passion, Gerald's first love was clearly for the fynbos and he had some amazing conservation stories to share. The most remarkable was about the marsh rose (*Orothamnus zeyheri*), a beautiful member of the protea family with a red, rose-like flower that has survived only in a few inaccessible mountainous peaks of the Kogelberg. The rare protea was nearly extinct when Gerald was managing Kogelberg Reserve – as far as they knew there were only 3 adult plants left. Then a conservationist read an account by the pioneering fynbos botanist Thomas Stokoe who described losing a colony of marsh roses to fire, only to find that they rose from the ashes. He realised part of the problem was the Department of Forestry's policy at the time of protecting fynbos from fire.

Fynbos has since proved to be not only fire-dependant, but a fire-evolved flora. After the first controlled burns carried out in Kogelberg as part of an emergency programme to save the marsh rose, more of the plants made an appearance. It was a poignant lesson in the role of fire for the survival of fynbos. 'It turns out the seed of the marsh rose – as with quite a few other fynbos species – has a little food source attached to it, the elaiosome, which triggers a powerful scent. Within seconds of seeds falling to the ground ants arrive and take them down underground and have a "Graça" party: the elaiosome sends them on a high! The seeds then remain under-

Pretty enough for a vase

Map-maker extraordinaire Peter Slingsby relates the tale of a picker collecting flowers for the Caledon Wildflower Show, who discovered a colony of marsh roses on the slopes the Perdeberg" above Kleinmond. He picked the lot, with long stalks and inadvertently wiped out one of the few remaining colony! Oops!

ground until fire breaks out when germination is triggered by the smoke.'

We contoured around to a lush kloof and Gerald pointed out where the Verreauxs' eagles were nesting. 'The parents are off teaching the young fledgling to fly in another area,' he informed us. 'They don't want it sticking around their patch.' He pointed to a rocky crag across the gorge: 'There's the nest they used last year; sadly it was destroyed by a typical Cape winter storm, so they've now chosen a more sheltered site.'

We continued along the path noting the rock elder, Cape beech and Cape fuscia trees growing in the pristine kloof up until where the path split. Today we would take the 'Hi' road. We hiked past some spectacular daisies, aromatic buchu and delicate little blue lobelias – 'cheery chappies' as he called them – then stopped in the shade for yet another fascinating anecdote, this time about the brown bearded protea, *Protea neriifolia*.

Apparently, before the growing of proteas became a major commercial concern, an American smuggled some seeds of these plants back to his ranch in Los Angeles. Having successfully grown them, he tried to persuade his local flower shop to stock the flowers. The florist wasn't convinced, particularly since the grower was unable to provide a popular common name for the protea. On his return home he saw his wife's lingerie out on the line and, inspired, rang the florist with the name *Panty Pinks* and the flowers sold like hot cakes. Panty Pink appears to be no longer the fashionable name in the States, but the flowers became known as 'pink mink' – much more marketable than brown bearded protea!

The trail contoured around, offering great views over Bot River and Niels Verberg's Luddite wine farm below. We passed yellow bushes of Cape gorse, big stands of fountain bush, some interesting cluster pin-

cushions (*Lecusopermum buxifoli)* known by pickers as 'buksies', the beautiful little pink flowers of *Pelagonium incarnatum*, which Gerald assured us means 'when God became a flower,' mountain cypress and the head-high daisy Leggie Lizzie (*Osteospermum polygaloides)*. 'That's my name for it, but I also know it as the "in your face daisy" as it doesn't have a well-known common name,' laughed Gerald.

Our journey was nearly at an end. After our final descent from the mountain we hiked along a short section of railway line to Beaumont Wines. Gerald paused before leading us up the last short rise. 'This is the end of the trail. Thank you, I hope you have enjoyed it as much as I have. Prepare yourselves for the view.'

We were not disappointed as we looked across a dam at a beautiful old farmstead, then made our way to the stoep of the wine-tasting room where an ice-cold jug of fresh lemonade awaited us. Lovely, lively Jayne Beaumont welcomed us in before leading us down to her house beside the water for lunch: a delicious feast of home-made soup, butter-bean pesto, quiche and a decadent dessert of pears marinated in Port, all accompanied by a wine tasting.

Before we left we toured the cellar and the old mill, which has been lovingly re-

Lunch on the stoep of Jayne Beaumont's wonderful home is a delicious feast washed down with wines from the estate.

stored by Andy Selfe, a local engineer with a passion for vintage machinery. We would have been happy just to check in to one of the beautiful self-catering cottages on this exquisitely beautiful farm and spend a couple of extra days hiking on the mountain – but our faithful taxi was waiting to transfer us back to our cars at Porcupine Hills. And that was probably just as well – the food was so delicious and plentiful that I put on 2 kg in just 4 days on the trail! But that's what slackpacking is about; I reckon this should be renamed the Green Mountain Gourmet Route.

In a nutshell · Green Mountain Trail

BOOKINGS Green Mountain Trail, 028-284-9827, 083-284-6226, info@greenmountaintrail.co.za, www.greenmountaintrail.co.za.
START/FINISH Porcupine Hills Guest Farm, Botrivier / Beaumont Wine Estate, Botrivier.
TRANSFERS Transfers back from the end of the trail to the start at Porcupine Hills are included in the package. Transfers to and from Cape Town can be organised on request.
HIGHLIGHTS The exceptional hospitality and guiding; topnotch accommodation and gourmet food; the wine tastings; the exquisite fynbos on the mountains; the game on the Paul Cluver Estate; the exclusivity of the trail.
LONGEST DAY 18 km.
SHORTEST DAY 11 km.
GROUP SIZE Minimum 2, maximum 10.
UP TO IT? This is a very straightforward trail, largely along jeep tracks or contour paths with some moderate climbs and descents. Nonetheless it requires a reasonable level of fitness particularly on day 1, which goes to the top of the Groenlandberg. Some of the paths will be slippery after rain so good footwear is important.
DON'T FORGET! Waterproof hiking gear, daypack, camera, binoculars – there's not much the trail organisers haven't thought of.
WHEN TO GO The trail can be hiked year round but spring (August–November) is wonderful as the weather is at its most predictable and the flowers are at their best. Autumn (April/May) is also a good time.
BEFORE AND AFTER Porcupine Hills, Wildekrans Country House and Beaumont Wines all offer accommodation to hikers wishing to extend their stay on the Green Mountain Eco Route. Visit www.greenmountaintrail.co.za for details on other activities in the area.
LOOK IT UP Peter Slingsby's map of the Overberg.

Survival Notes

- Water available at lunch stops on the trail.
- Wine, olives, jams and other delicacies for sale at the guesthouses.
- Shorter route options available.

9

Oystercatcher Trail

Western Cape

DISTANCE 48 km ◆ **DURATION** 5 days; with 2–4 day options ◆ **DIFFICULTY** 3
TRAIL TYPE Beach and cliff paths ◆ **LOGISTICS** Guided, luxury catered, bags driven
round ◆ **COST** RRRR ◆ **ACCOMMODATION TYPE** Guesthouses ◆ **AREA** Southern Cape

If slackpacking is the skill of backpacking without the schlep, then Fred Orban, the developer of the Oystercatcher Trail, is the master craftsman. He's thought of every possible way to spoil you, to make your life easier and to make hiking his trail a joy. If you want to walk for only 2 days rather than 5 – no problem. You want to stay put rather than overnight at the end of each stage – good idea. Of course it's also a stunningly beautiful trail, expertly guided, and highly educational and since some of your fee is ploughed back into conservation you feel you're making a valuable contribution to a worthy cause. And then there are the little touches: arriving at your home for the night to find the fire and candles lit; the welcome drinks and the input of local experts which ensure that whatever option you choose, this will be a memorable trail.

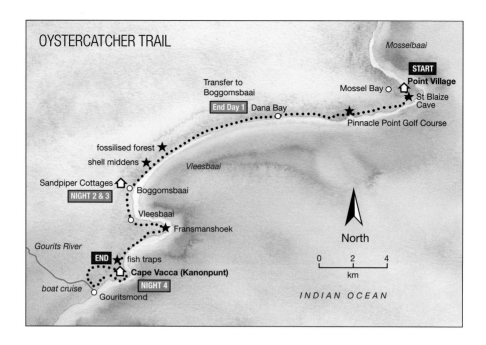

OYSTERCATCHER TRAIL

Mosselbaai

START
Point Village

Mossel Bay ○

St Blaize
Cave

Transfer to
Boggomsbaai

End Day 1 Dana Bay ○

Pinnacle Point Golf Course

fossilised forest ★

shell middens ★

Vleesbaai

Sandpiper Cottages ⌂ ○
NIGHT 2 & 3 ○ Boggomsbaai

Vleesbaai ○

Fransmanshoek ★

Gourits River

END ★ fish traps

⌂ **Cape Vacca (Kanonpunt)**

boat cruise **NIGHT 4**

○ Gouritsmond

North

0   2   4
km

INDIAN OCEAN

The trail starts at the St Blaize Point in Mossel Bay and heads west, along a wild, rugged coastline and along sandy beaches to the Gourits River mouth. Initially following the route of the St Blaize Trail, it takes in archaeological treasures such as the St Blaize Cave and ancient middens that reveal the lives of strandlopers (hunter-gatherer beachcombers), traverses precipitous orange, lichen-covered cliffs and one of the country's most dramatic – and, it should be noted, most environmentally controversial – golf-courses before winding its way through coastal fynbos and along sandy beaches – home to the endangered African black oystercatcher and a diverse array of other bird and marine life.

The trail is varied, and stunning, but perhaps the most appealing aspect for those who like their home comforts is the hospitality and the flexibility. Everyone involved goes the extra mile to ensure that you come away with a new understanding of the plight of the oystercatcher, but also of this unspoilt, wild piece of coast. You'll be treated to surprise lunches, oysters and bubbly and sauna and spa facilities at Boggomsbaai and, should you wish, massages can be arranged to refresh your weary legs. This is perhaps the epitome of the new slackpacking genre – a trail that traverses a spectacular natural environment, guided by people who are both knowledgeable and passionate about the coast, its flora and fauna, and hosted by a man who believes in the good things in life. Hard-core backpackers need not apply – they might end up converts!

Some of the revenue from the trail is used to protect the habitat of the trail's namesake, the endangered African black oystercatcher.

Day 1 follows the route of the St Blaize trail along the wave-cut coastal terrace west of Mossel Bay.

▶ DAY 1 Cape St Blaize to Dana Bay

15 KM ◆ 4–5 HR

The big, stylish self-catering units at Point Village are supremely well located – you wake to the light streaming in and a majestic view over the Mossel Bay point and the early surfers catching the waves. After a warm welcome and introduction to the trail we had enjoyed a superb meal at the Kingfisher restaurant downstairs the night before, and at breakfast a specially decorated table was laid specially for us trailists.

Our guide, Willie Komani, introduced himself and we set off to the trail head at the famous St Blaize Cave. There he explained the history of the area, the archaeological significance of the many similar caves in the rocky coastline and the strandloper customs. Then we were off along the cliff line enjoying awesome views of the craggy coast, the eroded stacks and caverns and the dramatic orange, lichen-covered rocks. Willie pointed out areas infested by alien vegetation – great patches of rooikrans – as well as those areas that had been cleared

and revegetated. An ex-Care for the Coast volunteer, he was outspoken about the destructive effect that humans can have on the natural environment.

We paused at a viewpoint on the cliffs where there were little memorials and names scribbled onto the rocks. Willie shook his head. Forlorn young people had hurled themselves to their deaths at these spots. 'Love-sick girls,' he noted philosophically. 'Boys don't do that!' We nodded our consent and moved on til we came to the edge of the Pinnacle Point golf course development. It was once all public open space, but trailists still have right of way around the edge of this beautifully manicured stretch. It's amusing to watch the golfers teeing off on what might well be the trickiest course in South Africa – particularly if there's any wind. We saw one poor woman send 3 balls down to the rocky shore below before she finally got one on to the fairway.

The trail then contours around the coastline, with an optional detour to one of the caves such as Groot Grot, which is being 'dug' by Professor Curtis Marean, Kyle Brown and other world-renowned archaeologists, that hikers can visit by special appointment. From there it was on to a pretty sandy beach where we stopped for a swim before regaining the path via a wide, golf-cart friendly boardwalk that has been constructed to give the Pinnacle Point residents access to the sea.

Then it was only a short walk through coastal fynbos to Dana Bay where a taxi was waiting to ferry us to Sandpiper Cottages a little down the coast at Boggomsbaai. A fire was blazing in our cottage, the candles glowed and there were cold beers in the fridge and red wine and sherry on the table; we made ourselves comfortable before wandering over to Fred's leisure centre for yet more welcoming drinks. (One of the options on the budget, self-catering version of the trail is to stay over in Dana Bay on night 1.)

After a tour of the leisure centre and spa we settled down to watch a video and listen to a short informative talk on the trail's namesake, the oystercatcher. Although numerous along the coast they're threatened beause of their nesting habits: their nests are mere scrapes just above the high-tide mark and unwitting beach users and their

Hikers can detour down to the beach to check out the massive archaeological caves.

dogs often disturb the birds, which then leave their nests and their young to their own peril.

We learnt that a pair of oystercatchers mates for life, and if one of them dies the other remains single, or may be seen on the beach enjoying safety in numbers by associating with other birds. Each female can lay up to 3 sets of eggs a season: if the first eggs hatch then she lays no more, but if the first, or second nest is destroyed for any reason, all is still not lost. It was a fascinating insight to the trail's raison d'être, which was followed by a real Cape dinner of bobotie and red wine. We booked massages for the following day, then admired the stars as we strolled back to our quaint fishers' cottages.

▶ **DAY 2** Dana Bay to Boggomsbaai

12 KM ◆ 4 HR

We were driven the short distance back to where we ended the trail the day before and set off along the beach to walk to Boggomsbaai. This was our first chance to really watch the oystercatchers we saw at regular intervals along the beach – apparently there are some 100 birds along the trail. Willie pointed out the nests and chicks and the brave aggression of the parent birds as they tried to protect their young. The tide was low and the oystercatchers were on the rocks picking at molluscs.

'That's how they mistakenly got their names,' explained Willie. 'Early observers saw the birds foraging on oyster-covered rocks and assumed they must be able to prise open the oyster shells. They can't, but the mussels from the same rocks are a staple in their diet.' We walked on in silence, noting the cerise beaks and legs and ever-watchful red-ringed eyes of the adult birds. A fretting seagull caught Willie's eye and he detoured up the beach to the piece of drift-

The first 2 nights of the trail are spent in the quaint Sandpiper cottages at Boggomsbaai.

wood that it appeared to be sheltering by. The poor bird was entangled in fishing line, trapped and unable to escape. He gently cut it free from the noose that would have surely signalled its end.

'I tell them all the time,' he said, 'but the fishermen say they don't just discard their line.' It was February when we were on the trail and not expecting to see whales, so we scanned the ocean for dolphins. From July to October this hike offers one of the most spectacular shore-based whale-watching experiences on the entire Cape coast. The sea was dark and grey and we were out of luck – maybe the following day. Willie pointed out a big midden of shells – more evidence of Khoisan people who had once roamed this coast – and pointed out the flints and other tools that littered the site.

We stopped for lunch at the Blinde Estuary, a closed river mouth, where Willie led us up to a higher plateau where he had a surprise in store ... I won't ruin it by letting out the secret! We continued along the beach, stopping for a final swim before cresting the dunes and walking through the lovely cluster of white Cape cottages of Boggomsbaai back 'home'. Development here is strictly controlled and the effect is impressive – the cottages are widely spaced, similar in size and design and, very importantly, have no external lights so it's as quaint as we imagined the old Cape fishing villages would have been before places like Paternoster got popular. In the evening the absence of light pollution meant we could see the moon reflected on the ocean, and the star-filled sky.

▶ DAY 3 Boggomsbaai to Kanonpunt

15 KM • 4-5 HR

We'd come armed with mussel permits for day 3 – friends had told us about the mine of white mussels and oysters we'd find on the beach. Willie obligingly showed us the drill and we were soon successful in the white mussel shuffle and our diggings in the sand. The oystercatchers also hunt for white mussels by digging with their bayonet-like beaks in the beach sand. Then it was along the beach again and along a path that led through the coastal scrub. We identified more ancient strandloper middens

Your guide will lead you to the strtandloper middens and fossil sites deep in the dune fields of Dana Bay.

and saw the unmistakable blow of a whale out at sea (probably Bryde's whales that stay year-round but are seldom seen from land), then paused at a rock pool to cool off while Willie collected some interesting urchins and molluscs to show us.

He was having fun introducing us to the fruits of the coast. Next he quizzed us about a familiar-looking plant – a tuber we guessed. Indeed, he rooted around and dug up what he calls African wild potato. Many of the species around have medicinal uses and Willie had given us a fascinat-ing insight, pointing out the various wild herbs and traditional uses of the leaves of the buchus, the poisonous milk of the asbos vygie – 1 of 5 poisons used by the Bushmen – and other succulents we'd seen along the way. But when he explained the significance of the prolific Christmas berry in his life we were transfixed.

As a young man he'd been in bad car accident which had left Willie seriously injured. His grandmother, a sangoma, had visited him in hospital and stuffed the ber-ries into the terrible wounds in his legs.

The silver star Oystercatcher

February 2010 saw the launch of a new, 4-night, 3-day, fully-guided and catered version of the more famous Oystercatcher Trail. The new silver star option allows hikers to enjoy the same high standards as on the standard trail, but is a day shorter and excludes drinks and airport transfers so is aimed at those on tighter budgets. Both versions of the Oystercatcher Trail can now be extended by an extra day. Instead of finishing at the Gourits River on the fourth walking day, hikers are ferried across the river and continue hiking for another 14 km along the coast to Rein's Nature Reserve where they can view plains game such as eland, kudu, springbok and zebra and then overnight in the beautiful chalets right on the seafront before being transferred back to the start. There are more stone fish traps to be seen there.

The deep scars are there today and he is missing part of a finger – but he believes the fruits saved him. He's inherited the healing knowledge from his gran and done his time living wild in the veld learning to survive off the land. We had many fascinating conversations about Xhosa and Zulu culture and beliefs.

Halfway between Vleesbaai village and Fransmanshoek we detoured up through the coastal thicket to Kapokbos, a beach shack with a wooden deck with a spectacular view over the coast – the perfect spot for a short break. Whales were again blowing out to sea and we could see right the way past Boggomsbaai to Dana Bay and the route back down our trail. Another hour of scrambling along the coast brought us to a gorgeous sandy cove where took a dip before climbing up to a historic fishers' hut on a promontory – and there a fabulous lunch of pasta, salad and koeksisters awaited us.

The stone building houses a small information centre with samples of the local fauna, flora and marine life displayed, as well as accounts of the French man-o'-war *La Fortune*, which sank off Fransmanshoek in 1763. Soon we were back on the beach and detoured up a high dune to admire the

Bring a mollusc permit and you can try to harvest your own supper.

view of this glorious stretch of coast before running down the steep sand for a welcome swim. The day ended at a magnificent Cape-style beach house at Kanonpunt – a private, deserted spot with awesome views. After enjoying a fish braai, which included our harvested white mussels, we fell asleep to the sound of the sea.

(Small groups of 6–8 hikers are sometimes accommodated in a beautiful, 4-star guesthouse, aptly named Dunen Haus, in the dunes just before Cape Vacca – both are simply gorgeous.)

▶ DAY 4 Kanonpunt/Dunen Haus to Kanon Village

5 KM/10 KM • 2 HR/3 HR

It's hard to leave this spectacular place but the last day on the trail, which stays on a path above the beach, has some interesting diversions. There is replica of a Dias cross at Cape Vacca and at low tide the old strandloper fish traps at were visible to the north, prompting Willie to explain their construction and the traditional methods of fishing by previous fossickers of the coast. The wild flowers were particularly striking along this section with brightly coloured aloes and pretty vygies providing wonderful photo opportunities.

Top Tip

Spoil yourself and book a massage at least once on the trail! Bring a mollusc permit (available at any post office) and you'll be able to collect wild oysters, white (sand) and black (rock) mussels to sample. Take time to visit the Post Office Tree Museum Complex, which includes the historic milkwood tree, Bartholomeu Dias' replica caravel and an excellent marine display.

On reaching the Gourits River estuary the path follows the river inland. After a swim in the river mouth trailists continue up-river for a short distance and then follow a footpath, which loops back over a hill and then meanders through the Cape Vacca private nature reserve. It has the most magnificent indigenous coastal thicket with stunning aloes, great views, a large variety of bird species and game such as bushbuck, grysbok, duiker and zebra. From there we were transported back to the Sandpiper leisure centre for a bubbly-and-oyster farewell.

In a nutshell · Oystercatcher Trail

BOOKINGS Sandpiper Safaris, 044-699-1204, stay@sandpipersafaris.co.za, www.oystercatchertrail.co.za.
START/FINISH Cape St Blaize, Mossel Bay / Sandpiper cottages, Boggomsbaai.
TRANSFERS Transfers back to the start or to and from George airport can be organised by Sandpiper Safaris.
HIGHLIGHTS Passionate guides who share their knowledge about this coast and the endangered African black oystercatcher; outstanding coastal scenery and landforms particularly on first day; empty swimming beaches and quaint seaside villages; dolphins, and whales in season; superb hospitality.
LONGEST DAY 16 km.
SHORTEST DAY 4 km.
GROUP SIZE Minimum 6, maximum 12.
UP TO IT? This is a straightforward, flexible trail that is ideal for novice hikers and family groups. The emphasis is on getting out and enjoying nature rather than on racing to the finish.
DON'T FORGET! A small day pack, warm and fully waterproof clothing and personal gear. A swimming costume – even if you don't brave the sea you might want to take a dip at the leisure centre!
LOOK IT UP A detailed map of the trail (also available on the website) along with a tide table and a check list of bird, reptile, mammal and marine species, is given out at the start.
LOGISTICS Luxury, catered guided hike staying in thatched Cape cottages. Bags driven around.
WHEN TO GO The trail can be walked year round except between mid-December to mid-January when all accommodation is otherwise booked. July to October is the best time for whale watching from the shores. The Mossel Bay area has been rated by the *Guiness Book of World Records* as having the second-best holiday climate in the world – much milder and more settled than that of Cape Town.
BEFORE AND AFTER Sandpiper Cottages, Boggomsbaai, www.sandpipersafaris.co.za

Survival Notes

- Drinking water not available on the trail.
- 2- and 5-night options available.

10

Garden Route Trail

Western Cape

DISTANCE 59 km ◆ **DURATION** 5 days ◆ **DIFFICULTY** 3 ◆ **TRAIL TYPE** Beach
LOGISTICS Bags driven around ◆ **COST** RRR ◆ **ACCOMMODATION TYPE** Chalets and cabanas
AREA Southern Cape

Most visitors to the scenic Garden Route, international and local alike, hit the
main tourist spots of Plettenberg Bay and Knysna, but tend to miss the treasures
in between. The Garden Route Trail opens up the rest of the area: the glorious
beaches, the lakes and vleis, the winding, reed-lined rivers, the fynbos and
indigenous forests and incredible coastal rock formations.

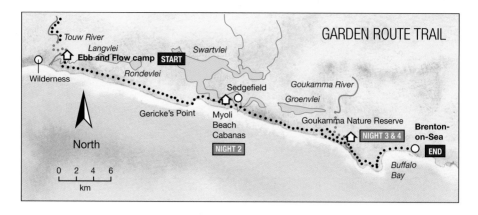

GARDEN ROUTE TRAIL

Touw River
Langvlei
Swartvlei
Ebb and Flow camp **START**
Wilderness
Rondevlei
Sedgefield
Goukamma River
Groenvlei
Gericke's Point
Myoli Beach Cabanas
NIGHT 2
Goukamma Nature Reserve
NIGHT 3 & 4
Brenton-on-Sea
END
Buffalo Bay

North

0 2 4 6
km

What makes this trail so special is the guiding. Mark Dixon, who developed and runs the trail, is as knowledgeable and passionate as any guide I've ever come across, so you'll finish the trail inspired and informed about the diverse and beautiful environment you usually whizz through on the N2.

The 5-day trail starts at the SANParks Ebb and Flow rest camp in Wilderness and finishes some 57 km later in Brenton-on-Sea just outside Knysna. It's a meander along the long, empty beaches of Wilderness, Sedgefield and Buffalo Bay, through coastal dune forest and up to tinkling waterfalls. Certain sections are covered by canoe, and all the time you're on the lookout for coastal and forest birds, and scouring the beach and rock pools for marine life. Although the beginning and end points are fixed, the trail is flexible and the route is chosen according to the weather, and with the interests and physical capabilities of the group in mind.

If you want a break you simply ask about a seashell, a plant or a bird and Mark will happily fill you in as you catch your breath. If want to sit with your binoculars for an hour, or take a quick dip, no problem. This is not just a trail, it's an immersion in the natural beauty of the Garden Route.

▶ **DAY 1** Ebb and Flow rest camp return walk

5 KM ◆ 2 HR PLUS 5 KM PADDLE

This is a great introduction to the area and the waterways that make the Garden Route so green and lush. We paired up and hopped into canoes and, after some brief instructions on paddle technique, headed up the Touw River. Soon we could no longer hear the traffic. The sound of birds and lapping water replaced the constant drone of modern life and we pulled over to look at the wonderful overhanging trees draped with old-man's-beard lichen and at colour-

The Garden Route Trail takes you along gorgeous beaches that most visitors never step foot on.

Crossing of the Swartvlei river mouth at Sedgefield doesn't always require the aid of a boat … but it's fun.

ful malachite kingfishers. A clever cormorant accompanied us the whole way, using the shadow of the boat to sneak up on unsuspecting fish, which it would then dart off and catch.

As the river narrowed we pulled our canoes to the bank and continued upriver on foot along the Giant Kingfisher Trail. The return hike to a waterfall was a full 5 km so we took it slowly, enjoying the damp, cool environment of the indigenous forest – a welcome escape from the summer heat. While striding along the recently completed boardwalk we watched out for forest birds: green wood-hoopoes, turacos and nesting paradise flycatchers. The spoor of forest folk was evident all around the pools – otter, baboon and bushbuck had been there not long before. We swam in the refreshing pools and rested awhile before heading back along the trail, amused by the antics of some shy vervet monkeys.

Wind conditions were condusive so that afternoon we set off paddling along the winding Serpentine. The narrow, heavily reeded channel was reminiscent of the Okavango delta and the twitchers in the group were, of course, in their element. We spotted malachite, half-collared and pied kingfishers, spoonbills and numerous waterfowl as we wriggled along the snaking channel, catching our paddle blades in the reeds and gliding slowly through the shallow water. The trips are well planned; after a couple of kilometres of gentle paddling upstream, just as we were beginning to tire, we turned around and floated gently back to the Ebb and Flow rest camp for a night in one of the comely chalets.

▶ **DAY 2** Wilderness to Myoli Beach Cabanas

21.5 KM ◆ 7 HR

Mark demonstrated his versatility by throwing together an excellent dinner, and then we breakfasted well at the rest camp before hitting the trail. Soon we were at the coast and paused at a lookout point on top of a dune overlooking a long stretch of golden beach. 'Welcome to my office! This is where we're going to do business today,' grinned Mark as we admired the bay and some precipitous cliffs of the fossilised dunes in the distance. Not too shabby a view from your office window, we agreed.

Our lunch spot, the rocky promontory of Gericke's Point, was visible 15.4 km away in the distance, but the tide was low so we hoped for an easy walk on hard sand.

The sandstone rocks and cliffs of this stretch of coast are actually eroded fossilised sand dunes.

'Look up!' someone cried as a paraglider swooped over our heads. Wilderness is a popular training ground for novice flyers as well as a playground for those who soar the on-shore updraft along the dune ridge.

We ran down like kids to the glorious expanse of Wilderness beach and it was good to feel the sand between our toes. After a short orientation around Mark's 'office' – a check on the tide table, discussion on dune formation and a quick toe in the water to test the temperature – we headed off towards Sedgefield. The beach was deserted, which, given that it was the height of summer, was not what we'd expected on the busy Garden Route. A couple of fishers were trying their luck just below the car park at Kleinkranz, but otherwise we had the place all to ourselves.

The ochre and orange dunes that flank the beach revealed the past activity on this stretch of coast, the great striations telling of periods of sedimentation and erosion by rivers and the sea. We spotted oystercatchers, some of which had chicks hidden among the rocks, and the fiercely protective adults bravely flew at us by way of diversion, so we gave the nests a wide berth and studied the young through binoculars from afar. A big translucent jellyfish lay stranded on the dry sand and Mark called us around to watch the fun. As he placed it close to the water the sand came to life as the beach cleaners appeared, scores of plough snails laboriously hauling themselves up for their next meal.

Next he picked up a white mussel shell and explained that these are not only prised open by oystercatchers but also attacked by octopuses. Apparently the octopus drills through at the thickest point to extract the mollusc's vital organs, leaving a telltale hole in the shell. We learnt about the bluebottles and jellyfish that line the high-water mark, about the oyster beds and how to judge the length of time rocks have been exposed or covered with sand (I won't steal Mark's thunder, but it has to do with the green shine of unicellular algae and the covering of tiny periwinkles).

It was lunchtime when we arrived at Gericke's Point and we sat in the shade of an undercut rock and wolfed our sandwiches. The tide was out and the rock pools deep and inviting so we donned masks and snorkels and swam through the narrow channels and deeply eroded caverns, admiring the tiny fish and colourful starfish, anemones and sponges. We even saw a big blue-and-black nudibranch – quite a treat for non-divers. The breakers crashed against the edge of the wave-cut platform, sending up spray that formed rainbows and showered us like refreshing rain.

We swam in the next bay, then headed on to Swartvlei where an open row boat awaited to ferry us across the river mouth. When the river mouth is closed or at low tide you can walk across, but that would be to miss out on an entertaining little crossing and the chance to chat to our quixotic ferryman, an old salty dog and fisher. (Sadly ferryman Cecil Salt died a while back so another local fisher, Mingo, has taken up the oars.)

Our overnight spot, the Myoli Beach Cabanas, lay just around a curve in the coast, above the restaurant in which we were to dine that night. We were intrigued by Mark's reports of sightings of ragged-tooth sharks in the estuary so we dumped our bags and headed back to the river. We took a fast drift on the incoming tide seeing a large number of mullet, grunter and a few colourful subtropical species. It was getting chilly by the time Mark signalled us over and, sure enough, resting among some large boulders near the edge of the river were 3 raggies: a beautiful, large grey adult that looked like a torpedo, and 2 smaller juveniles.

We dived down to get a better view; they were in only 3 or 4 m of water so we could get close enough to eyeball them and check out their fearsome-looking teeth.

If the tide is right snorkellers at Gericke's Point can observe fascinating marine life.

Then it was a short swim to the take-out point where Mark's father was waiting for us. A big swathe of sea grass covered the riverbed near where we were to clamber out and Mark urged us to keep our eyes peeled for seahorses. But if they were there they were well camouflaged – sightings of raggies would have to do for the day.

▶ DAY 3 Myoli to Goukamma Nature Reserve rondavels

14.5 KM • 5 HR

After a comfortable night in the cabanas and a morning swim, it was back to the beach for a 9 km beach walk to Oysterbed. We had been counting the number of African black oystercatchers and were now up to 25 – a healthy population, it would seem. However, Mark told us these apparently numerous birds are in fact listed as being the second most threatened South African species thanks to habitat destruction caused by the encroachment of housing and infrastruc-

Whale bones and other interesting specimens are often exposed on the beaches and guide Mark Dixon, a trained ichthyologist, will tell you all about them.

ture as well as unwitting beach users. We walked on, mindful of the need to tread sensitively along the coast. I asked Mark how he came by all this knowledge. Turns out that, in addition to being a trained ichthyologist who has worked as a scientific observer on the tooth-fish fishing boats off Antarctica, he's travelled the world on hikes and other adventures. It's experience that he's put to good use in devising this trail.

The final stretch of the day's walk started off along a shady 4×4 track through the coastal forest, then we broke out of the canopy onto a path that ran along the fynbos-covered spine of a fossil dune. The views over the coastal plain towards the beach and down onto a milkwood forest in the valley was stupendous. We stopped at the highest point to take in this magnificent stretch before continuing round a bend for yet another spectacular vista – the Goukamma River flowing into the Indian Ocean.

From here we followed the path down through the emerging dune vegetation

(slowly re-establishing itself after a controlled burn in March 2006) to river level for the final home stretch. All that remained was to cross the tea-brown river to the camp. It was a hot day so we donned swimming costumes and swam across: Mark had assured us he would pull a pont across the river should there be non-swimmers in the group or if it was too chilly for us. The evening was spent at the scenic camp, a cluster of 3 rondavels over-looking the river, while Mark prepared a potjiekos for dinner and recounted tales of his searches for the elusive and mystical Knysna forest elephants. It was a wonderful bush scene – the only thing missing was a herd of elephants drinking at sunset!

▶ DAY 4 Goukamma Nature Reserve

5–8.8 KM • 2–3 HR PLUS 3 HR PADDLE

Day 4 is a relaxed dream day for nature lovers and birders. After breakfast we set out for a 3-hour canoe trip on the Goukamma River in search of a resident pair of spotted eagle owls and a pair of African fish eagles that have been nesting along the river for decades. Mark told us floods in 2007 had felled the yellowwood they were nesting in, but they had started roosting in a stand of eucalyptus trees. We were in luck in spotting the eagle owls and were soon gliding just 3 m beneath them. The older bird sagely peered down at us while the younger one prepared to fly – very special indeed. As we meandered up the river Mark pointed out nesting burrows of swallows, kingfishers and martins before we turned around and headed back to the picnic site in the reserve.

From there we headed out on a circular walk, this time crossing the river by pont and immersing ourselves in the milkwoods of the valley where we lost all sense of direction and distance. After traversing a copse of false saffron trees, we unexpectedly

The guide has a tough job – the long, empty beaches around Wilderness and Sedgefield is his 'office'.

popped out on a 4×4 track. Mark suggested a couple of route options while we examined the profiles of a strandloper midden. 'Feeling tired? We can stick to the track and take the short route to the pont and back to the rondavels. Or would you rather have a swim? If so, let's head down to the beach, swim and make for the lagoon mouth to see terns and more oystercatchers.'

We opted for the latter, enjoying the flexibility offered by slackpacking trails.

Mark's culinary skills were evident again as he produced a gourmet meal of tuna kebabs, prawns, veggies and salads (some of which were grown in his own veggie patch) followed by another of his mother, Judy's, wonderful desserts. The views were endless, the landscape tranquil and pristine and we felt a million miles from busy Knysna. The gaggle of strangers who had gathered together in Wilderness had become a coherent group, united by a growing awareness of and passion for the unbelievably beautiful surroundings Mark was revealing to us.

▶ DAY 5 Buffalo Bay to Brenton-on-Sea

9.3 KM ◆ 3 HRS

The final day is a short one, allowing hikers plenty of time to either drive back home or to catch a flight from George airport. Initially we hiked along the bank of the Goukamma River to the mouth and then it was onto the golden sands of Buffalo Bay. Mark teased us with another choice – we could swim the 3 km across the bay or walk 5 km along the magnificent crescent-

Top Tip

Ask many questions and you'll come away enriched. Mark Dixon is a fount of information who really enjoys showing off the treasures of his backyard. Carry some money with you on day 5; a late lunch at Brenton-on-Sea before getting into the shuttle goes down a treat.

shaped beach and up through the fynbos to a viewpoint.

We enjoyed one last look back along the beautiful coastline before heading back to the beach for the final stretch to Brenton-on-Sea where our transfer to Wilderness awaited. The trail had been more than just a beach walk – rather it was a fascinating journey through beautiful, fragile environments that we now looked at with new eyes. So my advice, with the wisdom of hind-sight: next time you plan to pass through on the N2, consider taking a few extra days to really do the Garden Route.

In a nutshell · Garden Route Trail

BOOKINGS Mark Dixon 044-883-1015, 082-213-593, beachwalk@gardenroutetrail.co.za, www.gardenroutetrail.co.za.

START/FINISH Wilderness / Brenton-on-Sea.

TRANSFERS Transfers back to the start are included in the cost.

HIGHLIGHTS The standard of guiding; the diversity of the environments; empty swimming beaches; fascinating dunes; rock pools; indigenous forest and forest birds.

LONGEST DAY 21.5 km.

SHORTEST DAY 5 km.

GROUP SIZE Minimum 4, maximum 12.

UP TO IT? This is basically a beach walk, which averagely fit hikers will easily manage – 7 to 76-year-olds have.

DON'T FORGET! Swimming costumes, warm and waterproof clothing (including a backpack cover) and personal gear. Ponchos are provided in case it rains but a good waterproof jacket is always a good idea. The bird life is awesome so bring binos and bird books. Since there are a couple of outings onto the water, waterproof casings for cameras and/or cellphones are a bonus. There are wonderful rock pools and gullies to explore, so consider at least a couple of masks and snorkels for a group.

LOOK IT UP A map of the trail is provided at the start. Another excellent reference is Peter Slingsby's Garden Route map www.themaps.co.za/gardenroute.

WHEN TO GO The trail can be walked year round but winters are cool, if damp, and pleasant for hiking. Rain falls throughout the year on the Garden Route – though Mark claims the sun always shines when he has a trail going!

BEFORE AND AFTER There are numerous guesthouses in Wilderness, and chalets and camping are available at the Ebb and Flow rest camp, 012-428-9111, reservations@sanparks.org, www.sanparks.org.

Survival Notes

- Drinking water rarely available on the trail.
- Occasional shops on route.
- Duration is 5 days, but there are shorter and longer options available.

11

Donkey Trail

Western Cape

 DISTANCE 26 km ✦ **DURATION** 2 days ✦ **DIFFICULTY** 4 ✦ **TRAIL TYPE** Mountain, fynbos and riverside ✦ **LOGISTICS** Bags carried by donkeys for night 1 and driven round to Die Hel ✦ **COST** RRRR ✦ **ACCOMMODATION TYPE** Historic cottages and tents **AREA** Swartberg mountains

If you like a strenuous hike by day but a soft bed, good meal and a glass of wine in the evening, the Donkey Trail is one for you. It's a spectacularly beautiful route over the Swartberg, into the famous hidden valley of Gamkaskloof. While it falls squarely into the category of luxury slackpacking trails, the trail is also a real challenge: the first day is a demanding climb to the top of a mountain that is harder than any single day on any of the other luxury hikes on offer. The trail encapsulates a strong sense of history; walking with the donkeys takes you back to the days when there was no road to the isolated valley of Gamkaskloof and goods were carried over the mountains by trains of donkeys and their drivers.

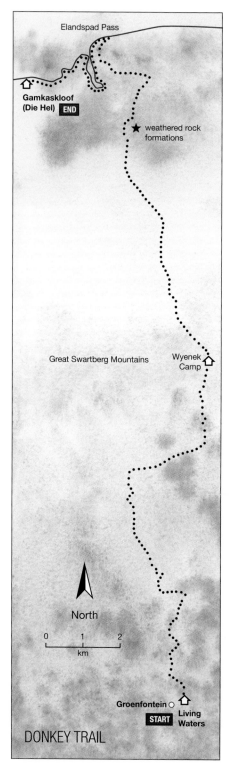

Elandspad Pass

Gamkaskloof (Die Hel) END

★ weathered rock formations

Great Swartberg Mountains

Wyenek Camp

North

0 1 2
km

Groenfontein ○ ⌂ Living Waters
START

DONKEY TRAIL

The fully catered and guided trail starts at Hans and Erika Calitz's farm, Living Waters Mountain Estate, in the Groenfontein valley about 15 km from Calitzdorp. It's a wonderful hike through magnificent fynbos and folded mountains, developed in partnership with CapeNature. The accommodation is delightful and even on top of the mountain you are treated like royalty. And on top of all that the trail has a real 'feel good' factor. It's very much a community project, which employs and empowers chefs, guides, donkey handlers and camp managers from the local settlements – people who have grown up in the valley and are happy to share their experiences along the way.

▶ NIGHT 1 Settling in

After a warm welcome at Living Waters we were shown to our en suite rooms in one of the renovated cottages on the farm. The historic buildings have been caringly furnished in traditional farmhouse style with old-fashioned gramophone players, kettles, cheese-making churns and big iron baths creating a sense of yesteryear. After a swim in the pool at the main house, we joined Hans and the guides for a briefing. A slide show included a detailed description of the trail, and the photos and route maps showed the unrelenting climb up to Wyenek and the overnight camp. We were left in no doubt about what we were in for but were assured that groups a lot older and less fit than ours had made it, so we should not be intimidated. We remained unconvinced!

Dinner that evening, prepared by Erika's mother Mimi and 2 local ladies, was an absolute feast that included pickled fish, vast platters of marinated chicken, marinated vegetables and fresh salads accompanied by delicious fresh bread. We barely had

The first night on the Donkey Trail is spent in a beautifully renovated historic cottage on Living Waters farm.

room for the sumptuous desserts but enjoyed our first taste of the local wines and Calitzdorp Port. Finally we waddled back to our rooms to pack our overnight bags – 1 to go to with the donkeys to the mountain camp and another for our arrival in Gamkaskloof – and to gather our strength.

▶ DAY 1 Living Waters Mountain Estate to Wyenek

15 KM ◆ 8 HR

After breakfast the next morning – another wholesome spread of fresh fruits, yoghurts, cheeses, eggs and freshly made breads, which we barely made an impact on – the donkeys were brought onto the lawn in front of the main guest area and loaded up. It turned out to be one of the unexpected highlights of the trail. The affectionate beasts, all previously abused animals from the De Rust Working Donkey Project, thoroughly enjoyed being the centre of attention and the petting they received as the panniers of overnight gear were strapped to their backs. We then set off with just rain jackets, cameras and water in our packs, and a spring in our steps.

The trail started off gently enough, and we had time to enjoy the mountainous landscape and the marked differences between the thicket of the west-facing slopes and the succulent Karoo vegetation, with its profusion of aloes, on the eastern slopes. All too soon, however, we were faced with a steep series of zigzags leading out of the valley. The community guides smiled encouragement as we looked daunted: 'It's not as bad as it looks. Just go slowly and stop when you need to. There's no rush.' After an hour of stiff climbing we stopped to look back. The farm was by now a tiny speck in the valley below – but the nek looked equally far away. The sight of a Verreauxs' (black) eagle soaring overhead inspired us upwards. We knew we would make it.

We kept climbing till we heard sounds approaching. 'Make way for the donkeys,' laughed Hans. We needed no second beckoning; the slope was steep and punishing so we willingly vacated the path to catch our breaths and let the beasts of burden pass. Under the watchful eyes of their handlers, Buddy and Thyme tiptoed through and we fell into line behind them and trudged on

After a night at Wyenek we said farewell to our 4-legged friends before setting out for Die Hel.

up, enjoying the natural rhythm of their steady pace and the companionship of the gentle Neds.

The path contoured round for a while through a renosterveld zone before descending into a steep river valley where the women in the group were invited to swim while the men modestly continued to another nearby stream to bathe. This second river crossing, one of the few places on the trail where there's shade, looked like a good lunch spot so we rested our weary legs as the guides unpacked the standard issue blue lunch boxes.

A steep climb out of the valley soon drove away our post-lunch lethargy, then we were pleased to find the trail actually descending for a while before rounding a spur to reveal magnificent outcrops of folded rock. The flowers were exquisite: pretty swathes of pink and purple ericas as well as tiny, delicate little blooms lining the path. We still had some way to climb and the day was heating up, so we took full advantage of the opportunities to ask the guides to identify this or that plant! The final section was a sustained climb up a series of zigzags to the saddle, with some interesting rock

formations to explore whenever we needed an excuse for a breather, and views all the way to the Red Hills and the Gamkaberg. A group of guides who had gone up the day before to set up camp stopped to check that we were all okay and offered to take any stragglers back down to Living Waters. We were strong, we assured them, trying to smile and look the part. In fact we were managing the long haul surprisingly well, thanks to the slow pace and the encouragement from Hans and his team.

Finally we reached the saddle and sat on the rocky outcrops like dassies soaking up the sun. We were now at 1 523 m having gained some 1 200 m so were pleased with our efforts – Living Waters seemed such a long, long way down in the valley. The scenery to the north was very different from the steep slope we'd just slogged up. Our path led down a gentle slope covered with big clumps of *Protea lorifolia*.

'Only an hour to go now,' the guides assured us. And in fact the hike down to the river valley and on to the overnight hut seemed even shorter than that. We admired the tumbling stream and were talking of swimming in its deep, inviting pools before spotting tents perched on a flat river terrace just ahead. We forded the river above a spectacular waterfall and were directed to the 'dining room' – a sheltered area of wooden tables and benches where tea was waiting. Hans introduced the camp manager who explained the set-up, the location of the loo with a view and how to get to the big swimming hole at the base of the waterfall just downstream, then we were shown to our larney tents.

I have to hand it to the camp team who, every time they have hikers, set up an *Out of Africa*-style bush camp on this high windy plateau. In our spacious canvas tent were 2 stretcher beds complete with mattresses,

No prizes for spotting the skull formation on this weathered rock on the second day of the trail.

sleeping sheets, warm sleeping bags and pillows as well as battery-operated lights, a basin, flask of hot water, soap, shampoo, body lotion and towels – and of course our personal gear in the panniers that had come up on the donkeys.

It was the first time I'd enjoyed such luxury on a mountain trail, and there was more to come. Once we'd bathed and sunned ourselves by the pool we dressed up warmly for sundowners. Beer and wine were retrieved from the 'fridge' in the river and we toasted our success, and an excellent day in the mountains, before tucking in to a hearty dinner. Although tired we sat out until quite late looking at the stars and discussing the history of the Donkey Trail and the hidden valley of Gamkaskloof (Die Hel) where we were headed the next day. Then happy, if a little weary, we retired to our tented suites.

▶ **DAY 2** Wyenek to Gamkaskloof

11 KM ◆ 6 HR

After breakfast and cappuccinos served in cute mugs painted with donkeys, we ambled around to the guides' camp to bid farewell to the donkeys, which were being loaded up for their return journey to the farm. It was a short climb up to the edge of the watershed from where we could see the long descent to Gamkaskloof. The guides identified the various ranges of impressive mountains laid out before us and strained our imaginations as we tried to find a formation resembling a skull and identify various animal likenesses among the weathered rocks.

The path to Die Hel was pretty much downhill all the way. As we lost height the views of the valley got better and better – a long green swathe in the otherwise barren landscape. The vegetational change was quite remarkable – suddenly we dropped out of the colourful aromatic fynbos into rather drab, scrubby renosterveld. Finally, as we neared the road into Die Hel, the slopes were covered with great towering aloes, which were irresistible photo models. The guides pointed out eland spoor on the path and we caught a glimpse of a pair of agile klipspringers on the rocky boulders just before we reached the dirt road that led down to the reserve entrance.

This section of the road, Elandspad, is incredibly steep – it was clearly quite a feat of engineering to open the kloof up to the outside world. We declined the offer of a lift and ambled down the road to the

Swartberg Shangri-la

Gamkaskloof (Die Hel) lies within the Cape Floristic Region World Heritage Site. It was first permanently inhabited by Dutch-descended farmers in the 1830s, but was only accessible on foot (or donkey) so was pretty much isolated from and unknown to the outside world until General Jan Smuts's commando stumbled upon it during the Anglo-Boer War. The gravel road and pass from the top of the Swartberg Pass was completed in 1962, and from then change came rapidly. By 1980 none of the valley dwellers remained.

No one is sure where the name Die Hel (hell) came from but one widely accepted version is that Piet Botha, a livestock inspector in the 1940s, had to travel to Gamkapoort every couple months, usually gaining access by a steep foot path at the far western end of the valley called The Ladder – a common access point until the road was built. He described the trip as 'hell'.

The overnight accommodation at Wyenek is more in keeping with that of a luxury bush camp than a hiking trail.

thickly vegetated valley of Die Hel where we lunched at the shady picnic site at the base of the tortuous, swithback pass. We had the option of continuing the hike along the valley floor but the hot sun and good food made us lazy so we were happy to be transferred by vehicle to our home for the night – one of the restored pioneer cottages in the valley. The specific cottage hikers stay in depends on group size and availability but the whitewashed, clay-wall dwellings are all full of character and the spirit of the hardy settlers who built them.

The day was still young so we dozed for a while until the sun had lost some of its intensity, then wandered around the grave-yard and the other cottages as the guides prepared the evening braai. The mountains glowed in the late light as we toasted our hosts with cold beers and wine. Again the food was superb, a selection of braai meats and boerewors, vegetable kebabs and imaginative salads. As we ate the guides regaled us with stories of the various characters who had lived in this valley, as well as their own lives in the neighbouring valley.

And there's even a deep natural rock pool just below the camp in which to bathe.

Not weary yet?

Before leaving Gamkaskloof in the morning you have time to fit in another short hike. The easy 6 km walk along the valley floor to the info centre should take no more than an hour and a half – alternatively, you can head out with a guide book on the Grootkloof interpretative trail, which takes roughly the same amount of time.

In the morning we rose early to visit the small CapeNature visitors' centre near the head of the valley. Gamkaskloof is an intriguing place and the interpretive boards and displays at the centre reveal much about its history, flora and fauna. After a stop to buy some home-made jams at the olde worlde shoppe on the property of the last remaining original resident of Gamkaskloof, Annetjie Joubert, we hopped into vehicles for the long climb out the valley, up the steep gravel road that joins Swartberg Pass and then back to Living Waters on the southern side of the range. It was an amazing journey. The road was dusty and precipitous, but we stopped several times to admire the wild flowers and to watch baboons or klipspringers bounding up the steep slopes. We'd been hiking only for a weekend, but it seemed like an eternity.

In a nutshell · Donkey Trail

BOOKINGS Erika Calitz, 083-628-9394, info@donkeytrail.com, www.donkeytrail.com.

START/FINISH Living Waters Mountain Estate, Groenfontein (15 km outside Calitzdorp)/Gamkaskloof.

TRANSFERS Transfers back to the start are included in the package.

HIGHLIGHTS High quality accommodation, guiding and attention to detail in every area of the experience; following the donkeys along the historical routes; spectacular mountain scenery; wonderful fynbos and game sightings; the night in the evocative, hidden valley of Gamkaskloof.

LONGEST DAY 15 km.

SHORTEST DAY 11 km.

GROUP SIZE Minimum 4, maximum 8.

UP TO IT? Overall this rates as a moderately strenuous trail. The hike up to Wyenek is strenuous but you're carrying only a day pack and you are free to take it just as slowly if you feel like.

DON'T FORGET! Perseverance for the big first day on the trail. Otherwise the trail organisers seem to have thought of everything.

TRAIL NOTES You stay in charming renovated, historic cottages on nights 1 and 3 (on night 3 you'll share a bathroom). The night on the mountain is in well-equipped, spacious 2-person safari tents and there's a shared portaloo.

WHEN TO GO The trail can be walked from mid-August to the end of June. Spring and autumn are probably the most pleasant for hiking, particularly since the temperatures are less extreme than summer or winter and many of the fynbos species are in flower. Summers in the valley are very hot, while winters are cold and snow is a distinct possibility on the peaks.

Survival Notes

- Guides carry extra drinking water.
- Longer hikes are available on request.

12

Dolphin Trail

Eastern Cape

DISTANCE 17 km ◆ **DURATION** 2 days ◆ **DIFFICULTY** 3 ◆ **TRAIL TYPE** Coastal, craggy, forest ◆ **LOGISTICS** Bags driven around ◆ **COST** RRRRR ◆ **ACCOMMODATION TYPE** Luxury chalets ◆ **AREA** Tsitsikamma coast

This luxury hiking trail is the perfect introduction to the delights of slackpacking, and a chance to intimately experience one of South Africa's most dramatic sections of coastline. The accommodation along the Dolphin Trail is luxurious and the trail is seen by many hikers as the 'alternative Otter Trail'. Like its famous sister, the Dolphin Trail starts at Storms River Mouth and the scenery is equally spectacular.

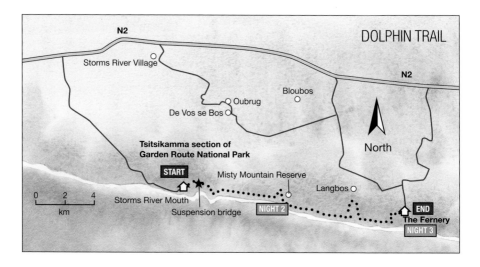

The 3-night, 2-day, 17 km Dolphin Trail – fruit of a partnership between the Garden Route National Park and 2 private-sector partners, Forest Ferns and Misty Mountain Reserve – starts at Storms River rest camp in the Tsitsikamma National Park and finishes a couple of days later at the privately owned Fernery chalets and nursery to the east. It's a wonderful, fresh coastal hike through indigenous forest, plantations and private farms that is spectacular but not unduly testing.

At times you're deep in the dense green forest admiring delicate ferns, at others

These wooden chalets overlooking the crashing ocean at Storms River rest camp were built specially for Dolphin trailists.

you're picking your way along through jagged rocks being showered with the spray of the sea or walking along a high path through sweet-smelling fynbos. The birds are spectacular and if you're lucky you'll see dolphins frolicking in the waves. You're spoilt with delicious meals, forest teas and beautifully decorated, up-market chalets. Best of all, unlike the Otter Trail, the Dolphin Trail is not yet booked up years in advance – but because it's a real hit with foreign visitors who don't have 5 days to spare for the Otter or other established slackpacking options, that may change. If you've limited time and/or like your creature comforts, this trail is just the ticket.

▶ NIGHT 1 Settling in

It's worth arriving early on the day before you start hiking to explore the magnificent Storms River section of the national park. There are few places in the world to match this setting – your chalet overlooks the ocean and the sound and smell of the sea will refresh even the most jaded soul. You can check in from noon, then head out on one of the trails or simply sit down at the coast among the aloes, staring out to sea. A

The narrow suspension foot bridge makes for an exciting crossing of the Storms River Mouth.

boat trip up the Storms River gorge is included in the trail package, and you'll also cross the famous suspension bridge so if you feel like a walk, rather head in the opposite direction and follow the Otter Trail for a few kilometres to the waterfall where you can swim and enjoy the spectacular scenery.

At 18h00 you'll be met by your guides and fellow hikers for snacks, a trail briefing and a short video on the Dolphin Trail before dinner is served at the Shark's Den. Then you can retire in anticipation of day 1.

▶ DAY 1 Storms River to Misty Mountain Reserve

7.5 KM • 4 HR

The leisurely pace of the trail is abundantly clear from the start – breakfast at the restaurant is at 08h30 so you've plenty of time for further exploration in the morning. Around 10h00 you hit the trail, along the boardwalk to Storms River Mouth and the Khoisan Cave. Here John, our guide, set the scene and offered something of the history and geology of the area before escorting us to the jetty for a river trip up the steep-sided gorge. As we motored upstream the

high cliff sides got closer and closer so that we felt as if we were entering a tunnel. The water was almost black, stained by tannins leached from the watercourse, and on our return trip against the incoming waves, they created a froth not unlike that found on a glass of freshly poured Guinness.

Once back on solid ground we headed for the narrow suspension bridge across the river mouth. The waves crashed below us and as we reached the other side the noise of rolling pebbles drowned out all other sounds. It was a steep climb from the beach to the lookout point at the top of the cliff – the hardest part of the whole trail – but we took it slowly and once on top we were rewarded with incredible views back over the Tsitsikamma coastline. The sea was rough so, despite our efforts, we saw neither whales nor dolphins, but John assured us that if the weather improved we might be in luck the next day.

Cheery voices greeted us from a Land Rover parked a couple of hundred metres further on – our first, unexpected refreshment stop where orange juice, coffee, tea and moist chocolate cake awaited us, along with our packed lunches. Revived, we gratefully accepted our freshly prepared sandwiches and followed the narrow trail along the cliff edge, enjoying the views before beginning a long descent through indigenous forest to a shady dell. The sun was shining so we rejected the offer of lunch in this cool place, preferring to continue to a big rock pool a little further on where we swam and lazed in the sun.

The next challenge was Steilkop (steep hill), a long, steady climb back up to the plateau. The views were incredible and we stopped often to admire the rocks – big, jagged orange teeth jutting out of the sea – and the ever-changing perspectives of this wild coastline. Before we knew it we were at the top and wandering through the plantation to Misty Mountain Reserve.

More refreshments awaited us, then we retired to our beautiful chalets, to a relaxing Jacuzzi bath and the opportunity to sit on the terrace admiring the views, the sound of the birds and the tranquillity of the lodge. The more active members of the group were soon enjoying the pool, while the twitchers had their binos out, scanning the dams and

From the moment you hit the trail at Storms River Mouth you enjoy the magnificent indigenous forest of the Tsitsikamma.

forest edges. Our group comprised mainly foreigners – Germans, in fact – who were blown away by the hike. As we sat over dinner that night, they explained how delighted they were with this short, accessible trail that didn't take up too much of their precious holiday time, yet allowed them to indulge in their favourite pastimes – hiking, and enjoying fine food and wine!

▶ DAY 2 Misty Mountain Reserve to The Fernery

9.5 KM ◆ 4 HR

We'd slept well, so set off enthusiastically down the steep path to the coast. The narrow track wove through rocky gullies and grassy flats and at times we found ourselves scrambling between big slabs of grey stone, where the sedimentary rock layers had been folded up into nearly vertical planes. We stopped to admire little clumps of colourful flowers and kept our eyes peeled around Otter's Alley for signs of Cape clawless otters that often frequent this section of coast.

We stopped for another swim in a rock pool before heading up again on our final climb. Then it was back into the indigenous forest where we admired and learnt the diagnostic features of the different types of ferns (tree ferns, sword ferns, river ferns, 7-week ferns and coral ferns) until suddenly we reached a clearing where lunch awaited – a huge buffet of fresh bread, cheese, ham and muffins all spread out on a trestle table. As I said, this trail is a spoil …

From there it was a gentle meander through the forest to the end of the trail at The Fernery. After welcome drinks, our haute cuisine menu was presented for us to choose from the various starter and entrée options and we were then shown to our beautiful chalets along the river. We declined the various adventure activities and

Ancient tectonic forces have folded the once horizontal beds of sedimentary rock into near-vertical planes.

Dolphin Trail **115**

opted to laze around the pool and browse the curio shop and nursery. Ferns, restios and other flowering plants are grown here for export to the European markets and the big, covered incubation areas had a wonderful peaty smell.

Dinner that night was a celebration. Although we'd only been on the trail for 2 days, we felt we'd had a much longer escape. We were in no rush to leave in the morning so we enjoyed a sumptuous breakfast before boarding a 4×4 for the trip back via the old Storms River Pass to our cars. We stopped at the bottom of the pass for a final indulgence – it was a wrench to leave this beautiful place.

In a nutshell · Dolphin Trail

BOOKINGS The Fernery 042-280-3588, info@dolphintrail.co.za, www.dolphintrail.co.za.

START/FINISH Storms River Mouth rest camp (Garden Route National Park) / The Fernery.

TRANSFERS The transfer back to your vehicle is included in the package.

HIGHLIGHTS Outstanding coastal scenery and landforms; wonderful rock pools; sightings of whales and dolphins; indigenous forest and ferns; turacos (previously known as Knysna louries) and other forest birds; superb accommodation and, at Forest Ferns, gourmet cuisine.

LONGEST DAY 9.5 km.

SHORTEST DAY 7.5 km.

GROUP SIZE Minimum 1, maximum 12.

UP TO IT? Anyone of moderate fitness will enjoy this stunning trail. Although there are some steep climbs and rocky sections, the distances are short so you can go at a slow pace, stopping as often as you like.

DON'T FORGET! Personal gear, including binos and field guides to the trees and birds if you're interested. There are a couple of wonderful rock pools to explore, so consider carrying at least a dive mask.

LOOK IT UP A map of the trail is available on the website.

WHEN TO GO The trail can be walked year round, but winters are cool and pleasant for hiking. The Tsitsikamma coast has a mild climate with most rain falling during April and October. If you go in summer, expect to get wet so waterproof your day pack.

BEFORE AND AFTER The night before the trail starts is spent in the stunning chalets in the Storms River rest camp. It's one of the most beautiful settings in the world, so enjoy it. The last night is spent at Forest Ferns, where you can happily spend a few extra days enjoying the magnificence of the Tsitsikamma mountains, cycling, fishing or lazing around the pool.

Survival Notes

• Ample drinking water available on the trail.

13

Diaz Cross Trail

Eastern Cape

DISTANCE 80 km ◆ **DURATION** 5 days ◆ **DIFFICULTY** 3 ◆ **TRAIL TYPE** Beach
LOGISTICS Bags driven around ◆ **ACCOMMODATION TYPE** Guest home and
guesthouse ◆ **COST** RRRR ◆ **AREA** Sunshine coast

It's hard to believe there are still totally empty stretches of coastline so close to a
major city, Port Elizabeth, and the popular resorts of Kenton-on-Sea and Port Alfred.
On the 4 days we spent on the Diaz Cross Trail we saw barely a soul outside our
overnight villages, save for the odd fisherman in the early morning or late afternoon.
The scenery along this luxury beach trail is inspiring in a lonely wind- and, wave-
tossed way – from the towering sand dunes of Woody Cape to the undercut rocks
of the Three Sisters – and since you never leave the beach and the distances are
never too taxing, it's a trail that even relatively unfit and novice hikers can enjoy.

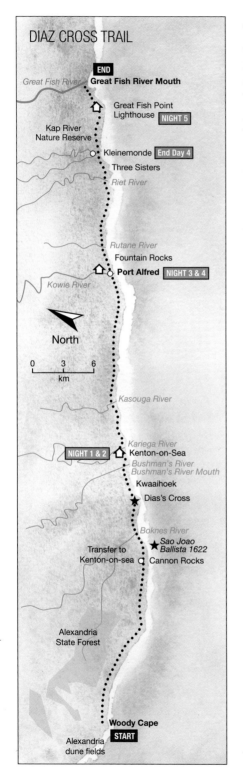

DIAZ CROSS TRAIL

Great Fish River — **END** Great Fish River Mouth

Great Fish Point Lighthouse — **NIGHT 5**

Kap River Nature Reserve

Kleinemonde — **End Day 4**

Three Sisters

Riet River

Rutane River
Fountain Rocks
Port Alfred — **NIGHT 3 & 4**

Kowie River

North

0   3   6
km

Kasouga River

Kariega River
NIGHT 1 & 2 — Kenton-on-Sea
Bushman's River
Bushman's River Mouth
Kwaaihoek
★ Dias's Cross

Boknes River
★ Sao Joao Ballista 1622
Transfer to Kenton-on-sea
Cannon Rocks

Alexandria State Forest

Woody Cape
START
Alexandria dune fields

This luxury hiking trail runs from the high dunes of Woody Cape (part of the Addo Elephant National Park, near Alexandria) to the Great Fish River Mouth. Your bags are driven to the private homes and guesthouses that serve as overnight spots, while David Lawson, one of the partners in Sunshine Coast Hiking Trails, acts as your guide, pointing out the shipwrecks, filling you in on the background to the area and taking you on local excursions. It's a trail you can do barefoot, carrying only a bathing costume, a waterproof and your lunch pack – and if you choose not to walk a section, no problem, you can catch a lift in the back-up vehicle. This is a hike to take slowly – to appreciate the solitude, to swim, explore the rock pools and to soak up the rays of the sunshine coast.

► DAY 1 Woody Cape to Cannon Rocks

14 KM ◆ 6 HR

The trail starts at Woody Cape, on the dune-field near Alexandria – the highest shifting dunes in the southern hemisphere we were led to believe. After buying your permits and checking out the maps at the rather quaint SANParks office, you drive down through the green coastal Alexandria forest to the trail head. This low-canopy forest is a unique mix of valley bushveld, lowland subtropical and Afro-montane temperate forest. A short walk takes you out of the canopy to a viewpoint overlooking miles and miles of empty sandy beach, with the sanctuary of Bird Island barely visible to the southwest in the curve of Algoa Bay.

Once down off the dunes you're in a different environment – a world of black oystercatchers, gulls and sand plovers, where shells are washed up on the beach along with the odd crate or other piece of flotsam. There are no other people, no dogs, no cottages, no roads – just your group and the backdrop of the magnificent forested dunes. Timing is everything on this hike, as you need to walk either side of the low tide to take advantage of the firm sand. We had timed our departure well so it was easy going, the sand was warm under our feet and we stopped often to swim and cool off. We briefly followed a cliff path past sea-shell middens, pump houses and reservoirs, lunched in a shady overhang and inspected the remains of a long-beached whale.

Eventually signs on the beach led us up to a settlement where a couple of cannons still stand sentinel over the ocean – Cannon Rocks of course. Oom Carel, our trusty logistics operator, picked us up here and took us to the private home of the Wilmot family, overlooking the Bushman's River where we readily accepted cups of refreshing tea before retiring for a short recuperative nap.

▶ DAY 2 Cannon Rocks to Kenton-on-Sea

12 KM ◆ 4 HR

We felt surprisingly sprightly after the moderate rigours of day 1 and once we were transferred back to the beach at Cannon

The Dias Cross you can hike up to on day 2 is a replica of that erected by the Portuguese explorer.

Dias crosses

The impressive cross on the promontory just south of Kwaaihoek is in fact a replica of the original stone cross, the Padrão de São Gregório, erected here in March 1488 by the famous Portuguese explorer Bartolomeu Dias. Dias, searching for a trade route to India, was the first Portuguese navigator to round Cape Point and sail east along the coast of what is now South Africa. The cross seen on this trail, erected on his homeward journey, is the most easterly of the *padrãos* that mark his route. It is believed he turned around at the Keiskamma River, where the sister hike to this, the Three Sisters Trail, ends. Other well-known Dias crosses can be seen at Cape Point and at Mossel Bay.

Rocks were soon into our stride. This was to be a short day, but we were looking forward to the highlight of the trail, the Dias Cross (the trail uses the old fashioned 'z' spelling so we'll stick with that name). We passed a recent shipwreck stranded in the sand and the big stone cross came into view on a high, grassy promontory at the end of the sweeping Boknes Bay. David suggested a swim in the sheltered lagoon, but since there was a chilly wind blowing we passed up the invitation and continued along the sand to the steps leading to the monument.

The view from the raised site is fantastic – back towards the Boknes River and Cannon Rocks and along the endless beach that lead to the mouth of the Bushman's River – so we ate lunch there while David recounted the historic voyage of Dias.

The effort of walking on sand was taking its toll and we took the next stretch easy,

Sea arches and other wave and wind sculpted rocks are a highlight of the trail.

stopping to admire pretty shells. We passed the charming bay of Kwaaihoek, then paused at the Norwegian barque, the *Volo*, which was wrecked near the mouth of the Bushman's River in 1896, before heading back 'home' to the Wilmots' where we had spent the previous night. Refreshed by a swim and shower, we finished the day with a sundowner cruise on the Bushman's, admiring the fish eagles and scouring the banks of the Emlanjeni Private Game Reserve in the (on this occasion, vain) hope of spotting white rhino and buffalo.

▶ DAY 3 Kenton-on-Sea to Port Alfred

28 KM • 9–10 HR but can be shortened

Kenton-on-Sea is a sleepy place for most of the year and, again, there were few other beachgoers as we set off for Port Alfred. We crossed the Kariega River by boat and were soon walking along jagged cliffs and past rocky outcrops, which formed the most interesting coastal scenery along the trail. The treacherous nature of the coast was again in evidence as we hiked past a polished granite memorial to 'Shelley', a young woman whose plane had crashed into the ocean off Shelley Beach, and later

Day 1 of the trail ends at Cannon Rocks where a couple of salvaged cannons stand sentinel.

the bleached skeleton of a large southern right whale half buried in the sand.

Oom Carel was waiting just before Port Alfred's blue-flag Kelly's Beach, ready to shuttle us to the Royal Guest House. That afternoon we were treated to a cruise up the Kowie River past the fading buildings of the Wharf, the town's oldest street, and the private jetties of the newer riverbank houses to a tranquil stretch just beyond what used to be the 43 Air School's crash-boat jetty, from which, if a plane went down, a rescue boat would immediately be launched! Sundowners were served and we were entertained by jumping mullet and fish eagles soaring overhead.

The river is a bird-watcher's delight – herons and egrets cruise by and pied and malachite kingfishers grace the river's banks, while gulls and cormorants like the jetties. The turnaround point on the cruise was Mantoni's tea gardens, with its beautiful cycads. In the 1930s and 1940s the older folk would go up the river on a barge to this charming spot, where they'd listen to a band as they enjoyed their tea! We, however, enjoyed slightly stronger stuff as we retraced our journey down the river and ended the day with a trip through the ingeniously designed Kowie Marina, before retiring to the chic Royal Guest House for the night.

If you're lucky you'll overnight at the Great Fish Point lighthouse on the last night of the trail.

▶ **DAY 4** Port Alfred to Kleinemonde

16 KM • 4–5 HR

Surfers were using the breakwater at the river mouth as a point break and early-morning joggers and dog walkers greeted us as we strode onto the beach east of the Kowie River on the morning of day 4. Within a couple of hours we'd reached one of the highlights of the trail, a beautiful site near the Riet River called Three Sisters. The scenery resembles that which you'd find in Zanzibar and elsewhere on the east coast of Africa – eroded, undercut limestone outcrops that sprout luxurious vegetation. We stopped for lunch on the rocks at the second sister and scrambled up to admire the view along this gloriously desolate stretch of coast. After lunch we swam and explored the wave-cut platforms before hitting the trail once again. An hour so later we came upon a cluster of cottages at the mouth of the Kleinemonde River, from where we were transported back to Port Alfred for another night.

Top Tip

Scour the beach for delicate nautilus shells, which are occasionally found at the high-water mark. You rarely need shoes – a pair of Crocs or slops tucked into your pack are ideal.

▶ **DAY 5** Kleinemonde to
Great Fish River Mouth

10 KM ♦ 2–3 HR

In the morning we were transferred back to the beach at the twin river mouths of Kleinemonde where early-bird fishers were already on their ways home, but otherwise we had the sands to ourselves. The Great Fish Point lighthouse towered on the cliffs above us as we rounded the rocky point. We were continuing along the beach to Great Fish River Mouth before being shuttled back to this spectacular spot for the night (unless the lighthouse accommodation is booked, in which case hikers overnight in Port Alfred) – a much better option than struggling up the steep steps from the beach!

Once again there was Oom Carel to pick us up at the mouth and after lunch at the lighthouse we drove to the nearby Kap River Nature Reserve for a canoe trip upriver. We paddled slowly, past cycads clinging to rocky cliffs and tiny kingfishers patiently watching among the reeds before diving for their prey. A trumpeter hornbill could be heard in the distance and we drifted between the river banks, soaking up both the scenery and the sun. It was a relaxing end to what had been a remarkable beach walk.

In a nutshell · Diaz Cross Trail

BOOKINGS Sunshine Coast Hiking Trails 046-624-5295, sunshinehikes@border.co.za, www.sunshinecoasthikingtrails.co.za; Wild Coast Holiday Reservations 043-743-6181, meross@iafrica.com, www.wildcoastholidays.co.za.
START/FINISH Woody Cape / Great Fish River Mouth.
TRANSFERS Transfers to the start of each day's hike and back to the accommodation at night are included in the cost of the trail.
HIGHLIGHTS Beautifully long and empty beaches; the dramatic undercut limestone rocks of the Three Sisters; views from the Dias Cross; whale and dolphin sightings.
LONGEST DAY 28 km.

SHORTEST DAY 10 km.
GROUP SIZE Minimum 2, maximum 14.
UP TO IT? The trail is flat, distances are modest and there's usually at least 1 bale-out option a day so it's a good trail for novice and averagely fit hikers and family groups.
LOOK IT UP A useful brochure with a map and details of the trail is provided at the start.
WHEN TO GO The trail can be walked all year round.
BEFORE AND AFTER Accommodation in Port Alfred and surrounds can be arranged through Sunshine Coast Hiking Trails 046-624-5295, sunshinehikes@border.co.za, www.sunshinecoasthikingtrails.co.za.

Survival Notes

- Drinking water rarely available on the trail.
- Occasional shops on route.

14

Three Sisters Trail

Eastern Cape

 DISTANCE 68 km ◆ **DURATION** 5 days ◆ **DIFFICULTY** 3 ◆ **TRAIL TYPE** Beach (north-eastward) ◆ **LOGISTICS** Bags driven round ◆ **ACCOMMODATION TYPE** Guest homes and guesthouses ◆ **COST** RRRR ◆ **AREA** Sunshine coast

If walking along beautiful empty beaches fringed by high dunes appeals to you, look no further than the Three Sisters Trail. Like the Diaz Cross Trail – with which it overlaps for the first couple of days – the Three Sisters Trail is a beach walk, albeit with a few diversions thrown in. The coast you walk along is even less developed than that which is covered on the Diaz trail, so between overnight stops in small hamlets you rarely see a soul.

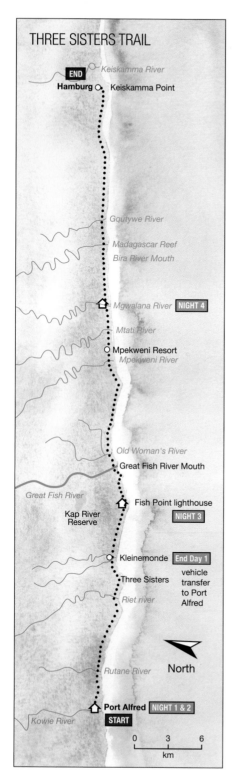

THREE SISTERS TRAIL

END
Hamburg ○ — *Keiskamma River*
Keiskamma Point

Gqutywe River

Madagascar Reef
Bira River Mouth

Mgwalana River **NIGHT 4**

Mtati River

○ Mpekweni Resort
Mpekweni River

Old Woman's River
Great Fish River Mouth

Great Fish River
Fish Point lighthouse
Kap River
Reserve **NIGHT 3**

○ Kleinemonde **End Day 1**
•Three Sisters vehicle transfer to Port Alfred
Riet river

North

Rutane River

Port Alfred **NIGHT 1 & 2**
Kowie River **START**

0   3   6
km

The trail starts in Port Alfred and heads northeast to Hamburg at the mouth of the Keiskamma River. It is along endless beaches flanked by vegetated dunes: the coast here has a stark, desolate beauty that is almost eerie in its emptiness, and you could be forgiven for feeling you were in a place a lot more remote.

The formula here is pretty much the same as on its sister the Diaz Cross Trail. Your bags are driven to the private homes and guesthouses that serve as overnight spots and, as on the Diaz hike, David Lawson guides you. You are also offered the choice to walk unaccompanied, with the back-up vehicle ferrying you around any necessary river crossings. So you can just kick off your shoes and take to the beach. The trail is flat and, with the exception of a long last day (which has a bale-out option if you tire!), the distances are short, so it's not unduly taxing.

▶ DAY 1 Exploring Kowie

AT YOUR LEISURE!

The trail starts in Port Alfred (also known as Kowie), a friendly little town on the Kowie River, among the country's longer tidal rivers. You kick off with a sunset cruise up the river, past the past-their-prime old Wharf Street buildings and larney houses, with their private jetties, to a spot several kilometres upstream where, if you're eagle-eyed, you'll spot cycads on the banks and fish eagles overhead. On your return you potter through the canals of the Royal Alfred Marina (a fascinating mini Fort Lauderdale kind-of-place), feast from the braai and retire to the wonderful Royal Guest House for the night. And if you still have time, other diversions such as golf, fishing, game drives, and water-skiing can be arranged, or you can simply relax at the pool or on the beach.

The trail starts with a leisurely cruise up the Kowie River, through the historic maritime town into nature.

▶ DAY 2 Port Alfred to Kleinemonde

16 KM ♦ 4–5 HR

Breakfast at the Royal Guest House was fresh and original. This is a real gem of a place, with airy, beautifully decorated rooms. Management has an eye for detail – scattered flower petals, carefully placed sprigs of lavender, the simple but tasteful décor and friendly staff contribute to a very special stay. Our guide David outlined the day ahead. After that we set off along East Beach past various local landmarks – Fountain Rocks, Oyster Rock and the Rufane River – before we stopped at the Riet River for a swim.

The highlight of the day was the wonderful rock formations from which the trail takes its name. The outcrops of the Three Sisters, with their blowholes, gullies and vegetated summits, sit on a wave-cut platform full of nooks and crannies. We enjoyed a long lunch break exploring and swimming in the warm tidal pools before continuing down the beach to Kleinemonde where our trusty driver Oom Carel from the Diaz hike before was waiting to lift us back to our overnight accommodation in Port Alfred.

▶ DAY 3 Kleinemonde to Great Fish River Mouth

10 KM ♦ 2–3 HR

The third day on the Three Sisters Trail is the same as day 5 on the Diaz Cross Trail:

The trail is named after a group of dramatically undercut calcrete rocks, the like of which are found all along the so-called Sunshine Coast.

The canoe trip on the seldom-seen Kap River is a treat, particularly for birders.

an easy beach stroll from the pretty bay of Kleinemonde past Clayton Rocks, Little Fish Point, the Palmiet River and Rocky Point to the lunch spot at the Great Fish River Mouth. Then you're transferred to the Kap River Nature Reserve for a canoe trip and birding adventure up the river. If it's not booked out, the overnight spot is at the historic Great Fish Point lighthouse, built in 1898. A night here is definitely one of the highlights of both this and the Diaz Cross trails: the view is breathtaking and the cottages (the lighthouse keeper's home) just super. It is a great and for most people unexpected treat that this scenic and very comfortable accommodation is available to the general public.

Oom Carel pointed out the steep steps coming up from the beach and recounted epic adventures he'd experienced here. After one particularly successful day's fishing on the point (and a few measures of medicinal spirits), he simply could not lug his load of fish, tackle box, rods and sundries up the path. He struggled and struggled, but eventually he gave up and had to resort to bribing his mate with bottles of whiskey to help him out. We felt for the man, having decided that even for us hikers it was too far to venture down to the beach for a swim. I wouldn't like to try to climb those steps with any load – they're seriously steep! We chilled out with our sundowners, enjoying the views over the Indian Ocean while David and his wife Lisa cooked up a storm on the braai.

▶ DAY 4 Great Fish River Mouth to Mgwalana River

16 KM ◆ 5 HR

We made a quick stop at the diner at the Great Fish River bridge before setting out on day 4 of the trail. This was the old Ciskei homeland border post until 1994, and the area has a fascinating history of frontier wars and settlers' tales. On the diner walls are photographs of huge fish that have been pulled out of the river – monster grunter and kob held aloft by proud fishers. But alas those kinds of catches are now very much a thing of the past – unless our marine stocks make a miraculous comeback.

From the river there were few distractions and the hike along the empty beach is elemental – miles and miles of just sun, sand, sea. We passed the mouth of the Old Women's River and David explained that the British Navy had landed a task force here to subdue the mighty Xhosa during one of the

Top Tip

Time your hike to take advantage of the low tides: walking on soft sand at high tide is very tiring! And be sure to keep your eye out for fragile nautilus (or pansy) shells on the last day.

Flocks of terns and other sea birds are usually your only companions along these long empty beaches.

8 frontier wars and, occasionally, wartime artefacts are still washed up on the beach.

We stopped to swim and lunch at Mpekweni River Mouth (in sight of the plush Southern Sun golfing hotel), then pushed on to Mgwalana. The warmth of our welcome at Mrs Bailey's cottage high on the dunes was quite a contrast to the stark, desolate beauty of this part of the coastline. Mrs Bailey clearly enjoyed having hikers invade her home and spoilt us with tea and cakes as she inquired about our experiences.

You might come across the odd holiday-maker at the caravan park near the Great Fish Estuary.

She has a veritable library of interesting books on the settlers and entertained us with stories of the tumultuous history of the region.

► **DAY 5** Mgwalana to Hamburg

26 KM • 8 HR

The last day was a long one and we barely saw a soul save for a few recreational fishers (an odd sight in this case as they had a wheelie trolley from which protruded what looked like a deadly arsenal of rods). We spotted dolphins surfing the waves just before reaching the Birha (pronounced *beega*, with a hard 'g') River, around which, since it was too high to wade, Oom Carel kindly ferried us. Back on the beach we passed a local eyesore, the gaudy buildings of the Sandcastle resort at the mouth of the Gqusha (you'll have to ask a local how to pronounce this one) lagoon, but our eyes were trained on the sand.

David had shown us some of the beautiful nautilus shells he'd picked up on this stretch, but we were out of luck. We walked past high dunes before rounding the corner to the Keiskamma mouth and small holiday fishing village of Hamburg. Wild, crashing waves pounded the sweeping arc of the beach, but we stopped anyway for a final swim before Oom Carel arrived to carry us away from it all. Although it had been a long and challenging day, we felt satisfied to have completed the trail.

In a nutshell · Three Sisters Trail

BOOKINGS Sunshine Coast Hiking Trails 046-624-5295, sunshinehikes@border. co.za, www.sunshinecoasthikingtrails. co.za; Wild Coast Holiday Reservations 043-743-6181, meross@iafrica.com, www.wildcoastholidays.co.za.

START/FINISH Port Alfred / Hamburg.

TRANSFERS Transfers to the start of each day's hike and back to the accommodation at night are included in the cost of the trail.

HIGHLIGHTS Beautiful, long empty beaches; dramatic undercut limestone rocks of the Three Sisters; dolphins, seabirds and, if you are very lucky, nautilus shells; overnight accommodation at the Great Fish Point lighthouse.

LONGEST DAY 26 km.

SHORTEST DAY 10 km.

GROUP SIZE Minimum 2, maximum 14.

UP TO IT? As with the Diaz trail, this hike is flat, distances are modest and there's usually at least 1 bale-out option a day; a good trail for novice and averagely fit hikers. You can opt to walk each day according to the prevailing wind, and as many or as few sections as you choose. And, should you wish, you can base yourself in the same overnight spot every night rather than pack up and move every day. This, and the wonderfully located, very comfortable overnight spots make it an ideal trail for families and those who enjoy leisurely hiking, as much as for the more energetic.

LOOK IT UP! A brochure with a map and details of the trail is provided at the start.

WHEN TO GO The trail can be walked year round, though March to the end of June are particularly fine months. But beware of the very high tides during the March equinox, which makes hiking a challenge! Winters can be cold so do go prepared.

BEFORE AND AFTER Accommodation in Port Alfred can be arranged through Sunshine Coast Hiking Trails 046-624-5295, sunshinehikes@border.co.za

Survival Notes

- Drinking water rarely available.
- Occasional shops on route.

15

Wild Coast Amble

Eastern Cape

DISTANCE 53 km ✦ **DURATION** 5 days ✦ **DIFFICULTY** 3 ✦ **TRAIL TYPE** Beach (southwestward)
LOGISTICS Bags driven around ✦ **COST** RRR **ACCOMMODATION TYPE** Hotels ✦ **AREA** Wild Coast

Building on the success of their Wild Coast Meander, Wild Coast Holiday
Reservations launched a second luxury hiking trail, the Wild Coast Amble. The
trail, which overlaps with the last day of the Meander, follows the route of the
Strandloper Hiking Trail but, instead of utilising overnight huts, offers comfortable
overnight accommodation on either a full-board or self-catering basis. As the name
suggests, it's a leisurely walk along beaches that the so-called strandlopers (Khoisan
or Xhosa beachcombers) once roamed, foraging and fishing from the rocks.

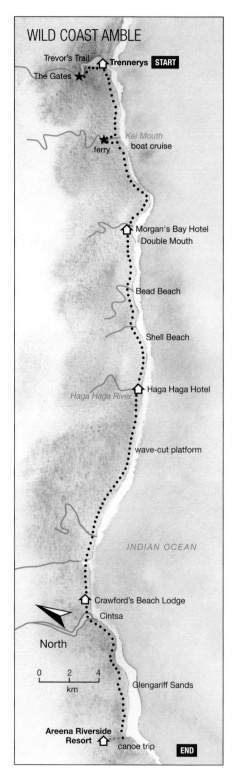

WILD COAST AMBLE

Trevor's Trail
Trennerys **START**
The Gates ★

Kei Mouth
ferry boat cruise

Morgan's Bay Hotel
Double Mouth

Bead Beach

Shell Beach

Haga Haga River Haga Haga Hotel

wave-cut platform

INDIAN OCEAN

Crawford's Beach Lodge
Cintsa

North

0   2   4
km

Glengariff Sands

Areena Riverside
Resort
canoe trip **END**

This trail starts at Trennery's Hotel a short way north of the Kei River and follows the coastline generally southwards to Areena River Resort just north of East London. It's roughly the same length and degree of difficulty as the Wild Coast Meander and, like the Meander, incorporates a number of interesting diversions: a visit to a local village, a cruise on the Kei (great) River and a canoe trip on the Kwelera River.

Just getting there is part of the intrigue – there's no bridge over this section of the old border between what was the 'independent homeland' of Transkei and the southern part of the Eastern Cape. You and your transfer vehicle are ferried across the river on a big yellow cable-drawn pontoon. Once you cross back over the Kei on day 2 the atmosphere changes a little, and the coast becomes less wild and more accessible, with long, empty beaches and the occassional holiday resort. It's a diverse, fascinating trail and, because it's so close to East London, it's convenient for anyone wanting an easily accessible escape without any schlep.

▶ **DAY 1** Settling in

OPTIONAL 3 KM CIRCULAR TRAIL ◆ 2 HR

Day 1 is geared to easing you into the easy pace of the Wild Coast. You journey from East London to the trail head via the old pontoon that bumbles across the Kei. The Kei was once the easternmost border of the Cape Colony and many battles between the British settlers and the Xhosa people were waged along its length. During the apartheid era (until 1994) the river was the southern boundary of the Transkei homeland, so it's not surprising that once you're over the river you still feel as if you're in a different country – even a different world. The roads are bumpier, the people are

You'll often encounter livestock grazing on the grassy section of trail between Trennery's and the Kei River.

friendlier and the place has a charming rural feel that is very different from the more sophisticated coastal resorts that you've left behind. By the time you reach the first overnight stop – that wonderful seaside abode of Trennery's Hotel – you'll be ready for the barefoot luxury that awaits you.

After lunch it's off on Trevor's Trail (see Wild Coast Meander, page 137) or to a nearby village where you meet a local Xhosa family. The order of the day varies, depending on who's around, but you'll be introduced to an *igqirha* (traditional healer) and be given a taste of traditional life in Xhosa homes – even in the 21st century.

The kids demonstrate how to make local food by grinding maize and kneading dough – and before you know it you'll be roped in, all the while being entertained by children dancing and singing as they carry out their chores. Nolokoza, the *igqirha*, performs a rite that is translated, with much empathy and sensitivity, by a Wild Coast veteran, Trevor Wigley. The experience offers a fascinating insight into rural life of the area.

Then it's back to the hotel for some chill time: to visit the gorgeous beach, wander in Trennery's lush, tropical gardens enjoying the birds, or sit out with a fine bottle of wine.

▶ **DAY 2** Trennery's to Morgan Bay

13 KM ◦ 4 HR (PLUS 2–3 HR CRUISE)

Our guide and porters were ready and waiting by the time we'd finished breakfast on day 2, so we packed water, cameras and rain jackets into our day packs and headed down to the beach. Our guide, Amos Nkonki, was smartly dressed in a collared shirt and chinos – very pukka for a beach walk! We were reluctant to leave the comfort of Trennery's, but it was an easy 6 km stroll to the Kei so we took our time. Goats grazed on the grass verges and warmed themselves on the sand, local women were out gathering shellfish from the rocks and

It's not all ambling along beaches; the section near Double Mouth involves some easy scrambling over rocks.

we poked around at the anemones, sea slugs and other marine life in the rock pools. It felt wonderful to be out, to be timeless, to be in such a beautiful place.

Around mid-morning we were back at the wide brown expanse of the Kei, which we followed inland over marshy mud flats to the now familiar pontoon. Once on the south bank we were escorted to another jetty to board the barge-like *Fish Eagle II*, and set off for a cruise up-river into the rugged interior where beautiful cycads clung to the cliffs and the big brown eyes of blesbok occasionally met ours.

The Trennery treat

Trennery's Hotel is something of a Wild Coast institution. It has been upgraded recently and we'd have happily whiled away a few days enjoying the empty beach, its lagoon and big swimming pool. I'd visited Trennery's many years before and remembered it as charming but rustic.

One incident, in particular, still makes me laugh. As I pulled back the bed cover on my first visit a little mouse shot out from the nest it had built in my pillow. I summoned the chambermaid, but when I moved the wardrobe to reveal the cowering little creature it promptly scuttled past her. The maid fled never to be seen again.

Somehow I can't see that happening now; the standards are topnotch and the staff extremely attentive! We celebrated starting the trail with oysters and sparkling wine served up by Pearl, our giggling, charming bar lady and were seriously impressed by the dinner menu – the chef serves up a choice of dishes that are more in keeping with a city restaurant than the sleepy Wild Coast.

Dredging for diamonds

There was a burst of prospecting activity on the Kei River in the 1900s. An old gentleman, Mr Bock, who lived on the northern side of the river, discovered diamonds – a lot of diamonds, in fact a jar full of them – over a very small area. The news went out and the rush was on with all sorts of fortune seekers arriving in the hope of finding precious stones. But to no avail. The old man was arrested and jailed for 3 years for fraud. But his extraordinary find had raised some suspicions: why were the diamonds only on his land?

After his death scientists discovered that the diamonds were, in fact, of South American and not South African origin. One mooted explanation is that that a survivor of the *Grosvenor*, the 741-ton British East India Company merchant ship, which ran aground at Lupatana north of Port St Johns in 1782, might have taken refuge, then died on the property having buried or lost his cache. Of the 125 survivors who made it ashore, only 13 are recorded as having made it back to 'civilisation'. Some survivors opted to chance their luck with local tribes and there are still places where their genes persist.

Our guide delighted the photographers and birders by throwing out a fish, which a resident fish eagle swooped down and caught, and entertained us with some local folklore. My favourite story was that of Huberta, the wandering hippopotamus that travelled some 1 000 km down the coast from KwaZulu-Natal. She lived in the river for a while at a spot called Third Cave and developed a taste for the local mealie lands. Not surprisingly this caused some upset and she was eventually chased away. She wandered on down the coast where she met a sorry end – shot at the Keiskamma River in the early 1930s. She is now preserved in the Amathole Museum in King William's Town.

I'd worked up quite an appetite after the morning's exertions, so the finger lunch went down a treat as we reversed our course back to the jetty. Then it was back on the trail. We were given the option of horse riding for the rest of the way, but the sun was shining and we all preferred to walk, opting to detour through the village of Kei Mouth for a visit to the interesting little shell museum rather than follow the coast the whole way. Once back on the coastal road we continued onto a jeep track, which we followed through the dune forest, past the Cape Morgan lighthouse and back down a forest path to a pump house. It was once part of old titanium mine that was operational there in the 1950s and which, before it was destroyed by storms, was used as an overnight stay on the Strandloper Trail.

The popular holiday resort of Morgan Bay was soon in our sights and we lingered on the beach, swimming and enjoying the views over towards the sea cliffs we'd be covering on day 3 before heading up to the Morgan Bay Hotel for a drink on the veranda. Oh, it's hard ambling along a beautiful coast!

▶ DAY 3 Morgan Bay to Haga Haga

14 KM • 5 HR

We knew day 3 was going to be more strenuous so we felt justified in tucking into a huge breakfast. Although we were given the option of continuing unguided (the trail is really straightforward), we were enjoying the information that walking with a local

The long stretch of beach before Haga Haga, the end of day 3 where we searched for washed-up beads.

brought. So, armed with tide tables – which we'd checked the night before as we'd planned our river crossings at low tide – and a packed lunch, we shouldered our day packs and strode out behind our leader. The trail led up to magnificent sheer cliffs off which, apparently, more adventurous types like to climb or to abseil. I can imagine it's hair-raising stuff – even looking over the edge at the exposed, rocky, wave-cut platform below is terrifying.

A goliath heron was also peering over the edge and the magnificent bird accompanied us for about 10 minutes, taking off as we approached and landing a few hundred

metres away before repeating its graceful flight. The next section of the trail along the grassy headland and over dark and brooding dolerite rocks was breathtaking and the wooden cabin and thatched rondavels of the beautifully located Double Mouth camp were soon in view. The path wound downhill to the Quko estuary, our first river crossing and our timing proved to be perfect. The water was not particularly deep, but we were taking no chances so stripped to our swimming costumes, balanced our packs on our heads and waded out into the swirling water. Then it was onto the beach for the rest of the day, admiring seashells, stopping to swim when we wanted to cool off and appreciating the solitude of this wonderful stretch of coast.

We lunched at Black Rock, a promontory where apparently numerous ships have come to grief, and scoured the beach like modern-day strandlopers. We were searching not for food but for beads, shards of Chinese Ming dynasty porcelain and other treasures that are regularly found washed up among the piles of shells. A local woman offered to sell us carnelian beads she'd collected and we chatted with her for a while before meandering down to the beautifully located Haga Haga Hotel for another classic evening relaxing by the sea.

▶ DAY 4 Haga Haga to Cefani

16 KM ◆ 5 HR

We were up and out early for this, the longest day of the trail, but the first little bay, Pullen's Bay, was so inviting we couldn't resist a brief stop to swim. Oystercatchers and other sea birds flitted about the rocks and our progress continued to be slow as we travelled across an exposed wave-cut platform, exploring small gullies and rock pools. On reaching the waterfall at Rooiwal we washed off the sand and salt of the sea in the fresh, clean water. The long beach of Cape Henderson stretched out before us, but we were advised to stop and swim at 1 of the 2 small beaches at the start because the steep slope of the main beach meant swimming would be dangerous there.

The rocks were covered by 'flatties', small oysters, and we spotted plenty of 'rollers' in the surf and washed up on the beach – big oysters that have broken off the rocks. Surprisingly many were still intact and, since we'd brought our oyster permits, we gathered a few to supplement our lunch.

The second half of the day was spent walking along a wide, sandy beach flanked by vegetated dunes – fairly strenuous walking even though it was low tide. We passed several lagoons in which children were playing. The lagoons were actually closed river mouths that burst open following rain. However, because it had been dry for some time, we had no further river crossings to contend with. Before long we were at the bottom of some steps on the beach that indicated the turn-off to our next overnight spot: the luxury, thatched cabanas of

Crawford's Beach Lodge, a private resort at Cefani, where we dined in style.

▶ DAY 5 Cefani to Areena Riverside Resort

12 KM ◆ 3–4 HR (PLUS 2 HR CANOE TRIP)

The final day of hiking was easy – the Amble is indeed the perfect name for this trail. After a slow meander along the rocks and narrow beaches, we arrived at Cintsa Bay. We were now re-entering the 'real' world of occasional shops and resorts, but in between there were lovely, empty, swimming beaches fringed with coastal forest. We rounded the rocky point off Glen Eden and splashed through the Bulura River to the sands of Glengariff. By early afternoon we were at the mouth of the Kwelera River ready for the final adventure – an easy 2-hour canoe paddle up river to the Areena Riverside Resort, our final night's accommodation.

After settling in to the lovely new chalets, we celebrated the end of the hike with drinks and a slap-up dinner. Some of our party had chosen an optional game drive at the nearby Inkwenkwezi Private Game Reserve the following morning: there is the option to enjoy an extra night or two on the reserve – a great value add-on if you

Trevor's Trail, an additional side trip offered to hikers, leads to The Gates – a steep-sided, hidden gorge.

fancy a bit of 'big 5' game viewing at the end of the trail. The others enjoyed sightings of plains game at Areena before being transferred back to East London.

Other options

Obviously you can walk this stretch of coast independently. If you prefer an unguided or non-portaged trip, but don't want the hassle of organising accommodation, transfers and the like, Wild Coast Holiday Reservations will happily take care of the logistics (this option starts at Kei Mouth). Variations include a night in the 'big 5' Inkwenkwezi reserve, staying in en-suite, luxury tented camps, enjoying game drives and viewing on quad bikes or on the back of an elephant, as well as a bush dinner.

In a nutshell · Wild Coast Amble

BOOKINGS Wild Coast Holiday Reservations 043-743-6181, meross@iafrica.com, www.wildcoastholidays.co.za.
START/FINISH Trennery's Hotel (Wild Coast) / Areena Riverside Resort (north of East London).
TRANSFERS Transfers to and from East London are included in the package.
HIGHLIGHTS Beautiful beaches; the dramatic cliffs between Morgan Bay and Haga Haga; a wide variety of seashells, birds and marine life; interaction with local Galeka – 1 of the 3 major clans of the Xhosa people; river cruise and canoe trip.
LONGEST DAY 16 km.
SHORTEST DAY 12 km.
GROUP SIZE Minimum 2, maximum 14.
UP TO IT? This really is an amble so it's ideal for novice hikers and family groups. Try to plan your beach walks around low tide – walking in soft sand can be very hard work!

DON'T FORGET! Swimming costumes, masks and snorkels, water bottles and personal gear. You may want to carry a small amount of change for a cool drink or snack along the way.
LOOK IT UP A great little map (and information brochure) is provided at the start.
WHEN TO GO The trail can be walked year round, except between the early December to mid-January holiday season and the Easter holidays when hotels are pre-booked. Winters are cool and pleasant for hiking. This section of the coast has a mild, humid climate, with most rain falling in summer. In summer you can expect not only rain but several river crossings, so it's worth waterproofing your pack.
BEFORE AND AFTER Meander Inn, East London 043-726-2310, meanderinn@telkomsa.net, www.wildcoastholidays.co.za/guest_houses.htm.

Survival Notes

- Water only occasionally available.
- Terrain largely beach walking, with river crossings.

16

Wild Coast Meander

Eastern Cape

DISTANCE 54 km ✦ **DURATION** 5 days ✦ **DIFFICULTY** 3 ✦ **TRAIL TYPE** Beach and coastal path **LOGISTICS** Bags carried by porters ✦ **COST** RRR ✦ **ACCOMMODATION TYPE** Hotels **AREA** Wild Coast

The Wild Coast is truly that – wild and empty. Fishers, cattle herders and curious local kids are generally the only people you meet outside the hotels, though at spring tide there are gaggles of cheerful women harvesting seafood from the rocks. The beaches are mostly deserted, the hills green and lush and the rock pools are perfect for snorkelling. All in all, the Wild Coast Meander is simply glorious; the fact that by hiring guides and porters you're creating jobs in an area that has a high rate of unemployment makes it really easy justifying not carrying your pack.

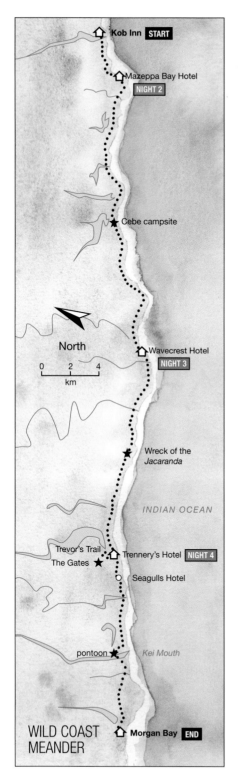

Kob Inn START
Mazeppa Bay Hotel
NIGHT 2
Cebe campsite
North
0 2 4
km
Wavecrest Hotel
NIGHT 3
Wreck of the
Jacaranda
INDIAN OCEAN
Trevor's Trail
The Gates
Trennery's Hotel NIGHT 4
Seagulls Hotel
pontoon
Kei Mouth
WILD COAST
MEANDER
Morgan Bay END

The hike starts at Kob Inn and finishes south of the Kei River at Morgan Bay, less than an hour's drive north of East London. Access to the area is limited to a few dirt roads that lead from the N2 to coastal villages and scattered resorts, so the only way to see most of the magnificent coastline is on foot or on horseback, along the sleigh tracks and cattle paths. As a result, the coast here is near pristine and still rather wild – a real nature lover's paradise. Hiking the long, lonely beaches allows you to appreciate not only the exquisite natural environment, but also gives you an insight into the unique culture of this remote part of the Eastern Cape.

For the local people life goes on, much as it has for centuries: the trappings of civilisation are few and the local people love the opportunity to interact with visitors. Along the way there are some interesting diversions and optional side trips that reveal the diversity of this coastline. They include a booze cruise or canoe trip on the Nxaxo River at Wavecrest, and Trevor's Trail into the forested gorge behind Trennery's. The Meander is not only the original slackpacking trail in this country, it's also – arguably – still the best.

▶ DAY 1 Settling in

AT YOUR LEISURE!

After the 2½-hour transfer from East London you get your first taste of the warmth of the Wild Coast in your welcome at the popular fishing resort of Kob Inn. The setting is superb and the resort boasts a big circular pool, spacious new rooms all with ocean views and a lively bar and dining area just metres back from the crashing waves, If the tides are right then after lunch it's into a boat for a cruise up the Qora River. The river's name means 'plenty of clay' and it was from the Qora that the clay to make the traditional pipes was extracted.

Sit back and relax as you learn about the fabulous bird life and the natural history of this beautiful area. The vegetation of the Wild Coast is surprisingly lush and sub-tropical; along the way you'll see cycads and, if you're fortunate to be there in spring, profusions of beautiful orange clivias. Silting up of the river limits the distance the cruise boat can go at low tide, in which case you can hop into canoes, head out on a forest trail along the river, or take a beach stroll north of Kob Inn before retiring to the bar for evening drinks and snacks.

The porters on the Meander are local women – some of whom carry hikers' bags on their heads in traditional style.

▶ DAY 2 Kob Inn to Mazeppa Bay

6 KM ♦ 2–3 HR

The hike to Mazeppa Bay on day 2 is short, so we decided to explore the coast to the north for a while. We passed Boulders Beach, with its small settlement of holiday houses, scrambled over some stunning red rocks and deep gullies and finally turned around at Julera, a wonderful estuary where we stopped to swim. Low tide (in other words, the easiest time for walking) was in the afternoon so we returned to Kob Inn for lunch and then set off for Mazeppa, heading up the hill behind the hotel and then descending to the river where we were shuttled across in a small rowing boat ferry.

It's truly a wonderful stretch of coastline with high dunes, pristine empty beaches and rocky headlands. We were astounded

In the beginning …

Slackpacking in South Africa began on the beaches of the Transkei as the brainchild of Nita Ross who, through her tourism business Wild Coast Holiday Reservations, now offers a number of trails along the Eastern Cape coast. Nita had been hiking this coast for years, but it was largely inaccessible and even frightening to outsiders. Then one day she had an idea: why not help to train up and employ local people as guides and porters and launch a multi-day, luxury trail on which visitors could enjoy the freedom of hiking with only a day pack, overnighting in the friendly, quaint Wild Coast hotels on the route?

At the end of the 1990s she did just that and the Wild Coast Meander has since gone from strength to strength. It's hardly surprising: not only is the scenery unbelievably beautiful, but this remote area of the country remains relatively untouched by the trappings of civilisation. There's no coastal road so at the start of each day the porters – all local women – walk down to the beach where they are allocated bags, which they then carry to the next overnight spot. The trained guides are also locals keen to show off the natural beauty of their land and to give you insight into Xhosa culture.

If there's no wind Shark Island across the bridge at Mazeppa Bay Hotel is a wonderful sundowner spot.

by the tropical feel, which is so different from the southern part of the Eastern Cape, and enjoyed picking our way along the green vegetated cliffs, around little coves and over rocky headlines. Birds flitted from tree to tree in the lush coastal bush; our guide informed us it is a transition zone where you find an overlap of both tree and bird species endemic to the Eastern Cape and KwaZulu-Natal.

Mazeppa Bay is another of the Wild Coast gems. The bay takes its named from a schooner that plied the coast in the 1830s and which brought the survivors of Louis

Small rowing boats serve as ferries over some of the larger Wild Coast rivers.

Trichardt's party of Voortrekkers from Delagoa Bay to Port Natal in 1839. It's one of the most remarkable settings you'll find along the coast, and you can't help but be seduced by the golden beach, swaying palm trees and azure blue sea – and there's even a little island linked to the mainland by a quaint suspension bridge, where you can chill out at sunset with a glass of wine.

▶ **DAY 3** Mazeppa Bay to Wavecrest

21 KM ◆ 7–8 HR

We ate well at breakfast in anticipation of the long hike to Wavecrest. Part-Nguni cattle on the beach were a gentle reminder that we were on the African mainland and not some tropical island. For most of the day we were on sandy beaches, often flanked by rippling dunes on one side and rocky wave-cut platforms on the other, or on grassy banks that led past natural springs and patches of indigenous forest. After about a kilometre we reached a wonderful little beach, crossed the closed mouth of the Gcina River and walked on the verge of a magnificent dune forest teeming with birds. The next reference point on our map was

Day 3 is a beautiful but long beach walk. It's a relief when Wavecrest finally comes into view.

simply named '2nd river' (actually the Nqg-wara) and we waded across its wide estuary before continuing past Stony Point to the forested hills bordering the Gqunqe River.

Our guide amused us with a tale that had clearly made an impression on the local population. Unexpectedly high rainfall in-land had once caused the Gqunqe River to flood so much the guide in charge of a hik-ing group decided it would be unsafe to try to ford it. The group retreated in the direc-tion of Mazeppa Bay, only to find that since they'd crossed the Nqgwara it too had risen dangerously high. The resulting evacuation (to Wavecrest) by helicopter was clearly one of the highlights of the trail's history.

Our lunch spot was at the Cebe River mouth, a peaceful place with forest on both sides. New guides and porters from Wavecrest took over from the Mazeppa-based crew at this, the half-way point – the day is simply too long for them to return home in time after a full day with hikers. With a new guide we continued along Sil-ver Bay where we stopped to snorkel in the rock pools.

It was a beautiful day and we quickly got into the groove of walking, losing ourselves in our thoughts and in the solitude of the long lonely beaches. Just before we reached our overnight spot of Wavecrest Hotel, we detoured through another pristine stretch of dune forest. More than 300 bird spe-cies have been recorded in the Wavecrest area, many of them forest birds. The guide identified – with binos or by call – narina trogons, green pigeons, forest weavers and turacos (louries).

Wavecrest Hotel sits on the southwestern bank of the Nxaxo lagoon and while we were being ferried across to the hotel jetty, our porters turned for home. It was an in-coming tide so, after dumping our bags, a few of us crossed back to the other side to swim in the ocean then rode the fast cur-rent back into the estuary. Later in the after-noon we took a river cruise to explore the mangroves, the most southerly in southern Africa and apparently the world, watch the birds and see as much as we could of this unique estuary.

Apparently mangroves are typically found no further than 23° south of the equator, but around here (32° 30' S) the Agulhas current is close to shore and coun-ter-current eddies break into the estuary

Sunrise at Wavecrest is magical – looking across the Nxaxo lagoon you can see most of the previous day's route.

so the water is around 5 degrees warmer than the surrounding coast. The twitchers were in their element; we sighted pied kingfishers, rare mangrove kingfishers, trumpeter hornbills, woodpeckers and crowned cranes as well as numerous other birds as we enjoyed sundowner drinks. Ihem island in the lagoon is one of the most important breeding grounds for rare southern grey crowned cranes in South Africa. The name of the island derives from their call.

We were soon regretting not having taken the option of a second night at Wavecrest – the setting is superb and our bird list indicated there were many water and forest birds that merited more attention. There's also horse-riding, fishing and other river activities offered and, if conditions are good, a boat trip out to sea to find dolphins and whales. The hotel has a lovely spa and we were very tempted by the thought of a gentle stroll, followed by a massage and a laze around in the jacuzzi and sauna. But all that would have to wait for next time: slackpacking is all about taking it easy but you have to know what and where!

▶ **DAY 4** Wavecrest to Trennery's

14 KM ◆ 5 HR

The twitchers were out early and were clearly sad to be moving on. Our route to the Gqobonqaba River took us past the local airstrip to the coastal forest where our guide explained many of the medicinal uses of the plants. 'This is the African potato. It has a yellow flower and we use the tuber mixed with calamine as sunscreen. And this is the elma thorn; we feed sick cattle with potions made from its bark,' he informed us. 'Over there is a crab apple, that great old gnarled tree is the forest mahogany, and this is the clinging bamboo which is made into baskets.'

Stay an extra day at Wavecrest if you can and enjoy the superb setting and facilities of this friendly resort.

We walked on, recognising more familiar species such as coastal silver-oak, acacia and ironwoods, until the guide stopped again. 'See this cut wood? It's an alien species, inkberry, that we are clearing.' A little further on we came to some tables and benches where we paused to enjoy the forest, tree orchids and the red fruits of the Natal plum. A Knysna turaco fluttered overhead and we saw vervet monkeys eating the fruit of the wild plum – it was a wonderful little diversion from the coast.

We emerged from the forest and headed back down to the coast. 'The tree up on the bank there is a coral tree,' we were informed; its soft branches are hollowed out and used as dagga pipes.

We waded across the Gqobonqaba where we were handed over to a new guide and group of cheery porters – part of the scheme to ensure that each community along the trail benefits from the trail. For the next half hour it was easy going along a jeep track, through an area with strelitzia palms, gazanias and other beautiful flowers along a slightly raised path that afforded superb views along the coast. Just before we reached

The wreck of the *Jacaranda* is one of the most iconic Wild Coast sights – but not for much longer.

the wreck of the *MV Jacaranda* we passed a deep shell midden that had been exposed when a road was cut down to the beach. We paused to learn more about the early people who had roamed this coast, then headed down to the wreck.

The *Jacaranda* was a Greek freighter that was wrecked southwest of the Gqobonqaba River on 18 September 1971, on a voyage from East London to Durban. The story goes that the captain was entertaining some East London lady, or ladies, and a cabin hand was in charge of the wheel. It was a dark and stormy night and the lad sailed the ship right up the beach, where it remains parked. Although rusted and decayed, she is still very impressive and well worth photographing – particular at low tide when you can walk right up to her bow, so we spent some time exploring during our lunch break.

The last stretch of coast to our overnight spot was equally dramatic: prominent rocky headlands we had to alternately scramble over and cross by cattle paths, separated by beautiful beaches. We had our cameras out to snap our favourite Wild Coast subject – cattle on the beach, this time next to a stream of fresh water. We then hiked the final stretch of sand and up through dune forest to Trennery's Hotel where we sat in the sun, quaffing sparkling wine and slurping down fresh oysters.

Top Tip

Be diligent about applying tick repellent – Bayticol is great for shoes, socks and clothes, while Tabard or Peaceful Sleep is kinder on your skin! Go slowly and get to know the local people and their customs. If you can, spend an additional night at Wavecrest or Trennery's so you can really relax and explore the Qlorgha region.

Transkei is a very special place that, despite the poverty, has an incredible charm of a precolonial Africa. But it won't remain unspoilt forever so enjoy these beaches and grassy hills while you can.

▶ DAY 5 Trennery's to Morgan Bay

13 KM ◆ 4–5 HR

After an early breakfast we joined our host for the morning, the enigmatic guide Trevor Wigley, for a tour upriver. Trevor's Trail, to the scenic gates on the Qolora River, is not included in the trail package, but it's worth every cent: not only is Trevor a raconteur of note, but the whole experience is fascinating. We hiked up through the forest to where a small motor boat was tethered in the Coca-Cola coloured river (the harmless colour derived from natural tannins in the forest litter), all the while Trevor and his young trainee pointing out endemic plants and their uses and entertaining us with local lore. The short boat trip took us through a narrow, steep-sided gorge festooned with hanging greenery – The Gates – to a waterfall where we changed into swimming costumes and leapt into the cool, refreshing stream, and then walked down back to the lagoon through rolling heathland that afforded wonderful views over the Qolora River mouth.

Then it was off on the final stretch of the trail. After about an hour's walking we crossed the mouth of the Gxara River and our new guide explained that one of the most significant sites in Xhosa history, the

From the Kei River lighthouse, the trail descends to the beach, then traverses around some cliffs to Morgan Bay.

Pool of Prophecy, lay just above the pool and falls where we had swum.

We continued southwards along the beach, past rocky outcrops and wonderful tidal pools, until we reached the mouth of the Kei. The rickety old pontoon was some time in coming, but we were happy to linger: the infrastructure is much better on the southern side of the Kei and the resorts more numerous and crowded. Once over the river a new guide (named Colonial, what a wonderful name!) took over and we followed him, alternating between the beach

The pool of fate

The legendary pool of prophecy was where, in 1856, the Xhosa maiden Nongqawuse had a vision and heard voices instructing her people to kill all their cattle and destroy their grain stores in the anticipation that the kraals and grain pits would swell a hundred-fold with new cattle and maize. Then all their dead ancestors would rise and in their tens of thousands and would drive the white colonists into the sea. Tragically, the people did as Nongqawuse advised and in the ensuing famine 40 000 Xhosa starved to death. Another 150 000 fled to seek help from other groups to the north or from the British authorities to the south, to whom they became indentured. This finally broke the military might as well as the cultural knot of the southern Xhosa people.

and coastal road until we joined the track leading to the Cape Morgan lighthouse.

A last meander through the lush coastal forest, and a short traverse of the grassy slopes below the lighthouse, and we were back on the sand for a windswept last stretch to the picturesque resort of Morgan Bay – a stunning place to hang up our boots. The food here is famously sumptuous and the welcome was so warm we felt positively spoiled from the first minute. From Morgan Bay you have the option of continuing down the coast for another 3 days on the Wild Coast Amble (see page 129) or staying on at Morgan Bay and enjoying the wonderful beach, cliff walks and water sports on the lagoon ... unless you have to get back to work, in which case you need to start making plans to escape the office for another hike along this glorious coastline!

In a nutshell · Wild Coast Meander

BOOKINGS Wild Coast Holiday Reservations 043-743-6181, meross@iafrica.com, www.wildcoastholidays.co.za.
START/FINISH Kob Inn / Morgan Bay.
TRANSFERS Transfers to and from East London are included in the package.
HIGHLIGHTS Stunning coastal scenery; beautiful beaches; river estuaries teeming with marine life; majestic views; knowledgeable and enthusiastic guides; Trevor's Trail at Trennery's; mangroves and outstanding birdlife at Wavecrest.
LONGEST DAY 21 km.
SHORTEST DAY 6 km.
GROUP SIZE Minimum 2, maximum 18.
UP TO IT? Definitely. This is a straightforward guided beach walk, easily accomplished by any moderately healthy hiker. And if you're only going to do 1 trail in this book it should probably be this. It's the classic.
DON'T FORGET! Swimming costumes, masks and snorkels, binoculars and bird book, water bottles and personal gear.
LOOK IT UP An informative trail map with a description of the trail is provided at the start, along with tree and bird lists.
TRAIL NOTES You stay in comfortable, characterful hotels and enjoy seafood night if you get the timing right.
WHEN TO GO The trail can be walked year round, except during the Christmas and Easter holiday seasons when the hotels are fully booked. Winters are cool and pleasant for hiking. This section of the coast has a mild, humid climate, with most rain falling during the summer, when you can expect both rain and several river crossings (so it's worth waterproofing your pack).
BEFORE AND AFTER Meander Inn, East London 043-726-2310, meanderinn@telkomsa.net.

Survival Notes

- Drinking water not available on the trail.
- Terrain largely coastal, with beach walking and river crossings (great for birders).

17

Wild Coast Hiking Trail –
Port St Johns to Coffee Bay

Eastern Cape

DISTANCE 64 km • **DURATION** 5 days, shorter options • **DIFFICULTY** 4
TRAIL TYPE Beach and hilly coastal path • **LOGISTICS** Porters available on request
COST R • **ACCOMMODATION TYPE** Village guest huts • **AREA** Wild Coast

Although the physical demands of the Wild Coast Hiking Trail are not to be underestimated, it is this wildness – steep hills, empty beaches and river crossings – that makes slackpacking here such an appealing option. This trail is very much a cultural experience: you'll be greeted like long-lost friends at every stop, put up by your community hosts in a clean rondavel and treated to local festivities.

A coastal hiking trail once ran the length of the Xhosa homeland of Transkei, from the Umtamvuma River 280 km south to the Kei River. Sadly much of the trail has been neglected, with only hardy, self-sufficient trekkers attempting the full trek. However, the stretch between Port St Johns and Coffee Bay – among the finest coastal walks in the world where the beauty of the deserted, white beaches, dramatic cliffs, ruggedly beautiful green hills and smiling, colourful people will blow you away – is still popular and do-able. You can do the trail in 5 days, but make no mistake it's a tough hike with steep hills, river crossings and long sections of soft beach walking.

Wild it might be, but it is not a wilderness. It is heavily populated, with villages – tiny clusters of thatched, circular 1-roomed rondavels – dotting every hillside. There are local shops at which to buy supplies, opportunist fishers who offer crayfish or their catch of the day, and enterprising women who produce crates of bottled beer from under their beds. Each evening we gathered to sample the local fare, samp and beans, or pap and sauce. The brave washed

And then there's Jimmy …

Although hardy hikers have been stomping the coastal sleigh paths for years, it's thanks to the efforts of an enterprising young guide based in Port St Johns that the trail is still operating as a comfortable, guided hike. Jimmy Selani first hit the headlines when he was awarded the title South African Tourism's 'Best Emerging Guide of the Year 2004' and his business has since gone from strength to strength. Charismatic and fluent in English, he's a fount of information on the area and its people – the perfect chaperone.

it down with the local millet beer, a thick, creamy concoction, while the timid availed themselves of the ample supply of Castles from the local stores.

Luxury it is not, but this is a trail you'll never forget. Port St Johns alone must be one of the most dramatically located towns anywhere, with a cool frontier vibe.

▶ DAY 1 Port St Johns to Madakeni

12 KM ◆ 5 HR

Once you're sufficiently chilled, and have linked up with Jimmy and the porters in town, it's a short walk to the trail head at the Silaka Nature Reserve, at the end of Second Beach. The path climbs through coastal forest to cliff-top vantage points from which you can survey the rounded promontories and sandy bays back towards Port St Johns. It then cuts briefly inland, through cattle-grazed rolling hillocks, to the pristine sands of Third Beach with its dramatic view of Bird Rock. Huge hardwood logs litter the coastline, washed up periodically.

The accommodation may be rustic but you'll be warmly welcomed by the villagers of the Wild Coast.

Carrying on past Bird Rock again you climb to a high spot overlooking the wave-battered headland of Sugar Loaf, following a track behind the coastal ridge until you descend towards Umngazi. The coast of the northern Transkei is extremely rugged, defined by dark dolerite cliffs and promontories that are extremely erosion resistant. Umngazi River Bungalows is a smart and extremely popular resort, but surprisingly welcoming to visiting hikers, so we enjoyed a cold drink in the bar and stocked up with snacks while waiting for the ferry across the wide river.

The pattern was pretty much set by now: another steep climb around a headland, followed by a punishing descent and we were finally walking on the flat beach to Mngazana and another ferry crossing. The river, with its great sweeping bends, mudflats and vegetated banks is typical of the area but an unusual feature is the 3 types of mangrove trees that occur – in most other estuaries along the coast there is only 1 species.

Our first night's accommodation was in the village of Madakeni on the south side and, after a welcome shower, we sat outside listening to the sounds of the crashing sea. If you still have the energy, there's the option of a canoe trip up the river but we were content just to sit and enjoy village life.

Cheeky kids poked their heads out from the kitchen while women with babies strapped to their backs smiled as they cooked and tried to teach us a few words of isiXhosa. Life is simple here – and tough. Overpopulation and poor agricultural techniques have resulted in large-scale soil erosion and Aids has hit the region hard, but looking at our happy, smiling hostess we felt the genuine welcome of these generous people. The grace, humility and sense of fun we associate with Nelson Mandela is evident throughout his homeland.

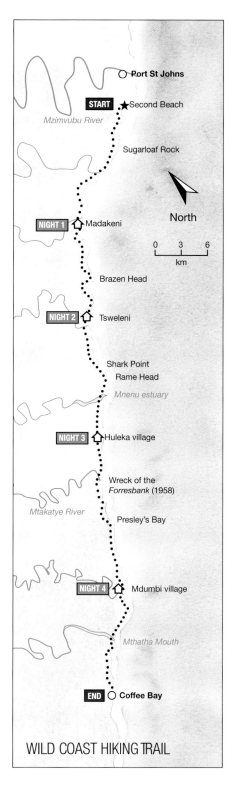

WILD COAST HIKING TRAIL

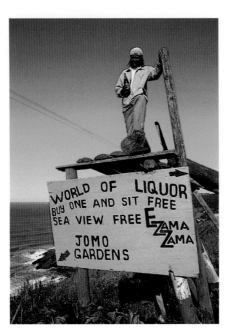

The trail starts in Port St Johns, a wacky town with a view to die for.

▶ DAY 2 Madakeni to Tsweleni

12 KM ◆ 6 HR

Day 2 was a tough haul. We left the coast behind and climbed steeper and steeper hills, the exertion of climbing – as much as the views – taking our breaths away. The vegetation varies enormously: the scrubby, dry, north-facing slopes contrasting with the lush, greener southern slopes and the verdant clusters of forest along the streams and rivers. In places the heavily grazed grasslands resemble mowed lawns, kranz aloes with their red-spike inflorescences in winter cling to the rocky cliffs and colourful ground orchids, daisies, and everlastings nestle among the tough grasses. The flora of the Transkei coast is extraordinary, with the intermixing of 3 floral kingdoms and close inspection reveals a profusion of tiny flowers amid the grasses.

Jimmy took us around the back of Brazen Head, the highest point on the trail, but we were feeling strong so scrambled up to the top to enjoy the incredible views of the coastline from the vantage of this massive dolerite intrusion. A few more hills and we were back at the coast strolling along Sinangwana beach. The kraals at Tsweleni Village, home for our second night, were visible from a long way off and, after the toils of the day, the sight of them was a most welcome relief.

All the villages are similarly structured: small distinct clusters of huts, each with its own fenced-off cattle pen and vegetable garden. Once you've settled in, you can wander

Get into the groove

The trail starts just outside Port St Johns, a sleepy, relaxed seaside town that has not quite emerged from the era of long-hair no-shoes flower power. It's worth spending a day here before you set off on Wild Coast time (read laid-back, man) to play in the gentle waves, take a sundowner drive up to the old airstrip on top of the vast rock plateau atop one of the great 'gates' that guard the seaward entrance to the town, or to explore the crags between First and Second beaches. The informal settlement up there must have one of the best views anywhere: you can enjoy a drink on the wooden deck of the ramshackle Millennium Bar perched out high above the crashing sea. Scramble down the rickety ladder and over to The Gap, a popular, but exposed, angling spot where many fishers have met their fate, then down to the gorgeous coves of Second Beach where hawkers proffer sizeable crayfish.

The extremely hard shale around Port St Johns results in some dramatic coastal landforms.

along the beach exploring the rock pools to what is left of the wreck of the *Aster*, which went aground at Sharks Point in 1999, or pay a visit to the local backpackers' lodge and tourists' drinking hole, The Kraal – a mini-fortress with commanding views over the crashing ocean. The welcoming bar, decorated with washed-out and washed-up driftwood, flotsam and shells, has the feel of a surfers' haunt. The food is excellent and a shuttle service from the N2 ensures that it's always full of travellers from all over the world who soon catch Pondo fever and stay for weeks, chilling out as time passes by.

► **DAY 3** Tsweleni to Huleka

14 KM ◆ 6 HR

Our first challenge of the day was crossing of the Mpande River – time to take off our shoes and wade. The cold, tannin-stained water came as a tonic for our weary feet, but we trod gently, mindful that hidden sticks and rocks could do damage. Many of the rivers along the trail are relatively shallow, but you still need to plan carefully and aim to cross at low tide. For most of the morning we followed sleigh paths over undulating hills, often encountering oxen

pulling their pre-wheel conveyances loaded with firewood and wide-eyed boys.

We watched impromptu soccer games on sloping fields with rickety goalposts, passed the burnt-out skeletons of cars and boats, waved to herd boys minding their flocks of sheep and goats, and experienced one of the classical Wild Coast sights: cattle strolling along the beach, as if taking an evening promenade. For the local people these tracks are their coastal highways and often a gaggle would fall in alongside us, chatting away merrily to Jimmy and trying to engage us with their few words of English. Horsemen slowed to ask where we were going and how we were enjoying their

If it's the crayfish season Jimmy often manages to rustle up some tasty treats.

Sadly the hikers' huts at Ncibe are in a state of dispair so the accommodation is in village rondavels.

beautiful land, and expressed their wish that we have the trek of our lives and take back happy memories of our stay.

The picturesque Mnenu estuary was the perfect lunch spot. Then it was back on the trail until we reached the Huleka Nature Re-serve with its wonderful stretch of coastal forest and elevated wooden chalets that are popular with fishers and families. In a land of continual eye delights, this bay is more picturesque than most, so we stopped for a final swim before heading inland to Huleka

The hardy hiker

You can still hike independently (for a paltry sum) but you'll need to be almost self-sufficient. Firewood can be collected and basic provisions bought at village stores, but bring a tent or simply rock up at a village with a smile: unless you're very unlucky you'll be offered a hut for a small sum and can experience Pondo hospitality at its best.

There are basic huts at roughly 12 km intervals, all in stunningly beautiful locations, and the occasional hotel or backpackers' lodge where you can get a meal or a bed, so if you choose the independent, self-sufficient route you are in for an incredible experience. And although your pack will be crammed with essential gear, the presence of local trading stores means you won't need to carry all your trail food. The route is reasonably well marked, with the location of the next hut-stop scrawled on rocks or signposts, but given the plethora of footpaths, you will probably end up getting lost on occasion. If in doubt, follow the coast – or ask the locals for directions to the next river crossing, village or store.

Permits/restrictions: Maximum of 12 hikers on each day section of the trail. Permits available through the Department of Economic Affairs, Mthatha. Contact Port St Johns Tourism for guides 047-564-1187, tourismpsj@ wildcoast.co.za, www.portstjohns.org.za.

village. We celebrated our third night – and breaking the back of the trail – with a visit to a shebeen where Black Label, Castle Light and Hunters Dry cider were proffered, and sat long into the night until the empty crates that served as seats became too uncomfortable to endure.

► DAY 4 Huleka to Mdumbi

19 KM • 9–10 HR

Just beyond Huleka lies the remains of the wreck of the *Forresbank*, a British freighter that caught fire and ran aground in 1958, a striking reminder of the dangers of this coastline. She's slightly off the trail, but if you're feeling fit it's an interesting detour. Not much of her remains – the proximity to the shore has resulted in large-scale scavenging, but the sight of the stem and broken wreckage in the spray and on the wave-cut platform is haunting.

Up and down a few more hills we went until we hit the wide Mtakatye estuary. Fish eagles soared majestically overhead, lifting our spirits and putting new fire into our tired legs. To our amazement, as we reached the far side of the estuary we came across some cyclists valiantly pedalling along the narrow path. Competitors on the Imana Wild Ride, one of South Africa's most gruelling off-road events, these madmen and women were busy cycling some 200 km from Kei Mouth to Umngazi River. The thought of navigating the steep paths, cliff-top trails and sandy beaches on bicycles made our efforts seem puny, so we simply squared our shoulders and tried to walk tall.

If you're hiking independently, the final overnight spot is at Ncibe. Unfortunately, the beautifully located hikers' huts – 4 rondavels facing the sea – are in a sorry state of disrepair so slackpackers now continue a further 5 km to Mdumbi village. In the early

Top Tip

Go with an open mind. This is not a luxury trail, but the local hospitality is fabulous. If you're invited to a shebeen, to see a sangoma or to join in any other festivities, be sure to seize the moment. You won't regret it.

days of the guided trail when he used Ncibe, Jimmy – enterprising as ever – would borrow pots and disappear to the local store for provisions, but the village is certainly a more comfortable option!

► DAY 5 Mdumbi to Coffee Bay

7 KM • 3 HR

The varied scenery on the last day was a fitting finale to this magnificent hike. We traversed dramatic cliffs, ambled down a long, empty beach and survived an exciting final ferry crossing across the Mthatha mouth in a rather shaky craft skippered by a lad. From the mouth the trail heads inland again over the grasslands until it comes to Coffee Bay – a major town (by Wild Coast standards) and popular holiday resort with gorgeous beaches and rolling surf. We stayed on a couple of extra days, preparing for our reintroduction to the real

Making friends along the way is easy if you have a digital camera to show the 'models'.

world, and to visit one of the country's most dramatic coastal landforms, the Hole in the Wall. This wave- and river-carved sea arch, a few clicks further south, is the focal point of another slackpacking trail, the Hole in the Wall Trail (see page 155).

In a nutshell · Wild Coast Hiking Trail

BOOKINGS Jimmy Selani 082-507-2256, jimmy.mbuyie@webmail.co.za, www.wildcoasthikes.com.

START/FINISH Port St Johns / Coffee Bay.

TRANSFERS Transfers back to the start can be organised through Port St Johns Tourism or the Coffee Shack (see below) and both are linked by a regular bus service to Mthatha.

HIGHLIGHTS Outstanding coastal scenery and landforms; empty swimming beaches; wonderful rock pools; fish eagles and forest birds; warm local hospitality.

LONGEST DAY 19 km.

SHORTEST DAY 7 km.

GROUP SIZE Minimum 1, maximum 22.

UP TO IT? This is a trail for fit hikers, but – even though it's steep at times and involves long beach walks – it's fairly straightforward, with no scrambling or exposed sections.

DON'T FORGET! Sleeping bags, warm and fully waterproof clothing (including a backpack cover) and personal gear. There are wonderful rock pools and gullies to explore, so consider at least a couple of masks and snorkels a group.

LOOK IT UP Maps of the Port St Johns to Coffee Bay section of the Transkei Hiking Trail, showing the trail, are available at the trail head at Silaka Nature Reserve.

TRAIL NOTES Hikers stay in village accommodation on DB&B basis.

WHEN TO GO The trail can be walked year round, but winters are cool and pleasant for hiking. The Wild Coast has a mild, humid climate, with most rain falling during the summer months. If you go in summer, expect to get wet so waterproof your pack. Occasionally the rivers get so high you have to resort to taking a taxi around to the other side!

BEFORE AND AFTER In Port St Johns, contact Outspan Inn 047-564-1057, outspan@wildcoast.co.za, www.wildcoast.com/outspan and Coffee Bay boasts a variety of accommodation to suit all tastes and budgets. Coffee Shack, where you can enjoy a final night in a rondavel, is a popular hikers' base and source of info and other adventures 047-575-2048, coffeeshack@wildcoast.com, www.coffeeshack.co.za.

Survival Notes

- Drinking water not available on the trail.
- Simple village-hut accommodation.
- Although duration is 5 days, linger if you can!

18

Hole in the Wall Trail

Eastern Cape

DISTANCE 31 km ◆ **DURATION** 3 days ◆ **DIFFICULTY** 3 ◆ **TRAIL TYPE** Beach and undulating cliff paths ◆ **LOGISTICS** Porters carry bags ◆ **COST** RRR
ACCOMMODATION TYPE Hotels and private cottage ◆ **AREA** Wild Coast

If the Wild Coast Meander is the classic, then the Hole in the Wall Trail is the pretender. This trail, along South Africa's most attractive and varied stretch of coast, is a relatively new kid on the block, but it's an absolute gem. And, best of all, it's short enough to manage over a long weekend yet make you feel that you've managed to escape the madness of the rat race. Sign up now before the secret's out – I have a feeling that this is a trail that is going to catapult into the headlines.

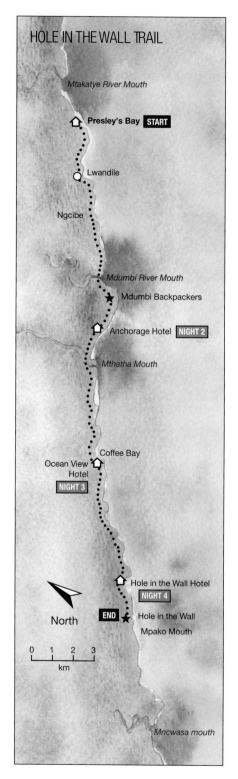

HOLE IN THE WALL TRAIL

Mtakatye River Mouth

Presley's Bay **START**

Lwandile

Ngcibe

Mdumbi River Mouth

★ Mdumbi Backpackers

Anchorage Hotel **NIGHT 2**

Mthatha Mouth

Coffee Bay

Ocean View Hotel
NIGHT 3

Hole in the Wall Hotel
NIGHT 4

North

END ★ Hole in the Wall
Mpako Mouth

0   1   2   3
km

Mncwasa mouth

This hike overlaps with the last day and a half of the Wild Coast Hiking Trail (Port St Johns to Coffee Bay, see page 147), but this trail continues to 1 of the country's most iconic land-forms – the dramatic sea arch of the Hole in the Wall. This is an un-tamed area regarded by many as the Eden of the Wild Coast. You walk along long empty beaches, over green rolling hills and past stands of aloes clinging to dramatic, precipitous cliffs. There are wide rivers to be crossed on local ferries while fish eagles soar overhead.

But it's not only the physical beauty that makes this trail so magical. Hikes are often run at spring tide so the exposed tidal plat-forms are alive with women and children harvesting redbait, oysters and limpets or gathering seaweed. They'll happily show off their meagre catch and amuse you by guzzling redbait and swallowing oysters with gusto. And you'll overnight in some of the most beautifully situated accommo-dation you could ever imagine. If wander-ing along a rugged coastline and a room with a view is your thing, this is your trail.

▶ NIGHT 1 Settling in

AT YOUR LEISURE!

We spent the night before we were due to embark on the trail at Presley's Bay, and when we saw the view from the deck of our pre-trail seaside cottage we thought twice about the prospect of leaving.

We'd arrived early so we strolled north to a lovely beach – why on earth hadn't we booked to stay a couple of days, I won-dered? The braai rustled up by Andy and her assistant Shirley gave us a taste of what was to come on the rest of the trail and we savoured some fresh seafood as we chilled out on the timber deck before retiring. And, as it turned out, things only got better ...

Lush vegetation and dramatic coastal scenery along the Hole in the Wall Trail are hard to better.

▶ DAY 1 Presley's Bay to Anchorage Hotel

12 KM ◆ 4–5 HR

On the morning of day 1, surfeit after a hearty breakfast, we packed our lunch into small day packs, handed over our overnight bags to our porters and followed Cedric, our guide, down to the beach. This is a glorious stretch of coast, with white sand beaches, tidal pools and pulsating gullies, which you hug all the way to the Mthatha River Mouth. On the way, you pass the small hamlet of Lwandile, the hikers' huts at Ncibe – 4 little rondavels on the river where

Top Tip

Stop and talk to the locals along the way. The Wild Coast is incredibly special – there is little privately owned land so people still live off the land and the shore, collecting the fruits of the sea and grazing their animals on the adjacent hills.

kids bathe and sit on driftwood – and the wide open sands of Mdumbi.

We'd been asking Cedric where we could swim but he'd kept us waiting for this point: 'You can swim here!' he proudly announced, 'This is one of the top 10 beaches in South Africa.' I'm not sure who the accolade is attributed to – Mdumbi was rated as an 'unbeatable beach' by *Getaway* magazine – but it's certainly a great spot. We waded across the Mdumbi River, had a most welcome swim and body surf, and then opened up our packed lunches. Crayfish sarmies – what a treat! If I needed any more convincing this was going to be an awesome trail, that was it.

The afternoon stroll (we were getting into Wild Coast pace already) took us onto the rocks, around Whale Rock, where we spent some time rooting for shells. Cowries, baby toes and Venus ears were there aplenty. Once past the small settlement of Tshani we were yet again on pristine beach until, quite unexpectedly, we saw a sign directing us up to our overnight spot at the Anchorage

Hotel, a fishing resort that offers comfortable accommodation in an outstanding setting. We celebrated our efforts in the pub before the sea air and our exertions drove us to our chalets for an early night.

▶ **DAY 2** Anchorage Hotel to Coffee Bay

8 KM • 3 HR

It's a short walk along the beach from the Anchorage to the Mthatha River. As we waited for the ferry to arrive – a rowing boat, powered by a strapping young man – we checked out the mangroves and the island in the wide, muddy estuary. From the far bank you can choose your route to Coffee Bay: the gentle gradient of the road or over the steep, green hills that follow the coast. The coast changes in accordance with the tides and river flow – apparently the island we observed is a new feature following recent floods. We climbed again, past bushy aloes to a plateau that used to be an old airstrip and there sat a gaggle of young men outside a wooden shack. They beckoned us in.

Their shebeen had only warm beer, which the storekeeper clearly thought we would

baulk at, but I assured him that this was the norm in my native Britain and shared a bottle with my fellow hikers as we chatted to the curious youngsters outside. A youth stuck his head out of a nearby rondavel, white clay covering his face and his torso naked. Cedric explained that he was an *umkhwetha*, an initiate, who was undergoing the several-weeks-long rite of passage – a traditional practice of circumcision, education and survival in a hostile environment that is still an important part of a boy's journey to manhood in this part of the world.

The trail then clings to the hillside, offering dramatic views the whole way. The adventurous can scramble down to some caves cut by the waves into the dolerite cliffs where ANC cadres used to stash their arms caches during the liberation struggle. If you don't fancy the scramble, stay high and keep your eyes peeled for whales and dolphins until you reach the lunch spot at the tranquil Mapuzi Point.

You climb again and round the hills on a contour path until you can see the way down to the sands of Coffee Bay. It's a steep, slippery descent, followed by a scramble over a wave-cut platform and round the headline to the beach if the tide is low enough, while the higher route brings you out behind your home for the night,

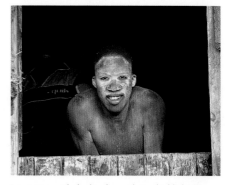

Interaction with the local people is a highlight. This youth is an *umkhwetha* – an initiate.

The last day of the trail starts at Coffee Bay where you might be joined by some unlikely companions ...

the Ocean View Hotel at Coffee Bay. This is considered one of the most luxurious and popular hotels on the Wild Coast – and deservedly so, as you'll appreciate from the awesome setting, warm welcome and excellent food.

▶ DAY 3 Coffee Bay to Hole in the Wall

11 KM ◆ 4 HR

The next morning we stepped out of Ocean View straight onto the beach to be greeted by a classic Wild Coast sight: a herd of Nguni cattle and a couple of young herd boys chilling out on the sand. Beside them sat 3 figures clad in black neoprene: surfers waiting for the waves to start pumping. Once over the river, the trail led through a dune forest on the leeward side of Sugar Loaf hill down to an even more secluded, even more beautiful beach. This is the kind of trail that just makes you want to stop and swim all the way, so plan accordingly!

You pass Coffee Shack and Bomvu Backpackers, then climb across and around the

hills to Hole in the Wall. Keep looking out to sea, particularly if you are walking during June/July, the season for the annual sardine run. As the vast slicks of silvery fish cruise by, the Cape gannets fall like comets into the water, dolphins frolic in the waves, whales blow and dense shoals of sardines and predatory game fish result in spectacular feeding frenzies. Recognised as

... and ends at the magnificent Hole in the Wall.

the world's biggest migration, the sardine run is an awesome time to be on this part of the coast.

From here the trail descends to Black Rock, and from then on you're on the wave-cut platform or on the beach all the way to the recently renovated Hole in the Wall Hotel. Dump your bags, then hike round to check out the awesome sea arch before returning to the beach for a final dip in the Indian Ocean and the end of an amazing hike.

In a nutshell · Hole in the Wall Trail

BOOKINGS Wild Coast Holiday Reservations 043-743-6181, meross@iafrica. com, www.wildcoastholidays.co.za.
START/FINISH Presley's Bay / Hole in the Wall.
TRANSFERS Transfers to and from Coffee Bay, Mthatha or East London can be organised through Wild Coast Holiday Reservations.
HIGHLIGHTS Outstanding coastal scenery and landforms; long, empty beaches, where you'll often see herds of Nguni cattle, goats and cheerful local folk, especially at spring tides; fish eagles and black oystercatchers; local hospitality.
LONGEST DAY 12 km.
SHORTEST DAY 8 km.
GROUP SIZE Minimum 6, maximum 12.
UP TO IT? Moderately fit hikers will take this in their stride. Distances are short and although there are a few steep hills, they're never unduly strenuous.
DON'T FORGET! Warm and fully waterproof clothing (including a backpack cover), water bottles and personal gear. Insect repellent to ward off ticks. A permit for collecting shells

and crayfish permit if it's the season and you wish to dive for them! Both can be obtained from any post office. Some change for a beer or snack at the shebeen or at the backpackers.
LOOK IT UP Hikers are issued with a detailed map. The Port St Johns to Coffee Bay section of the Transkei Hiking Trail (the old name, but still labelled as such on many maps) is also an excellent reference. You can still buy them at the Silaka Nature Reserve in Port St Johns, but I've never seen them anywhere else.
TRAIL NOTES Like most of other Wild Coast slackpacking trails, you stay in the endearing Kei hotels.
WHEN TO GO The trail can be walked year round but winters are cool and pleasant for hiking. The Wild Coast has a mild, humid climate, with most rain falling during the summer months. If you go in summer, expect to get wet and waterproof your pack.
BEFORE AND AFTER Meander Inn, East London 043-726-2310, meanderinn@telkomsa.net.

Survival Notes

- There's no water on the trail so fill your bottles before setting out each day.
- Liberally apply tick repellent to shoes and legs (also clothes).

19

Wartrail Skywalk

Eastern Cape

DISTANCE 54 km ◆ **DURATION** 4 days ◆ **DIFFICULTY** 4 ◆ **TRAIL TYPE** Mountain
LOGISTICS Bags driven round ◆ **ACCOMMODATION TYPE** Guesthouses, farm cottages
COST RRR ◆ **AREA** New England, Ben Macdui

This spectacular mountain trail traverses the remote and beautiful farms of the Wartrail and New England area of the northeastern Eastern Cape above Rhodes village. Incredible views, sandstone gorges, tumbling streams, outstanding rock art, wild flowers, mountain wildlife and the warm hospitality of your hosts make for a fascinating journey through a little-known but exquisitely beautiful part of South Africa. If you're a mountain lover in need of a complete escape, this trail should Dubbin your boots.

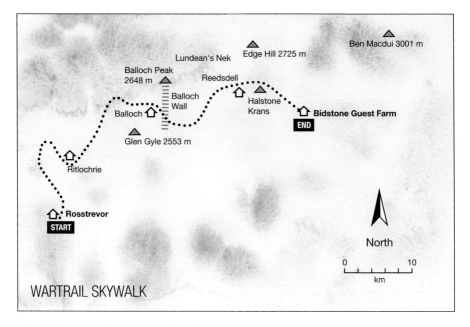

WARTRAIL SKYWALK

This fully catered and guided trail starts just outside Barkly East and takes hikers through the wild mountain country of the southern Drakensberg. There are some steep climbs and descents and you reach altitudes of 2 500 m on some of the passes, so you'll feel the effect of the rarefied air. But since average distances are only about 15 km a day you can take it slowly. The accommodation is in cosy guesthouses where you'll be welcomed as a friend and fed delicious home-made meals, so though you hike hard you finish the trail feeling healthy and spoilt. The area was originally farmed by the 1820 settlers and virtually all the host families and guides are descendants who enthusiastically share their knowledge and passion for the mountains, flora and fauna.

Along the way you'll see soaring eagles, delicate Afro-alpine flowers and various small antelope so there's plenty to distract you as you climb. And don't be intimidated if you're not super fit. The trail can be tailored to the fitness and interests of the groups, allowing strong hikers to take the high road to the peaks described below, while there are plenty of low-level options for those wanting a more sedate outing.

► NIGHT 1 Settling in

The journey to Rosstrevor Guest Farm, the trail head, some 20 km from Barkly East, was an adventure itself, the highlight of which was the drive from Elliot over the 2 012 m Barkly Pass. This was our first taste of the massive sandstone cliffs and spectacular mountain scenery we were to enjoy along the trail.

Dancing 'therianthrope' figures in the Stowe rock-art site on day 1 of the trail.

Phil Harrison and Kate Nelson, our hosts, welcomed us to the area and showed us around the place. After settling into our rooms in the big old Victorian farmhouse, we gathered for a briefing. We were feeling fit and the weather forecast was good so, after pouring over the map, we opted for the most strenuous trail option that would afford us the best views. Dinner that night was a surprise: Phil, previously a restaurateur in Port St Johns, is a chef of note and we feasted on juicy locally grown steaks. We were clearly going to be fed well on this trail.

The trail starts with a fairly gentle hike along the sandstone cliffs of the Diepspruit River.

► DAY 2 Rosstrevor to Pitlochrie

15 KM ◆ 5–6 HR

We rose early to the sound of birdsong and took the opportunity to try our hands at fly-fishing. Sadly we weren't able to land our own trout for the pan, but Phil was on standby with a delicious farm breakfast. We'd been briefed that this first day was very much a warm-up – a chance to acclimatise before the more challenging days ahead, so we took it easy heading up the Diepspruit River between the sandstone cliffs that characterise this part of the world.

Our first stop was at the first of a series of rock-art sites where we admired a 4 m-long serpent painted in such a way that it disappears into, and emerges from, cracks in the rock face. The water serpent was of great spiritual importance to the San, representing potency and fertility. We left the river and climbed up Baboon Rocks, followed the east side of the river for a while before crossing over some stepping stones and enjoying a mid-morning swim in a refreshing pool.

Phil led us to the nearby Stowe rock-art site, which is famous in archaeological circles as a place revealing something of the daily life of the San. There are various types of stone tools and ashy deposits from a hearth still remain on the floor of the cave. We discovered paintings at different levels and identified eland, other antelope such as rhebok, figures portraying various dance postures and Nguni cattle.

We crossed the river and walked under great undercut sandstone cliffs for a while before leaving the gorge and cutting across the top of Laureston farm to Queensbury Bridge where we stopped for lunch at the riverside beach. The swirling pools were inviting so we enjoyed a natural Jacuzzi before pushing on over Maarman (skinny man) Hill. From there it was downhill to beautiful Pitlochrie farm where Joe Sephton and his dogs greeted us warmly and showed us to the cosy cottage in the trees where we'd be staying.

Trainspotter alert

Barkly East is known for its railway system. The 117 km stretch of railway from Aliwal North to Barkly East has numerous stone arch bridges and 8 reverses, which trainspotters from all over would come to *ooh* at. Must have been an interesting journey when it was still operational!

The trail traverses well-tended farms, originally settled in the 1820s.

After tea we wandered around the woods and well-tended gardens until suppertime. Joe, a Jamie Oliver fan, served up just about the largest and most deliciously flavoured chickens I've ever enjoyed (locally produced by his cousin, he proudly announced) and we had a wonderful evening learning about the history of the area before retiring early. It had been a glorious start, the sandstone gorge and paintings were awesome, while the relatively flat terrain on the day meant no-one was feeling the effects of altitude.

▶ DAY 3 Pitlochrie to Balloch

18 KM ◆ 8 HR

Joe brought us each coffee in bed, then over a hearty breakfast and more strong coffee (what a treat, how I wish every trail guesthouse offered 'proper' coffee) we discussed the day's hike. We could see the route over the mountain and it looked quite challenging – 'around 800 m of height gain,' Joe mentioned. Initially the gradient was gentle as we walked across the farm, crossing a couple of streams on the way (be prepared to wade after rain). After a couple of hours the slope steepened and we followed a bri-

dle path up to the top of Skidaw, stopping often to catch our breaths and admire the striking gazanias, delicate blue moraea lilies and pink-purple ericas. Joe pointed out a few flowers that we didn't know including purple aster *Felicia filifolia*.

At the top we followed the fence line along the ridge and Joe outlined our options – we could either head down along a stream into Balloch Valley, or carry on to the top of Glen Gyle Peak. It was a glorious day so we continued up to the 2 553 m summit – a perfect lunch stop while we took in the 360° view. We descended the ridge enjoying the unbelievable views over the sandstone gorge and wind- and water-sculpted sandstone boulders. Joe pointed out the route ahead – the famous Balloch Wall that would be our challenge the next day.

Now heading down the valley we followed the river, stopping to swim in a deep pool. Scenically this was the most spectacular part of the hike so, despite the long, strenuous day, we arrived at Balloch with a spring in our step. Our home for the night, Willowstream Cottage, was simply divine and roomy with a fire in the ceramic fireplace just needing a match to get blazing.

We sat out in the sun taking in the view of the grand sandstone formations while Joe explained that our host, Margy, had done all the woodwork herself. When she arrived we discussed plans for the next day and she pointed the way to one of the rock-painting sites in the area. We immediately scrambled up behind the cottage to the overhang, enjoying the ever-improving views of the pretty valley. The paintings, which included a large cat, some delicate antelope and some hunters, were striking. It always amazes me that there are such well-preserved works of art in such accessible locations on the farms of the Eastern Cape and this is certainly a highlight of Balloch – it's the kind of place

The trail follows the river into Balloch Valley allowing plenty of opportunities for a quick dip.

that demands you return to and take time to explore and enjoy its natural abundance.

When we returned to the cottage our supper had been prepared and the table laid so we uncorked a bottle of wine that we'd brought with us and tucked in. The farms are so far from the local shops that everything is home made – a real treat for us city types.

▶ DAY 4 Balloch to Reedsdell

6 KM • 4 HR (or longer but more moderate contour 12 KM • 4 HR)

We were due to meet Margy only at 11h00 so had time to explore more of the area, to swim and to wander between the boulders before strolling down the road and over a swing bridge to the dressed sandstone farmhouse. In front of us loomed the infamous Balloch Wall: a steep climb to a nek at 2 395 m followed by a knee-jarring descent. Accompanied by the farm dogs we started off from the gorgeous old red-roofed farmhouse, through a couple of gates and fields of Bonsmara cattle, before starting the climb in earnest.

It was a strenuous route but we stopped often to look at frogs in the grass, pretty blue flowers and shiny stones. Halfway up we stopped for a breather and looked back at the dramatic sandstone formations along the previous day's route. On our left were the Tandjies (teeth) jutting out on the skyline over which a lammergeier (bearded vulture) soared just as we were watching. We felt we were deep in the mountains here, miles from civilisation. We continued up to a saddle from where the views were even more incredible. Margy pointed out soaring Avoca and Snowdon peaks in the distance and traced the line across the other high peaks joined by the famous trail race in the area, the Skyrun. And we marvelled at how much height we had gained. A few hours before, when we left the valley, the sandstone cliffs and domes of Balloch seemed massive, now they were little pimples below us.

We crossed a fence marking the top of the farm, then dropped below the ridge to eat our lunch out of the wind. Reedsdell guest farm was way below us and we could see the route of the final day's hike heading out beyond it. The initial descent over rocks and

The steep ascent of Balloch Wall is the major challenge on day 4, so stop often to admire the view.

grassy tussocks was really steep, uneven and taxing. We took it slowly, often resorting to sliding down rather inelegantly on our backsides, and it was not long before we were on the gravel road approaching the farmhouse. Our home for the night was another lovely old 2-bedroom sandstone cottage with a roaring log fire, balcony upstairs, sun terrace below and lovely farm-style furniture, including a big old-fashioned bath.

Reedsdell breeds emus, so on our way to the river for a swim we checked out the big birds in their enclosure. The emu products made on site are sold in the 'Woolly's in Wartrail Craft Shop' on the farm, along with knitted beanies, scarves, children's jerseys and other products made by the Masibambane Knitting Project – an initiative that encourages local women to start their own businesses by supplying them with skills training, equipment and an outlet for their products.

In the late afternoon our hosts, Chris and Kath Isted, drove us up Lundean's (also Lundin's) Nek Pass for sundowners.

From our high vantage we could see over the mountains of Lesotho and the southern Drakensberg and down into deep river gorges and we soon realised why the region has been dubbed Wild Mountain Country.

Chris elaborated on the history of the region. 'Wartrail, the area below Lundean's Nek, was the old border between the former homeland of Transkei and Lesotho,' he explained. 'Its name comes from the days when King Moshesh and Chief Moorosi of Lesotho sent cattle-raiding parties over the nek and through Moshesh's Ford to rustle the stock of the Southern Nguni and Sesotho people living down around Elliot.'

As we surveyed the tranquil surroundings it was hard to imagine such a tumultuous past. The light was amazing: as the sun sank lower the peaks changed from golds and oranges through gradations of blue. Back at the cottage we found our dinner on the table and tucked into an amazing meal of fresh farm produce. After that we sat out under the stars looking at the outlines of the high peaks before retiring for the night.

▶ DAY 5 Reedsdell to Bidstone Guest Farm

15 KM ◆ 6 HR

We were up bright and early and enjoyed a lavish, beautifully presented breakfast of fresh fruits, yoghurts, home-made bread and a fry-up. Our guide, Tskholo, arrived sporting a wonderful hat made out of bright blue twine. He pointed out the route for the day, over the dramatic peak of Halstone Krans which, at 2 464 m, looked quite daunting. As we followed him across the farm he stopped often to point out various plants and their folk uses.

'This is ouhout, *Leucosidea sericea*, the only indigenous tree found in the area. It produces nectar utilised by bees and other insects. The wood burns slowly and produces a lot of smoke like old and decaying wood and this, together with the appearance of the dark, flaky bark, has given rise to the tree's common name meaning "old wood". Local people hang the branches and leaves as charms to protect the inhabitants of homesteads, and also to make knobkerries,' he explained.

'During initiation ceremonies in Lesotho, a young boy would come back from

The accommodation is in cottages and renovated sandstone farmhouses such as this at Reedsdell.

his 3 months in the bush carrying a large and a smaller knobkerrie, thereby delivering the message to his mother and the village that he is now a man. The Zulu people use a paste made from the crushed leaves of *mtshitshi* for treating ophthalmia.'

In spring cattle and goats browse the flowers and young shoots of this plant, which then spreads to form dense thickets on overgrazed, eroded or otherwise disturbed areas. So it performs an unwitting but vital environmental service – even though some farmers perceive it in a negative way.

We passed some bright orange flowers. 'When I was a young shepherd I'd eat these gazania flowers, and these too,' Tskholo proffered some white flowers from a nearby acacia. They tasted good – a bit like raw bean sprouts.

We continued along a jeep track, then veered off right to start the ascent of Halstone Krans. Initially it was a gentle hike up the side of a stream, but then the climb began in earnest and we were breathless by the time we reached the saddle at the top of the farm. A final push and we were on the summit where our guide for the second half of the hike, Andy Viedge, and his 5 dogs greeted us.

The wrap-around view from the rocky summit was amazing; a great precipice dropped away on one side and we could see back to Reedsdell where we'd started out a few hours earlier, down to Bidstone Guest Farm, our home for the night, and across to Ben Mcdui, at 3 001 m, the highest peak in the Eastern Cape. After enjoying lunch on the top we headed down, traversing great slabs of rock shot through with white quartzite and other minerals. Cattle were grazing on this high plateau and the Afro-alpine flowers included pretty little blue moraeas and everlastings.

After wandering along the ridge for a while we cut down steeply to the dirt road that leads up to Tiffindell, the on-off-on again ski resort, then down a path to Bidstone. Janet welcomed us into her home and after a very welcome cup of tea and large slice of chocolate cake we installed ourselves in yet another lovely cottage. This one overlooked a dam and we could gaze at the mountains we'd come to know and love over the past 4 days. It had been a stiff hike at times, but we felt strong and refreshed. We'd had virtually no contact with the outside world, our cellphones were useless and we'd not seen a newspaper or TV; I felt I could happily have just gone on walking and living healthily in Wild Mountain Country.

In a nutshell · Wartrail Skywalk

BOOKINGS Wild Mountain Adventures 079-536-3996, wildmountain@polka.co.za, www.wildmountainadventures.co.za.
START/FINISH Rosstrevor / Bidstone Guest Farm.
TRANSFERS Transfers back from the end of the trail to the start are included in the package.
HIGHLIGHTS Warm and welcoming hospitality; the farmers (and farm dogs) that guide you; far-reaching views; awesome sandstone boulders and cliffs; delicate montane flora and the bird life; rock art shelters.
LONGEST DAY 17.8 km.
SHORTEST DAY 6 km.
GROUP SIZE Minimum 4, maximum 8. Smaller parties may be able to join a scheduled trail.
UP TO IT? This is a demanding, high-altitude trail with some steep climbs and descents, which requires a good level of fitness – but there are low-level options for those who want a more leisurely walk. For much of the way you are on cattle paths or on rough terrain so sturdy footwear is important.
DON'T FORGET! Waterproof hiking gear, day pack, camera, binoculars, snacks and your favourite tipple.
WHEN TO GO The trail can be hiked year round, but spring (August–November) and autumn (April/May) offer the most pleasant hiking weather.
BEFORE AND AFTER All the guesthouses offer accommodation to hikers wishing to extend their stay in the area. Visit www.wartrail.co.za for more detail.
HARDY HIKER OPTION The Wartrail and New England area is a paradise for self-sufficient hikers. Simply book into one of the guesthouses to use as your base, or speak to the farmers and head for the hills.

Survival Notes

- Drinking water is available on the trail.
- Catered accommodation in very comfortable farmhouses and cottages.
- Easier route options available.

20

Mehloding Hiking Trail

Eastern Cape – *by Prof Leon Hugo*

DISTANCE 61 km • **DURATION** 4 days, 5 nights • **DIFFICULTY** 4 • **TRAIL TYPE** Mountain
LOGISTICS Bags driven to huts • **COST** RR • **ACCOMMODATION TYPE** Village guest huts
AREA Southern Drakensberg

The Mehloding Hiking Trail is run by the Mehloding Community Tourism Trust in the mountainous foothills of the southern Drakensberg. This fairly strenuous trail leads through relatively unexplored mountains with little-known rock-art sites and passes through villages where there are opportunities for cultural visits; it's as much a taste of local life as it is a spectacular walk.

On this trail you'll explore the diverse natural and cultural heritage of a corner of the Maloti-Drakensberg World Heritage Site that used to be called East Griqualand. You'll discover San rock art, enjoy the magnificent proteas, tree ferns, indigenous forests, wild flower gardens and rare birds. At the end of each day you'll be welcomed into clean and comfortable chalets where you'll enjoy a hot shower, African cuisine and an inviting bed.

▶ NIGHT 1 Settling in

As we were bumping and shaking and trying to stay on our seats in the 4×4, I was tempted to ask myself: 'What on earth am I doing here?' We were driving from Matatiele, 30 km inland from Kokstad, towards the start of the Mehloding Hiking Trail – a community tourism project that has been running since 2001 and which is still relatively unknown among the general hiking public. Apart from hiking for the inherent pleasure of it, I had a job to complete: our group was there to audit the trail according to the prestigious Green Flag Trails accreditation system.

To complicate matters, thunderclouds were gathering ominously over the Drakensberg escarpment where we were heading.

Colourfully decorated huts are your home for the nights on the Mehloding Hiking Trail.

Not that I cared about getting wet, but I knew how terrifying lightning storms in this part of the world could be. I was entering a wilderness area and had no idea what the facilities and emergency back-up systems would be like – and the first concern of the Green Flag system is that the trail needs to be verified as being safe!

My concern was somewhat put at rest when we arrived at the start of the trail: a brand new and beautifully decorated group of 3 Xhosa huts where we were each handed a cup of hot tea. We were overwhelmed by the welcome of the personnel – such friendly welcome have I seldom experienced before and definitely not on any hiking trail. Little did I realise that this would be the norm at all of the overnight accommodation stops, and indeed a highlight of the hike.

After a nice warm shower to wash off the dust (and some of the stress), I was surprised with a dinner that could hardly be improved on in a standard restaurant in town. Then it was off to bed, which was already made with immaculately clean linen. Outside it was pouring with rain. Before dozing off I remembered the suggestion of our guide and trail manager, Robert, that we should start early in the morning as summer thunderstorms tend to come at 15h00. I nevertheless slept like a baby and was awakened with a cup of coffee and a healthy breakfast … and beautiful clear skies.

▶ DAY 1 Malekhalonyane to Makhulong

14 KM ◆ 6 HR

We started walking with only our day packs – our heavy load stuff was being transported for us to the next overnight hut. To our left rose the majestic Drakensberg escarpment and to the right were rolling

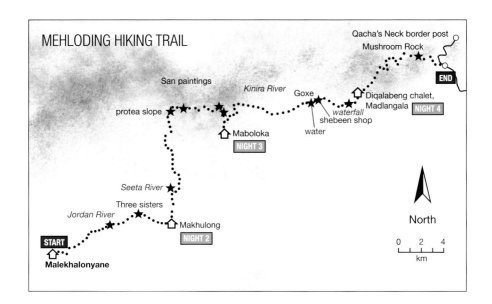

MEHLODING HIKING TRAIL

Qacha's Neck border post
Mushroom Rock
San paintings
Kinira River
Goxe
Diqalabeng chalet,
Madlangala
NIGHT 4
protea slope
waterfall
shebeen shop
water
Maboloka
NIGHT 3
END
North
Seeta River
Three sisters
Jordan River
Makhulong
NIGHT 2
START
Malekhalonyane
0 2 4
km

green foothills dotted with villages. Hiking past the kranzes, we were told by our guide of the enormous outflow of volcanic material that had spread over the subcontinent during the time (around 100 million years ago) when the ancient continent of Gondwana started breaking up and South America, Antarctica and India started drifting away from Africa.

Beneath this massive, uppermost basalt layer lie the sandstone layers of the Karoo sedimentary rocks, which are being exposed by the erosion of the overlying layers, presenting us with the most beautiful yellow kranzes with caves and undercut mushroom-like formations. We also enjoyed learning about all the medicinal uses of plants and the building use of ant heaps from our very capable guide. As a result our hike changed from a physical exercise into a truly enlightening experience.

We felt relaxed when walking with the guide. It was a joy not to have watch the map in case the trail markers were obscured or missing – we had no worries that we were on the wrong track. But half an hour after we started Robert sat down next

to a raging mountain stream and start taking off his shoes, adding nonchalantly that he was wondering last night if we would be able to cross the river. But I have learned after many years of hiking that any trail that is worthwhile must have some places where you experience something of a challenge.

We crossed the Jordan River (this is no reference to the Israelites) safely, holding onto each other, which enhanced our camaraderie if nothing else.

After crossing open grasslands and a large marshy area we forded yet another swollen river (the Mokopo, or Pumpkin, River) before arriving at the small town of Masupa where we were swamped by local kids. It had been a fine walk, but sadly the infestation of wattles and the erosion created by cattle left us with a feeling of despondency at the degradation of this beautiful area.

▶ DAY 2 Makhulong to Maboloka

20 KM ◆ 8 HR

This day had us descending steeply through Mpharane village to cross the Seeta River, which in summer can be so deep horses are used to assist hikers across. A steady climb, on heavily eroded footpaths and sled tracks, brought us onto a watershed with excellent 360-degree views. We stopped to admire the views of The Twins – the Maka-lane peaks – then walked through a nek and onto a contour path to a protea-filled valley where the path meanders through open grassland with streams and incised valleys. Towards the end of the day's hike we passed by remarkably well-preserved San paintings in a valley full of swimming holes. It was so beautiful we felt we could sit there forever taking in the wonders of nature and ancient humankind.

By midday the clouds were already build-ing up ominously over the escarpment behind us. A thunderstorm was brewing and lightning flashed at regular intervals, followed disconcertingly soon afterwards by deep rolling thunder. Robert pointed out a small plant and proffered some insider knowledge. 'The locals believe that if you smear it over your body it will protect you from lightning strikes,' he told us. Maybe so, but he was not convincing enough to settle my nerves.

The views across to the Makalane peaks, often known as The Twins, are a highlight of day 2.

A final moderate climb and we saw the Maboloka chalet in the distance. Our host-ess was standing outside and waving us in, then revived us with a plate of hot vetkoek (deep-fried doughnut-style bread), tea and cold drinks. What a treat. And that was the pattern for all the days to come: lovely views of the majestic Drakensberg, numer-ous crossings of mountain streams, meet-ing local people busy with their everyday chores and, for 4 days, completely forget-ting all the hassles of our city lives. As we entered the overnight hut the storm broke in its full force. Experiencing such a storm is a truly remarkable African bush experi-ence – difficult to describe but exhilarating to experience; especially when you are safe in a cozy, warm hut, sipping your tea and looking forward to a nice hot shower afterwards.

▶ **DAY 3** Maboloka to Madlangala

13 KM • 7 HR

The first stretch took us, after a moderate climb along stock paths, up an easy incline with interesting sandstone features, past Robert's Table (be sure to ask your guide to point it out and explain the name). Then we descended to the Kinira River and followed undulating terrain through Goxe and Pepe-la villages, where there is clean drinking water, and, to our delight, a shebeen with cold beer. Here you can see a unique fusion between Xhosa, Pedi and Sotho style houses with ever-encroaching and incongruous-looking Western influences.

We crossed the Makomoring stream, the banks unfortunately infested with wattles, then detoured a few hundred metres to a beautiful waterfall and huge pool where we rested for a while. This is the nicety of walk-ing with a guide on a slackpacking trail; there is no rigid route. For the rest of the

Although mountainous, this is certainly not a wilderness area and frequently you'll be walking through villages and interacting with the local people.

day we contoured around or meandered over rolling hillsides, crossed streams, hiked through a small village and met local herdsmen with their cattle and groups of boys with their lean dogs. A group of young men, clad in colourful blankets, passed on their way to an initiation school – chanting and singing as they went.

Earlier in the day Robert lost the sole of his shoe and had to walk 10 km barefoot over the rocky path. He told us it was no problem for him – in his childhood he used to take the cattle out early mornings in winter (barefooted of course) and warm his feet in the fresh, warm cow dung. 'Those were better days,' he reflected, 'when we were care-free and people were still trustworthy.'

I fully agreed with him and it sparked a lively debate about the price we are paying for development and about what we understand by 'quality of life'. We had witnessed a state-driven programme of using enormous tractors to plough large tracts land in order to enhance the food production of farmlands reclaimed through the process of land restitution, and were left with many questions in our minds. Was it really en-

hancing the capacity of the local farmers to become better custodians of the land?

▶ DAY 4 Madlangala to Qacha's Nek road

13 KM ◆ 6 HR

The last day's hike was a pleasant walk through patches of indigenous forest, protea groves, fascinating sandstone features and mountain grassland. We stopped at a huge mushroom-shaped rock, an hour's walk from the end, to enjoy our final lunch while absorbing the impressive landscape: layers of yellow-white sandstone resembling giant steps rising above the valleys below us. From there it was just a stroll through a pretty section of veld alive with wild flowers and twittering birds to the end of the trail near the Qacha's Nek border post with Lesotho. There we were collected by vehicle and taken back to Matatiele where our cars were safely parked.

As we journeyed we reflected on the previous few days. It had been a thoroughly enjoyable trail. Every night we had a lovely dinner and a hot shower and there were even magazines to read. In in the mornings we breakfasted well and were then issued with a tasty lunch pack each. But the route, though beautiful, highlighted some problems inherent to many wilderness areas. What was particularly disconcerting was the excessive erosion. The trail follows cattle paths, many of which are heavily eroded.

In many places patches or relic indigenous forest surviving in the deep valleys are being pushed back by the aggressive infestation of wattles. While there is a programme of alien vegetation eradication in place, the scars on the environment are extremely obtrusive. We also saw herdsmen from adjacent Lesotho living in the high mountain with their cattle and their half-wild dogs and heard of the problems they create.

Life is not easy in harsh environments and often leads to conflict between humans and nature and among humans. The only animal life I saw along the trails was 1 reedbuck … probably one of the last few left in the southern Drakensberg.

In a nutshell · Mehloding Trail

BOOKINGS Mehloding Community Tourism Trust, 039-737-3289, masakala@telkomsa.net, www.mehloding.co.za.
START/FINISH Malekhalonyane chalet to Qacha's Nek.
TRANSFERS Transfers back to the start are included in the trail fee. Transfers from Matatiele, the gateway to the area, can be arranged for a small extra fee.
HIGHLIGHTS Spectacular mountain scenery and views; interactions with local communities; rock art sites; indigenous flora and fauna; warm local hospitality.
LONGEST DAY 20 km.
SHORTEST DAY 13 km.
GROUP SIZE Minimum 2, maximum 12.
UP TO IT? This is a moderately difficult hike in the mountains with some steep climbs and occasional river crossings that is suitable for averagely fit hikers and families.
DON'T FORGET! Waterproof hiking gear, swimming costume and kikoi, day pack, camera.
TRAIL NOTES You sleep in rondavels and eat and commune in a central building.
WHEN TO GO The trail can be hiked year round but winters are intensely cold while in summer expect thunder storms.
BEFORE AND AFTER Hikers wishing to extend their stay can book into the chalets through the Mehloding community trust www.mehloding.co.za.
LOOK IT UP A new map of the trail is available from the organisers.

Survival Notes

- Drinking water not available on the trail.
- There is a risk of bilharzia in the larger rivers so swim only in fast flowing mountain streams.
- Self-catering and shorter trail options also available.

21

Giant's Cup Hikeathon

KwaZulu-Natal

DISTANCE 43 km ◆ **DURATION** 3 days ◆ **DIFFICULTY** 4 ◆ **TRAIL TYPE** Mountain
LOGISTICS Bags driven around ◆ **COST** RRR ◆ **ACCOMMODATION TYPE** Guesthouses and lodge
AREA Drakensberg foothills

The Giant's Cup Hikeathon is a gem of a slackpacking trail, following a well-marked, hiking trail along the base of the southern Drakensberg. Largely contouring around the sandstone hills of the Little Berg, the trail affords wonderful views of the high mountains, game sightings and big mountain pools in which to cool off. Because there are no sustained climbs, it's surprisingly non-strenuous. At night you're ferried a short distance to a lodge or private guesthouse where you can enjoy the views and the setting sun with a cold beer in the knowledge that a comfortable bed awaits.

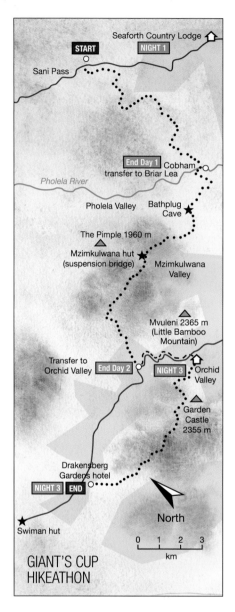

START
Seaforth Country Lodge
NIGHT 1
Sani Pass

End Day 1 Cobham
transfer to Briar Lea
Pholela River

Pholela Valley   Bathplug
Cave
The Pimple 1960 m
Mzimkulwana hut
(suspension bridge)   Mzimkulwana
Valley

Mvuleni 2365 m
(Little Bamboo
Mountain)

Transfer to
Orchid Valley   End Day 2   NIGHT 3   Orchid
Valley

Garden
Castle
2355 m

Drakensberg
Gardens hotel
NIGHT 3   END

North

Swiman hut

0 1 2 3
km

GIANT'S CUP
HIKEATHON

Overnight hiking in the Drakensberg is definitely not for sissies. The trails are tough and rugged, the weather unpredictable and the few overnight huts in the wilderness area are basic and unmanned. So I was most relieved to discover that Paul Colvin, of SA Adventure Trails, offers a comfortable alternative. If you love the mountains but thought that hiking in the Berg was for hardy mountaineers only, then check out this trail – you're in for a pleasant surprise!

The Hikeathon follows part of the route of the established Giant's Cup Hiking Trail, from Sani Pass to Drakensberg Gardens hotel. This is effectively the first 4 days of the Giant's Cup Trail (the full, 5-day, 60 km, hutted trail continues beyond the resort to Bushmans Nek.) Bags are driven between each overnight spot so slackpackers are able to cover the second and third days of the Giant's Cup Trail in a single 18 km push, making the Hikeathon an extremely accessible trail that's perfect for a long weekend. The route is through some of the finest scenery of the uKhahlamba Wilderness Area (a World Heritage Site) and is surprisingly underutilised – we didn't see another hiker in 3 days.

▶ **NIGHT 1** Settling in

The night before the trail starts is spent at Seaforth Country Lodge, a grand, gracious lodge with views to die for. If you have the time, arrive early and enjoy the farm – the Marching Men of Katanga rock paintings are an 8-hour return hike, but worth every bead of sweat. Your guide, Matthew Wiggell, usually calls in that evening to introduce himself and to provide a bit of background on the trail and the rock-art of the area. He's an accredited rock art guide and is clearly not just well informed but also passionate about the topic. The first and last days of the Hikeathon are short and straightforward so we opted to walk unguided, but Matthew would be escorting us on the long, 2nd day.

▶ **DAY 1** Sani Pass to Cobham

13 KM • 4–5 HR

After breakfast on the morning of day 1 we were transported to the start of the trail,

The trail starts at the bottom of Sani Pass, winding its way through protea grassland and around sandstone cliffs.

at the bottom of the Sani Pass. It's a short, scenic drive, although the last stretch of the road will make you grateful you're not in your own vehicle! As we set off up the first hill we soon realised this was a trail where we'd have to watch our step. Rows of upright stones and wooden poles lie across the path to channel rainwater – but as they're often hidden by the long grass you find yourself regularly tripping over them. We were soon into the groove, however, and enjoyed the patches of colourful everlastings, which had turned their open faces to the sun. The terrain is undulating and the path very well marked so we took it slowly, enjoying the changing views and the dramatic sandstone cliffs.

Once over the ridge between the well-wooded Mkomazana and Gxalingwa valleys (and not much tree cover after that) we wound downhill before the steep descent to the Ngwenwa Pools. A big, deep pool convinced us it was time for a swim and a lunch stop and we baked on the rocks for a while, contemplating the steep climb out of the valley. It wasn't so bad, and after the ascent the trail meandered along a contour path and over a couple more streams before following gurgling Trout Beck down to Cobham conservation station in the beautiful Pholela Valley.

We had time for another quick dip in the pool at the suspension bridge before we were picked up at the trail head and transferred to the overnight spot – the lovely old stone farmhouse of Briar Lea just down the valley. The rooms here are old fashioned and comfortable, but what Briar Lea lacks in sophistication it certainly makes up for in the form of Jocelyn's cooking. Paul laughed as he showed us around: 'All the hikers leave here raving about Jocelyn – it makes it a very hard act for me to follow tomorrow!' We were not disappointed – this was country cuisine at its best.

▶ DAY 2 Cobham to Orchid Valley

18 KM ◆ 7–8 HR

Matthew arrived early to guide us on this, the longest day. The prospect of an 18 km walk was quite daunting, but he oozed confidence – we would make it, he assured us, we just needed to take it slowly. After our transfer back to Cobham, we set off up the Pholela Valley again, past paddocks of grazing horses before attacking the ridge to our left (south). The views back along the river and up towards the Giant's Cup and Hodgson's Peak were stunning, so we stopped often to catch our breaths and take in the magnificence of the escarpment.

Familiar barking sounded not far away – a big troop of baboons was silhouetted on the ridge above us and, as we rounded the corner, they strode up in single file, almost parallel to us, then turned and spread out as if daring us to come further into their territory. Not that we were worried; the path was leading us in the other direction, up the Siphongweni Ridge and past Tortoise Rocks, but their display was entertaining nevertheless. We detoured to a big cave above the trail and a wonderful glade of lush trees where a small river cascaded through an opening at the far end – hence its name, Bathplug Cave. We spotted some clear, but rather poorly preserved paintings of human figures, eland and other antelope but those in the next cave just below the trail were even more impressive so we spent some time here as Matthew pointed out the various figures and animals and explained the theories on their interpretation. From there it was only a short contour through some wonderful groves of proteas and open

On a warm day the Ngwenwa Pools are inviting – be warned it's a steep climb out.

grassland, where we startled a few antelope into the Mzimkulwana Valley.

The Giant's Cup Wilderness Reserve camp, nestling beside a dam below us, looked a perfect escape from civilisation so, before we began the descent to the river, I made a mental note to revisit the place. The Mzimkulwana Hut – usually the overnight hut on day 2 – was visible from a long way off. Its setting, beneath sandstone cliffs on the banks of one of the tributaries of the Mzimkulu River, is quite superb and we decided it would be a good spot for a break. The hut, like that at Pholela, is really top-notch – clean, with good ablutions and comfortable mattresses so even regular hikers are a little spoilt on this trail!

The water in the pool at the hut was clear and inviting, but its icy temperature was a shock to our systems when we dived in! Nonetheless it is the perfect spot to laze and enjoy the mountains that rise all around. After our dip it was back on the trail. The first challenge after lunch was the suspension bridge, which aids the crossing of the Mzimkulwana River – as you step onto it, it sinks and sways disconcertingly! Then it's the real challenge of the day, the long climb up towards Little Bamboo Mountain. But when you get to the top you're rewarded again with incredible views back down to the river, and there's a shallow tarn, Crane Tarn, in which to freshen up.

Matthew pointed out the remains of petrified trees and rued the fact that there were no cranes to be seen, then led us down to a lower valley. Here we picked up the Killiecrankie Stream and had a final swim in a deep pool before descending a steep slope to the tarred road where Paul was waiting to ferry us up to the magnificent Orchid Valley Lodge for the night. This luxurious, privately owned lodge perched high on the upper slopes was a highlight of the trail.

The Mzimkulwana River crossing is quite exciting – the suspension bridge sways disconcertingly as you go.

The huge bedrooms are magnificent, all with big bathrooms – one of which had a jacuzzi bath – so once we'd cleaned up we sat outside enjoying the wonderful views as Paul tended the braai.

▶ DAY 3 Orchid Valley to Drakensberg Gardens Hotel

12 KM ◆ 4 HR

We opted to hike out directly from Orchid Valley along the flanks of Garden Castle and pick up the trail above Winterhoek Hut, instead of the slightly shorter option of being transferred back to the road. After a great breakfast of fresh pawpaw, yoghurt and bacon and eggs, we filled our water bottles – there's no water on this section of the trail – and strode out up the hill behind the house. A couple of mountain reedbuck bounded away as we climbed the first ridge and Paul pointed out the tell-tale white stains of a Cape vulture colony on the upper cliffs of Garden Castle. Some big eland bulls stared at us from the edge of the plateau – apparently the stately antelope are often spotted, sometimes in big herds, on this section. After an hour we saw the familiar white footprints marking the hiking trail and so waved Paul goodbye as we started the ascent up the steep Black Eagle Pass. It was a lovely walk though, with glorious views – arguably the best of the hike – down into Mzimkulwana Valley and Drakensberg Gardens to the right and all the way up the valley to Rhino Peak and Mashai Pass.

At the top of our pass the vistas changed as we looked south, down to the more expansive Mzimude Valley, with its lakes and farms. The horn of Rhino Peak is clearly identifiable from here, and we were quite tempted by the option of conquering this dramatic peak the following day. We descended towards the golf course and villas

Top Tip

Stay for an extra day at the end of the trail to climb one of the Berg's most iconic and accessible peaks, Rhino Peak (a 3 000 m peak that is a 21 km, 10 hr return guided hike with a vertical ascent of 1 000 m), or to visit the outstanding rock art of the area with a specialist guide.

of the Drakensberg Gardens hotel, then left the main trail (which continues to the Swiman Hut a little further up the valley) to rendezvous with Paul at the golf club.

The sun was shining and we toasted this fine setting from the terrace – if only all Drakensberg hikes had luxury options such as this.

In a nutshell · Giant's Cup Hikeathon

BOOKINGS SA Adventure Trails 033-343-1217, reservations@trails.co.za, www.trails.co.za/kzn/hikeathon.

START/FINISH Sani Pass / Drakensberg Gardens hotel.

TRANSFERS Transfers to the start and back to your cars are included in the trail cost.

HIGHLIGHTS Spectacular mountain vistas; wonderful swimming pools; lammergeiers, Cape vultures and other birds of prey; eland and other antelope; the superb lodges on day 1 and day 3; rock art interpretation.

LONGEST DAY 18 km.

SHORTEST DAY 12 km.

GROUP SIZE Minimum 4, maximum 9.

UP TO IT? This is a great trail for moderately fit and fit hikers. There are a few steep hills, but the trail is largely along a contour path so is never unduly strenuous. The many pools, game sightings and rock-art sites give you plenty of chance to catch your breath and if you tire on day 2 you can organise a pick-up from the Mzimkulwana Hut halfway!

DON'T FORGET! Warm and fully waterproof clothing (including a backpack cover if it's likely to rain), water bottles, binoculars and personal gear.

LOOK IT UP Hikers are issued with a detailed map of the Drakensberg Hiking Trail – Giant's Cup Section, and Ezemvelo KZN Wildlife's *Hiking in the Berg* guide at the start of the trail.

TRAIL NOTES Luxury accommodation, partially guided, fullly catered hike.

WHEN TO GO The trail can be walked year round but the weather is most stable between March and November. The autumn and spring months are ideal for hiking in the Drakensberg as it's not too cold or dry, so SA Adventure Trails offers scheduled hikes from March to May and from September to November with other dates according to demand.

BEFORE AND AFTER Underberg Hideaways will organise self-catering or guesthouse accommodation in the area, 033-343-1217, pc@hideaways.co.za, www.hideaways.co.za.

Survival Notes

- Drinking water available on all but the last day.
- 2- and 4-day options available.
- Winters will be extremely cold, so go prepared for the Poles; in summer expect serious thundershowers.

22

Amphitheatre Heritage Hike

Free State/KwaZulu-Natal

DISTANCE 28 km ◆ **DURATION** 3 days ◆ **DIFFICULTY** 4 ◆ **TRAIL TYPE** Mountain
LOGISTICS Bags driven around ◆ **COST** RRRR ◆ **ACCOMMODATION TYPE** Bush camp and hotel
AREA Drakensberg mountains

This hike takes you right up onto the edge of the Drakensberg escarpment and is
simply mind-blowing. The iconic Amphitheatre is undoubtedly the most recognisable
and dramatically imposing feature of the entire Drakensberg range. The great wall
of basalt rises over 1000 m from the Thukela (previously the Tugela) valley to the
watershed plateau that fans out below Mont-aux-sources (3 282 m) – a sheer, grey
wall in the shape of a natural, symmetric amphitheatre wall that extends for some
5 km from the Eastern Buttress to the Sentinel Peak on your right looking west.

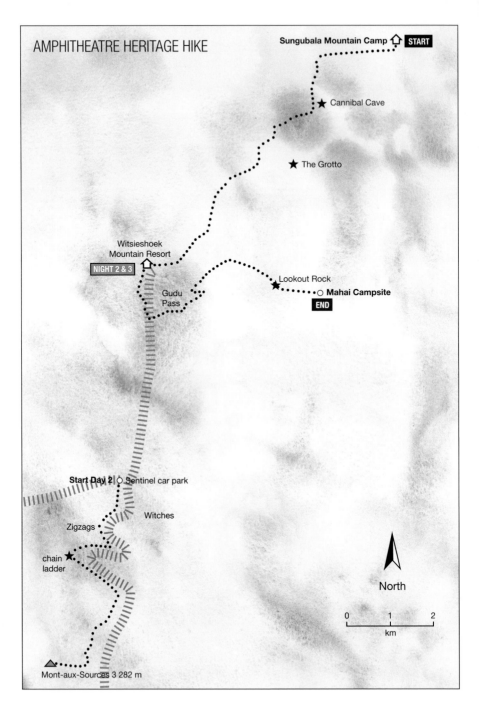

AMPHITHEATRE HERITAGE HIKE

Sungubala Mountain Camp ⌂ START

★ Cannibal Cave

★ The Grotto

Witsieshoek
Mountain Resort ⌂
NIGHT 2 & 3

Gudu
Pass

Lookout Rock ★
● **Mahai Campsite**
END

Start Day 2 ○ Sentinel car park

Witches

Zigzags

chain ★
ladder

Mont-aux-Sources 3 282 m

North

0   1   2
km

At the risk of being branded a mountainist, this has to be the most dramatic and scenically varied hike featured in this book. It starts with a beautiful ridge walk to Witsie-shoek, a recently revamped mountain hotel in a superb setting where you spend 2 nights, and ends with a spectacular walk down to one of the Berg's nicest campsites at Mahai. But it's day 2 that you will remember most. The walk past the daunting bulk of the Sentinel to the foot of the chain ladders, the vertiginous climb and the awe-inspiring views from the Mont-aux-Sources plateau south over almost all the northern Drakensberg range are images that will remain vivid for years and years. This is a place where you can look down on soaring raptors (lammergeiers if you are in luck), a place where the air is thin, can be sprinkled with snow even in summer, and which most regard to be the preserve of mountaineers. If the weather is kind, this is 1 of the most magical hikes in the world. If it is not, it will be one of the most memorable anyhow.

▶ **NIGHT 1** Settling in

AT YOUR LEISURE!

The night before the trail is spent at one of the most scenic locations in the northern Drakensberg, the beautiful Sungubala Mountain Camp, on a private farm just outside the Royal Natal Park. After we were shown to our remarkable 2-bed safari tents, we simply stood around trying to take in the magnificence of the camp at the foot of the towering peaks of Hlolela and Sungubala, surrounded by 500 ha of pristine wilderness. Cyndi, the owner of Sungubala, welcomed us and spoilt us with superb food, then we sat out around the fire staring up at the starlit African sky and agreeing that there could be few more perfect places to start a trail.

▶ **DAY 1** Sungubala to Witsieshoek

9 KM • 4–5 HR

We were met on the morning of day 1 by our guide, Godfrey, and after packing our lunches and wet-weather gear into our day packs we set off on the trail. A fairly stiff climb brought us out at the top of Sugar Loaf Gap, where we were greeted by breathtaking views. The route continues on the borderline between KwaZulu-Natal and the Free State, along Cold Ridge and past Broome Hill, with wonderful views in all directions and frequent sightings of vultures and eagles.

Finally we could see our home for the night, the superbly situated, community-owned Witsieshoek Mountain Resort, high

The mighty uKhahlamba

Such is the outstanding natural beauty and cultural significance of the uKhahlamba-Drakensberg Park that, in 2000, it was declared a World Heritage Site. This is a place where lammergeiers (bearded vultures) soar overhead, where the magnificent Thukela River cascades off the Great Escarpment and where the cliffs look so perilous it seems that no-one with just average fitness could possibly reach the top of this mighty natural fortress to survey some of the finest scenery in the world. In awarding its World Heritage Site status, uKhahlamba-Drakensberg Park was recognised both for the exceptional natural beauty of the Berg's soaring basaltic buttresses, golden sandstone ramparts and pristine, steep-sided river valleys; the diversity of habitats that protect a high level of endemic and globally threatened bird and plant species; as well as the overwhelming importance of the San rock art here that constitutes the world's largest and perhaps most important outdoor art gallery.

The famous double set of chain ladders allow even slackpackers to easily reach the roof of Africa.

on a ridge straddling the divide between KZN, Free State and Lesotho. From the watsonia- and helichrysum-covered ridge behind the resort you can see right across to the Amphitheatre, to the dramatic block of the Sentinel and to the precipitous cliffs

History carved in stone

As important as the natural splendour of the uKhahlamba-Drakensberg Park is its cultural heritage. The Berg's many caves and rock shelters harbour the largest and most concentrated group of paintings in Africa, made by the San people over a period estimated to be 4 000 years. The rock paintings, which represent the spiritual life of the San people who no longer live in this region, are outstanding in quality and diversity of subject and in their depiction of animals, humans and animal-human 'therianthropes'.

you'll conquer the following day: take a short stroll along the ridge line to whet your appetite before settling in.

To be honest, I've stayed at the resort on numerous occasions but in the past few I've been somewhat disappointed by the slightly rundown air and lack of enthusiasm of the staff. But you'll get a cold beer, a reasonable meal and a comfortable bed – and rumour has it that an improvement is imminent with the recent change in ownership. A bonus is that carcasses are often left out on a flat area behind the hotel as a 'lammergeier restaurant', so you might be in luck.

▶ DAY 2 Witsieshoek to the Escarpment top

12 KM ◆ 6–7 HR

We were shuttled the steep 7 km from Witsieshoek to the Sentinel car park, where we signed the mountain register and began the gentle climb up towards the magnificent, sheer rock face of the Sentinel. The well-maintained path ascends gradually towards the Witches, then zigzags almost to the base of the rock face. From there we swung right and followed the contour path below the western buttresses, enjoying the far-reaching views over the Malutis and the Witsieshoek plateau and listening to the bark of the resident baboons. This path used to be known as Coventry's Path, after Walter Coventry who cut it in the early 1900s. His family opened the first hotel in the Drakensberg, named Goodoo, where the park offices are now.

We reached the chain ladders in a couple of hours and steeled ourselves for the climb. Although only 30 m or so in length, the 2 parallel sets of double ladders are quite intimidating, particularly when the rungs are touching the rock and you move from one ladder to the next. The first set was installed in the 1930s and remains the easiest way – and for unfit hikers probably the only way – to reach the top of the escarpment.

Once at the top, though, you can pat yourself on the back and enjoy the incredible views, then take the short walk to the head of the Thukela Falls, where the river drops into the gorge below: the longest single drop is 614 m, which would make it the fourth highest fall in the world; taken together the 948 m plunge is the world's second highest falls. It's a great spot for lunch if it's not too windy or cold and, since most of the guided hikes take place between autumn and spring, you're quite likely to see snow up here – a very special experience.

If the group has made quick progress and the weather is good, there are several options for exploring the plateau. We opted for the very scenic, moderately strenuous, 8 km return hike along the escarpment to Rainbow Falls and a close-up view across the Devil's Tooth to the the the Eastern Buttress. I have also enjoyed the more demanding, longer hike to the summit of the highest peak in the area, the 3 282 m Mont-aux-Sources. By early afternoon we had retraced our steps down the chain ladders and were back at the car park, ready for the transfer back to Witsieshoek.

▶ **DAY 3** Witsieshoek to Mahai

7 KM ◆ 3 HR

After the excitement of day 2, the easy walk from the resort down the Mahai River valley was a breeze. Fortunately, the beautiful valley and the outstanding views ensure that it's not an anticlimax. We walked unguided, rock-hopping several times as the path crisscrossed the stream, and stopping frequently to dip in the pools. The path divides several times, with the easiest route being on the left bank of the stream, but

The magnificent view from the top of the Drakensberg escarpment is reward for your efforts on day 2.

all routes are well trodden and if you keep to the riverbank you'll emerge at Lookout Rocks. It was a very pretty day out in the mountains. The vegetation and topography change dramatically as you descend and we passed tumbling waterfalls, admired the eroded sandstone cliffs and wandered through small patches of pretty indigenous forest before reaching the trappings of civilisation, the stunningly situated campsite and finally the visitors' centre of the Royal

Top Tip

The top of the Drakensberg is a magnificent, but hostile terrain where weather changes can be swift and dramatic. Ensure you are well prepared for all weather conditions and allow sufficient time to get back to your lodge by early afternoon as storms and mist often descend later in the day. It's worth packing a good-quality camera to record the spectacular scenery from the top of the Amphitheatre.

Natal Park. From there we were met and transferred back to Sungubala where our cars were waiting. We opted to stay on an extra night and celebrate our achievement – after all, it's not every day you get to stand on the roof of Africa.

In a nutshell · Amphitheatre Heritage Hike

BOOKINGS SA Adventure Trails 033-343-1217, reservations@trails.co.za, www.trails.co.za/kzn/amphitheatre.

START/FINISH Sungubala Mountain Camp / Mahai (Royal Natal Park).

TRANSFERS Transfers back to your cars are included in the cost of the trail.

HIGHLIGHTS Spectacular mountain vistas and unforgettable views from the top of the Berg; Cape vultures and other birds of prey, possibly lammergeiers; eland and other antelope; bush camp experience, including dining out under the stars.

LONGEST DAY 15 km.

SHORTEST DAY 7 km.

GROUP SIZE Minimum 4, maximum 9.

UP TO IT? The trail is suitable for hikers of any age with an average level of fitness. Distances are not great but there are significant climbs on the way, so a degree of altitude acclimatisation is recommended – go slowly, with frequent stops to catch your breath. Those with a fear of heights would be better off staying on the ground – the chain ladders are likely to be daunting!

DON'T FORGET! Warm and fully water-proof clothing (including a backpack cover if it's likely to rain), water bottles, binoculars and personal gear.

LOOK IT UP Hikers are issued with a detailed map from the new KZN Wildlife series of maps covering the Royal Natal region of the Drakensberg Park, as well as a guide, *Hiking in the 'Berg*. David Bristow's *Drakensberg Walks* (Struik) is the definitive Drakensberg hiking guide.

WHEN TO GO The trail can be walked all year round but the weather is most stable between March and November. The autumn and spring months are ideal for hiking in the Berg as it's not too cold or dry. SA Adventure Trails offers scheduled hikes from March–May and September–November, or on request.

BEFORE AND AFTER There is a number of well-located hotels, B&Bs and self-catering accommodation places in the Northern Berg. Check out the Drakensberg Tourism Association 036-448-2455, www.drakensberg.org.za.

Survival Notes

- Drinking water available at least once a day.
- The weather on the summit can be extreme, and can change in minutes, from hot sunshine to icy snow storms: you must go prepared for the worst.
- The trail is partially guided on days 1 and 2.

23

Kosi Bay Trail

KwaZulu-Natal

DISTANCE 31 km ✦ DURATION 2 days hiking, 3 nights ✦ DIFFICULTY 2
TRAIL TYPE Beach, coastal bush and wetlands ✦ LOGISTICS Bags driven around ✦ COST RRR
ACCOMMODATION TYPE Chalets and safari tents ✦ AREA Maputaland coral coast

The Kosi Bay Trail takes hikers through the pristine and spectacular northern corner of Maputaland abutting the border with Mozambique. It's a total escape in one of the most inaccessible and diverse regions of South Africa, part of the iSimangaliso Wetland Park, South Africa's first World Heritage Site. The trail can be tailored to suit the time available and the age, fitness levels and interests of the group and allows hikers the opportunity to indulge in a range of activities along the way.

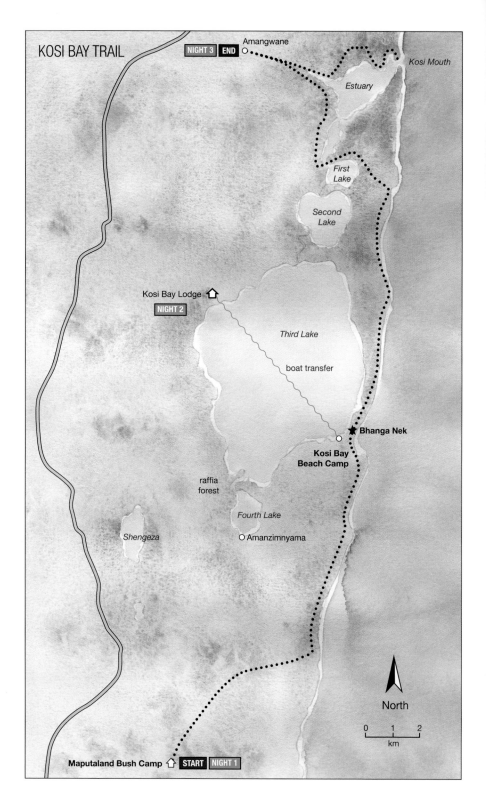

KOSI BAY TRAIL

NIGHT 3 END Amangwane

Kosi Mouth

Estuary

First Lake

Second Lake

Kosi Bay Lodge
NIGHT 2

Third Lake

boat transfer

Bhanga Nek

Kosi Bay Beach Camp

raffia forest

Fourth Lake

Shengeza

Amanzimnyama

North

0 1 2
km

Maputaland Bush Camp START NIGHT 1

The long history of conservation (read old-style), the use of community facilities and the remoteness of the area means this is not a typical luxury trail: although en suite, some of the accommodation is more rustic and comfortable than 5-star. However, but the standard of hospitality is second to none, the guiding is superb and the biodiversity, the fish traps, incredibly diverse bird life, marine mammals and the turtle nesting beaches that you experience en route make this an extraordinary outdoor experience.

The trail starts south of the Kosi lake system at Maputaland Bush Camp near Black Rock and winds its way through savanna, wetlands, coastal dune forests, along isolated beaches and past the much-photographed fish traps of the Kosi lakes estuary. The 3-night trail is described below, but hikers have the option of taking different routes and you can spend 4 or 5 days hiking and enjoying the area.

Daily hiking distances are typically around 15 km so you are usually at your overnight spot by lunchtime, giving plenty of time to enjoy activities such as canoeing, horse riding, turtle tours (in summer), snorkelling, boat trips, fishing and visits to local homes and shebeens in the afternoon. Or you can simply enjoy the unique trail environment. The trail is led by passionate and knowledgeable guides from the local communities who happily share their heritage so you come away not just refreshed but enriched.

▶ **NIGHT 1** Settling in

We were transferred by 4×4 from Manguzi Town to Maputuland Bush Camp, the home of Willie and Isabelle Labuschagne – a wonderful open-plan house on a ridge which has views in all direction. The guest bedrooms are in individual thatched cottages but since the bar, lounge and dining area are in the main house it's very much home-stay style. I headed out to explore the area on horseback while some of the chillers (or sinners) sat on the deck admiring the panoramic views. Being a Sunday, others walked down to the local church.

In the late afternoon we all strolled down to the Hippo Pools for sundowners before returning to the Bush Camp for a briefing on the trail. As with many of the slackpacking trails, the Kosi trail is flexible so we listened to the options and expressed our

A place of miracles

In 1999 iSimangaliso (previously Greater St Lucia) Wetland Park was designated the first UNESCO World Heritage Site in South Africa. Its inclusion was due to its unique diversity and scenic beauty: this includes the undeveloped sandy beaches, vegetated dunes, wetlands, grasslands, forests, lakes and the pristine Indian Ocean.

It provides habitat for large numbers of nesting turtles, migrating whales, dolphins and whale sharks off-shore, large breeding colonies of storks, pelicans, herons and the vast numbers of other waterfowl. Thanks to the coastal setting and location in the transition zone between subtropical and tropical Africa, 5 interconnected ecosystems provide habitats for exceptional species diversity. Within the World Heritage Site 4 sites – Kosi Bay, Lake Sibaya, the St Lucia Estuary System and the turtle-nesting beaches – are also designated as Ramsar Wetland Sites of International Importance.

The trail on day 1 takes you through coastal forest and along beaches where turtles nest in summer.

interests. Many of the groups, particularly those from overseas, focus on the cultural and historical aspects of the area so Willie gave us a run-down on the history of Maputaland and its people and explained how it was central to the area having been declared a World Heritage Site.

The first day at least would be ad hoc: we had a choice of walking all the way to the next overnight stop through the savanna and forest, of visiting local people in their homes, or of spending time on the beach. The evening ended in style with Isabelle,

Crossing the sand dunes is the only major challenge on this straightforward trail.

who is Belgian, serving a superb dinner of beef fillet and potatoes accompanied by a scrumptuous salad.

▶ DAY 1 Maputaland Bush Camp to Kosi Bay Lodge

±15 KM ◆ 4 HR

After a hearty breakfast we set off on foot from the camp following tracks across what was once a wetland area but is now, apart from the Hippo Pools, open savanna. Our guide informed us the Kosi hike is part of an initiative between local communities and tourism operators, known as Siyazenzela ('we help ourselves'). He led us into one of the homes along the way so we could meet some of the people and appreciate their simple lives; we were amazed how they managed with so little.

The trail then led into a bushier area and we admired the numerous cycads by the path and expressed our surprise that these rare plants still occured in such big numbers. 'The area is accessible only by 4×4 and has been protected for a long time,' explained our guide, 'so it's still pristine'. And wild, we thought. We continued along the trail until we came to the 'God knows tuckshop' shebeen where we made our second stop of the day.

The trail, which largely follows hippo paths, then wound towards the sea, taking us through lush coastal forest and over undulating dunes. Our guide pointed out a beautiful orange-flowered bush. 'That's the swamp hibiscus. The local people harvest it to make rope for fish traps.' He pointed out the other prolific plants, albizia and waterberry trees, the fruit of which is turned into tasty jams. We emerged from the forest to a splendid sight – rippled sand dunes covered with coastal vegetation. We sprinted down the dunes to the sea for a swim then, refreshed, set off along the beach until our guide indicated some tracks in the sand.

'This was where a leatherback turtle came up to nest last night,' he explained. 'You can tell by the pattern and the width of the tracks. Leatherbacks pull themselves up using both their front flippers simultaneously, so the tracks are regular on both sides. The smaller loggerhead turtle moves 1 front flipper at a time to haul herself up the beach.'

The last stretch of the trail along the beach was short but we took our time, looking at the shells, stumbling upon dried out eggs that turtle hatchlings had vacated the previous year and stopping often to swim so it was lunchtime by the time we arrived at Bhanga Nek. This was the end of the hike for the day so we headed away from the beach, across the narrow spit of land that separates the sea from the Kosi lake system, where a boat was waiting to take us across to our home for the night, Kosi Bay Lodge.

After lunch it was back in the boat for a trip on the lakes, the highlight of which was meandering through the narrow channels that link the 3 lakes. We heard the haunting call of a fish eagle and, to the delight of the twitchers, spotted a Pel's fishing owl – 1 of the most prized birding treats in southern Africa. We were also treated to a close-up look at the ancient Thonga fish traps for which the lakes are renowned. Our guide explained how the intricate traps work by funnelling fish into enclosures, how they are maintained and each is passed down from father to son.

We were lucky to be there on a low, outgoing tide so were able to follow the fishers out as they inspected their traps. It wasn't a lucky day for those we met. No fresh fish were speared for their suppers – we were the lucky ones to be able to return to the restaurant at Kosi Bay Lodge where fresh fish was only 1 item on the extensive menu.

▶ **DAY 2** Kosi Bay Lodge to Amangwane

±16 KM ♦ 4 HR

We set off early the next morning enjoying the short walk through the coastal forest and along the lake again. Tree ferns grew out of the albizia trees and a little red duiker scuttled away as we passed. An early morning mist was rising on the lake, silhouetting the reeds at the water's edge. As we motored back to Bhanga Nek we were told about another route option, with less

The accommodation at Maputaland Bush Camp is rustic but comfortable.

beach time: a visit to the most southerly stand of raffia palms in Africa.

The raffia-palm forest is found further inland, past Lake Amanzimnyana where it is fed by the Siyadla River. It is a rather boggy area around the inlet and the palms are the feeding and nesting ground for a colony of palm-nut vultures so the chance to observe this bird at the southern end of its range is a major attraction. The palm leaves – the longest of any plant in the world – are also used extensively in house building, while the trunks are tapped for sap that makes a vicious local fire water.

Once on the other side of the lake we retraced our steps to the beach past the Bhanga Nek community campsite. Our guide indentified the Ezemvelo KZN Wildlife turtle research station at the end of the beach and the marker posts that we passed at 500 m intervals. The conservation work being carried out here is of critical importance in preserving both species.

Female turtles that are born here return when they are sexually mature and come up the beach to lay their eggs. After laboriously hauling their massive bodies above the high-water mark, they use their hind flippers to dig a pit in the sand. It takes some time, with lots of resting, and she then deposits around 100–120 eggs each roughly the size and shape of a ping-pong ball.

The transfer form Bhanga Nek to Kosi Bay Lodge includes a boat cruise on the Kosi lakes.

We learnt how the sex of a hatchling is determined by the temperature of the sand, as is the case for many reptiles; that the last eggs laid, the ones on top, are foul-tasting to discourage predators; the way that the young hatch, then orientate themselves; and about the frightening gauntlet they have to run between emerging from the nest and reaching the sea. Between November and March turtle viewing is a major tourist attraction along this coastline.

We stopped often to watch women gathering shellfish, to photograph scuttling ghost crabs and to peer at the marine life in the rock pools. Many were circular and deep, natural rim-fill pools which the surging tide gave the appearance of inviting Jacuzzis. Our guide bade us try the different sea grasses that covered the rocks in a brilliant green. Most were slightly salty, but one, we all agreed, tasted distinctly of oysters. After about 5 km we left the beach and climbed a dune past great swathes of colourful vygies (succulent 'sour figs'), prickly pears which are invaders, and the fluffy white flowers of the waterberry trees. Halfway up we stopped for a final view back along the coast and our guide pointed out the silver oak, wild date palm and lala palm trees, many of which had been burnt. 'The local people burn the palm and then extract the sap to make palm wine,' he explained.

The next vantage point was on the inland side of the dunes where the magnificent panorama of the entire lake system, with its maze of fish traps, was breathtaking. We descended to Second Lake and waded through the shallow water to the other side, stopping to inspect the elaborate stick-and-grass fencing that channelled the fish into the circular central corrals of the fish traps. We were assured there were no crocodiles in the salty water, but it was slightly nerve-wracking nonetheless. Our route then took

The viewpoint near Amangwane camp is the perfect spot for sundowners and to see the network of fish traps.

us through beautiful coastal forest, dells of lichen-covered trees and verdant ferns, and alive with birds.

Before leaving First Lake we stopped to talk to the fishermen and inspect their catch – bundles of stumpnose fish hung from the trees and we were tempted to buy some for supper. Another short wade and a stretch of coastal bush took us to a path heading up – after an almost flat hike the last 20-minute pull up the hill to Amangwane camp seemed quite strenuous! The sight of houses and the sounds of villagers going about their daily business were also a bit of a shock: apart from the odd fisher we had seen little sign of people or habitation on the trail that day. We were soon having tea in camp, before being shown to our rooms – en suite safari-style tents each with a wooden deck.

The day was still young so, after a filling pasta lunch, we set off for Kosi Mouth armed with our binoculars, as well as snorkels and masks provided by the lodge. The path followed the lake shore, past more fishers laboriously working on their traps to Kosi Mouth. The mouth was even more beautiful than I had imagined it would be. A palm-fringed beach of rippling sand curved around to the mouth itself while

the estuary was a tangle of plaited, golden sandbanks and fast-flowing channels. The gentle waves were perfect for body surfing, while on the seaside of the mouth a small reef inhabited by lots of small tropical fish made for lovely snorkelling. After returning to camp to shower we hiked back to a viewpoint for sundowners and tried to capture the incredible scene of the zigzagging fish traps for posterity before a superb dinner of prawns and fresh fish.

▶ DAY 3 Transfer back to Manguzi

We were up at dawn to enjoy a final walk down to the mouth and for a swim before

As you wander the lake shore you'll learn more about the traditional fish traps from local fishers.

our transfer back to the real world. It had been a magical hike (the name iSimangaliso means 'place of miracles') and insight into a culturally and ecologically incredibly rich part of Africa that few outsiders have the privilege of seeing close up.

In a nutshell · Kosi Bay Trail

BOOKINGS Jacana Marketing & Reservations, 0861-JACANA (0861-522-262) or 011-656-0606, bookings@jacanacollection.co.za, www.jacanacollection.co.za or Siyazenzela 072-727-3079, info@kositourism.co.za, http://hiking.kositourism.co.za.

START/FINISH Manguzi, Maputaland. Transfers are included in the cost of the trail.

HIGHLIGHTS The diversity of the places you pass through; the empty golden beaches; the fish traps and fisherfolk of the Kosi lakes; loggerhead and leatherback turtles nesting and hatching in season; the bird life; the cycads and raffia palms; the pristine wilderness; the wonderful hospitality at the camps.

LONGEST DAY 16 km.

SHORTEST DAY 15 km.

GROUP SIZE Minimum 4, maximum 12.

UP TO IT? Although there are no significant hills, you do need to be reasonably fit to enjoy this hike as walking on sand is quite tiring. But since the trail can be adapted to the fitness levels of the group – and there is vehicle back-up – even sedentary types can enjoy it.

DON'T FORGET! Swimming costume, snorkel gear, camera, bird/plant guides, waterproofs, mosquito repellent, binoculars and snacks. There are no shops along the way but beers, wine and cool drinks can be purchased at the overnight spots. Light shoes or sandals are ideal footwear.

STYLE Fully catered guided hike staying in comfortable chalets or safari style tents.

WHEN TO GO The trail is open year-round except from 15 December to 15 January. April–September is probably the best time for hiking as summers are hot and humid. If you want to see turtles go in November or February/March – but be warned, February in particular can be very hot.

BEFORE AND AFTER All the accommodation on the trail can be booked for extended stays and there's plenty to do in the area, so factor in a bit of extra time to go on an ocean safari, to scuba dive or snorkel on the pristine reefs or go for a game drive in Tembe Elephant Reserve.

Survival Notes

- A malarial area, so do take precautions, especially in summer.
- Drinking water not available on the trail.
- Longer and shorter route options available.

Hoerikwaggo Tented Classic

Western Cape

DISTANCE 25–36 km • **DURATION** 2–4 days • **DIFFICULTY** 4 • **TRAIL TYPE** Mountain, fynbos, forest, beach • **LOGISTICS** Currently guided and portered, self-catering, bags driven around **COST** RR • **ACCOMMODATION TYPE** Comfortable safari-style tents • **AREA** Cape Peninsula

Much of the appeal – apart from getting access to the inner sanctums of iconic Table Mountain – is that it is a hike somewhat in the traditional style, with a fairly strenuous hike each day and staying on a self-catering basis in (albeit extremely comfortable) overnight huts. The route takes you through areas of the mountain that are not open to the general public … and the huts are exceptional.

NOTE: Trail logistics have changed over the years, and are mooted to change again, so be sure to get an update from the trail organisers.

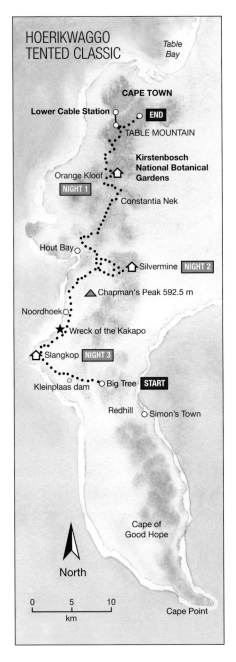

HOERIKWAGGO
TENTED CLASSIC

Table Bay

CAPE TOWN

Lower Cable Station

END

TABLE MOUNTAIN

Kirstenbosch
National Botanical
Gardens

Orange Kloof

NIGHT 1

Constantia Nek

Hout Bay

Silvermine   NIGHT 2

Chapman's Peak 592.5 m

Noordhoek

Wreck of the Kakapo

Slangkop   NIGHT 3

Kleinplaas dam

Big Tree   START

Redhill

Simon's Town

Cape of
Good Hope

North

0   5   10
km

Cape Point

The Hoerikwaggo Tented Classic Hiking Trail was planned to run for 97 km or the full length of the Cape Peninsula. At the time of writing (early 2010) 4 stages and 3 tented camps were open, so hikers could walk from Big Tree on Redhill all the way to the Lower Cable Station. The Hoerikwaggo Tented Classic has 3 options: Slangkop – 2 days, 33 km; Silvermine – 2 days, 36 km; and Orange Kloof – 2 days, 25 km.

The Hoerikwaggo Tented Classic also can be walked as separate 1-night guided and portered mini-hikes. Whichever you go for, I can guarantee you'll be blown away by the privilege of hiking and overnighting on the mountain, by the quality of the guiding and by the unique tented camps. Just don't expect a walk in the park – the distances are taxing and there are big hills to climb. But when you arrive in camp at night you'll do so with a sense of satisfaction, and with a new appreciation for the magnificent Table Mountain National Park. The trails run south–north. At the time of writing the plan was for the trail to be guided and portered only by arrangement.

Slangkop Trail

▶ DAY 1 Big Tree, Redhill Road to Slangkop camp

12 KM • 5–6 HR

This is the easiest day of the Hoerikwaggo Tented Classic. From the Big Tree, near the Signals School, high in the mountains above Glencairn, the trail initially follows the Kleinplaas Dam trail – a fairly flat, undemanding route through the fynbos on the top of Red Hill. The vegetation is sparse and the views are extensive so we stopped often to look at these unfamiliar vistas down to Cape Point and north to Chapman's Peak; to the big peak of Karbonkelberg above Hout Bay, and even as far as the main table. The trail skirts Grootkop, and since it was an easy day we took a short diversion to climb this 390 m peak. The trail then veers right around the dam, with the boggier sections protected by a boardwalk, before continu-

The first section of the Slangkop trail takes you into the mountains on top of Red Hill.

ing to a second dam where, since it was a hot day, we stopped for a refreshing swim.

The fynbos, particularly the wonderful ericas, on the good, undulating, path towards Slangkop, was stunning so we stopped often to admire and photograph the colourful plants. Soon the shaggy settlement of Ocean View came into view and beyond it stretched the great white expanse of Noordhoek Beach – part of our route for the next day. The water was brilliant blue and looked inviting; we were looking forward to reaching the sea.

We passed a water tank on the top of the mountain. 'This is a watering station placed here to encourage the baboons to stay high in the hills during the dry summer months, rather than come down to the residential areas where they make a nuisance of themselves,' explained our guide.

After lunch at the derelict buildings of the old observatory station on Slangkop, we headed down to the coast. Far below we could see the village of Kommetjie (its more recent sprawling, affluent extension out of sight around the mountain spine to

our right), the Slangkop lighthouse and our home for the night, Slangkop tented camp.

The steep downhill hike didn't take long and we were soon crossing the tarred road onto a boardwalk that took us through magnificent lichen-covered milkwoods behind the camp. The trail leads onto another boardwalk that crosses low dunes to a coastal track, then onto a path made of boulders

All the camps on the Hoerikwaggo Trail are superbly designed and well equipped. The one at Slangkop has lights built into whale vertebrae.

The overnight camp is right on the sea in the shadow of the Slangkop lighthouse.

to the camp gate. As we approached through the indigenous garden we passed an enormous whale bone. The camp is close to an old whaling station and the coastal theme is evident in construction and décor.

The design of the Slangkop camp is quite different to Silvermine and Orange Kloof camps. The braai area is enclosed, while the tents are domed (in contrast to the A-frame structures at the other 2 camps) – apparently to reflect the movement of waves and wind as well as to encourage the prolific coastal vegetation to creep over and act as camouflage and protection against the wind. As with all the highly imaginative and beautifully constructed Hoerikwaggo camps, there are lots of inspired touches such as overhead lighting concealed in whale vertebrae, as well as great views from the decks of the tents and the main area.

After a cup of tea the brave members of the party strolled to the beach for a quick, chilly dip then we wandered down to the lighthouse for sundowners. The sounds of the sea were all we could hear when we

retired to our tents – we were on the edge of a city, but it felt like we were miles from civilisation on a wild, windy shore.

▶ DAY 2 Slangkop camp to Silvermine dam

21 KM ◆ 8–10 HR

Since this is the longest, toughest day of the Hoerikwaggo tented camp trails we were up early, with plenty of food and water packed. After rejoining the coastal path for a short while, we stopped for a breather at the wreck of the *Kakapo*, which ran aground one misty night in 1900 having just left on its voyage from Cape Town to Sydney. The skipper apparently mistook Chapman's Peak for Cape Point and his easterly turn took him not into False Bay but up the beach. 'Fortunately, the Slangkop lighthouse ensured that there were no further beachings after 1919,' laughed a guide. Horse riders cantered past as we carried on along the beach right to the far end, where more surfers were lying on their boards in the clear, blue water, and then it was up a steep little path through coastal forest to Chapman's Peak Drive.

A sturdy wooden ladder aided the first steep section of the climb, then we contoured and climbed gradually on a gentle track heading north towards Hout Bay. It is a fantastic path, specially constructed for this trail by a largely female workforce funded by the Department of Environmental Affairs and Tourism (DEAT) Social Responsibility Projects. The guides called a break at a lookout over Hout Bay, from where we could see the brooding bulk of the Sentinel, the famous Dungeons wave and the flotillas of surf skis, fishing vessels and cruise boats moving about in the bay. Then it was the final push up to the summit of Chapman's Peak. The peak is one of my favourite short hikes, but I'd never been up from the south side so I thoroughly enjoyed the unfamiliar path and vistas.

We lunched on the summit, sunning ourselves like dassies on the warm rocks, before winding our way down to the saddle between Chapman's and Noordhoek peaks. The climb up Noordhoek Peak was more direct and – in the heat of the afternoon – more taxing, but we stopped frequently to admire the delicate blue disas that had sprung up next to the path and to take photos. After a brief spell on a 4×4 track we were deep in fynbos again, heading towards the Silvermine dam. The red-tasselled erica were magnificent and as we brushed against the bush along the path the scent of buchu

Enjoy the long empty sands of Long and Noordhoek beaches – there's a steep climb ahead.

Nature's way

The ethos behind the trail camps is to 'touch the earth lightly'. Development is designed to have the least possible impact on the natural and cultural landscapes, and to reflect both internally and externally the sense of place. Emphasis is placed on new and innovative ideas and approaches to energy-efficient design and on encouraging responsible custodianship of the resources by hikers.

The tented camps have been built almost entirely of alien vegetation chopped down within Table Mountain National Park. Not only does this create work for disadvantaged communities and aid fynbos restoration, but it saves around 30 per cent of the timber costs commercial wood retailers would charge. The tents are built on wooden decks with connecting boardwalks, so scarring the ground is minimised by the approach of 'poles in holes'. No concrete is used; only light cement mixes are used where absolutely

necessary, otherwise it's all crushed and compacted stone.

Planning the trail has been restricted to using only previously disturbed areas for camps, but both the Silvermine and Orange Kloof camps are ingenious and unique. The theme behind the Silvermine camp is mountain fynbos – and the camp looks out over False Bay and the fynbos-covered slopes.

In deference to one of the main attractions of the reserve, the rock climbing on the crags, the walls of the communal lounge/kitchen building are a mini climbing wall so enthusiasts can hone their skills on this funky bouldering wall. The buildings are constructed from alien vegetation, cut and sawn on site, using wire mesh cages packed with broken stones.

The guides pointed out an unusual little touch – lights made from burnt protea wood … which was their lead into an interesting discussion on the regenerating, essential role of fire in the fynbos ecosystem.

was unmistakable. Our overnight base beckoned in the distance and we quickened our step on the steep downhill, past the dam and down to the tented camp's boardwalk.

Silvermine Trail

▶ **DAY 1** Slangkop Point to Silvermine camp

21 KM ◆ 8–10 HR

The Silvermine Trail begins at Slangkop Point, next to the Slangkop lighthouse, a Peninsula landmark and a fitting backdrop for this section of the trail. Our guides gave us a short, upbeat briefing before we took the boardwalk down to the beach. The lighthouse, they informed us, has been operational since 1919 and is the tallest cast-iron tower on the South African coast, more than 30 m from base to its balcony.

We strode out along the beach, envious of the owners of the beautiful houses that hugged the shore, passed little boats bobbing in the bay at Kommetjie and surfers

The one in Silvermine complements the opportunities for rock-climbing in the reserve by offering bouldering on the walls.

Be prepared

It may be a walk in 'a park for all, forever' – as the marketing slogan for Table Mountain National Park proclaims – but don't forget Table Mountain is a big mountain. In fact it's only 300 m lower than Ben Nevis, the highest peak in the UK! So go prepared. Even if it's baking hot when you start, remember the weather on top will probably be colder and windier – and can change alarmingly quickly. Sturdy footwear (with a good grip), warm and wet-weather gear (at least a fleece and rainproof jacket), sunscreen and a sun hat are essential. Carry plenty of water as there is little to be had on the mountain.

at Sunset Beach before scrambling over the rocks to the glorious expanse of sand of Noordhoek. Walking on the sand was hard work, but we kicked off our shoes and enjoyed the freedom of walking barefoot – and, in any case, the views more than made up for our toil. This part of the walk – along Noordhoek beach and the climb up Chapman's Peak is the same as for the second day of the Slangkop Trail and, since nothing had changed, the trail description on page 198 applies here.

Note that access to the path up Chapman's Peak from the south is restricted, as is that through Orange Kloof and Disa Gorge, so you can't walk this trail independently without a special permit. These can be obtained by calling the SANParks at 021-701-8692 or 021-689-4441. The other sections can be done as day hikes – more information is available from the books and maps listed in the 'In a nutshell' section on page 204, or by visiting www.tmnp.co.za.

The trail follows a path up the southern side of Chapman's Peak affording great views over Hout Bay.

We dropped our packs in our tents, beautifully done with big wooden beds, and a small 'lobby' area to take off and hang your kit – very useful if it's been raining – before sitting around the big fire in the shade of a yellowwood tree, and getting the braai for supper started.

▶ DAY 2 Silvermine to Constantia Nek

15 KM ◆ 7 HR

We started out early on day 2, having risen at dawn so the climb up from the camp to the nek between Noordhoek Peak and Constantiaberg was not unduly taxing. The trail skirts around Constantiaberg – easily identified by the radio mast on its top – to a lookout above Blackburn Ravine where the views over the Constantia Valley and Cape Flats were simply incredible. We continued along the contour, stopping for lunch at a waterfall close to the path before climbing briefly again and then descending the slopes of Vlakkenberg through a rather unsightly area of recently cleared alien vegetation.

Much of the alien vegetation that dominated the flanks of the mountain has been cleared and although it was untidy then, new shoots suggested it would not be long before the area recovered and was recolonised by fynbos. By the time we reached Constantia Nek we were tired but happy campers. It had been a wonderful couple of days in the mountains.

Orange Kloof Trail

▶ DAY 1 Silvermine dam to Orange Kloof camp

15.5 KM ◆ 5 HR

The first day of the Orange Kloof Trail was the same as that of day 2 of the Silvermine Trail, except that from the nek we entered the restricted area of Orange Kloof (where a permit is necessary), a magnificent wilderness area that contains the best-preserved indigenous forest found on the main table. It was only a short walk to our overnight spot, a wonderfully secluded setting where the noise of the birds and the stream was

The indigenous forest of Disa Gorge, the start of the final day, is accessible only to those on the Hoerikwaggo trail or permit holders.

all we heard. The camp, in the shadow of the towering Eagle's Nest and Constantia Ridge, is so cleverly designed you feel as if you're deep in the cradle of the mountains and it's hard to believe it's just a 20-minute drive to the centre of Cape Town.

Although built on similar principles to Silvermine, Orange Kloof camp, on the banks of a tinkling stream in a dank forest, has a very different feel. We headed to a raised lookout deck for sundowners – cold beers, how civilised it is having fridges in these camps! Again we were impressed by the eco-friendly touches – funky recycled glass jars used for lighting and 4 different recycling bins – and the showers were an absolute highlight. We spent a peaceful evening around the glowing embers of the fire, talking to the guides and marvelling at this little piece of wilderness.

▶ **DAY 2** Orange Kloof camp to Lower Cable Station

9.5 KM ◆ 4–5 HR

We'd been looking forward to the final day – it was a real privilege to be able to hike up

Disa Gorge, and the guides emphasised the importance of this relic of indigenous forest. The trail was shady to start as we wandered beneath the canopy of yellowwoods, milkwoods, red alder and Cape beech and up verdant kloofs adorned with ferns.

It was a stiff, steady climb up Disa Gorge, but we stopped often to look at the mosses, the ferns and a clump of stunning scarlet *Disa uniflora*, the Cape's most famous flower. Commonly known as the Pride of Table Mountain, the red disa is the emblem of both the Mountain Club of South Africa and of Western Cape sports teams. Once common, the population of this colourful orchid has been decimated by collectors and is now endangered and protected, but the bright red flowers can occasionally be seen in the lesser-known ravines and on waterfall cliffs between January and March. Another rare inhabitant of the Disa River is the Cape clawless otter, a mainly nocturnal animal that feeds mainly on fish, frogs and crabs. Keep your eyes peeled for their droppings – which often contain bits of crab material – as you climb.

The path narrows near the top of the gorge and is quite precipitous, so tread carefully. Then it's a short hike to the bottom of the dam wall, which holds back the water of the Woodhead Reservoir, built in 1897 to supply water to the burgeoning city below. Day-trippers watched us from the path on top of the wall as we climbed

Top Tip

Carry plenty of water – it can get very hot on the climbs, particularly during the summer months. Take a flower book, too, although the guides are very knowledgeable about most of the 9 000-odd species in the Cape Floristic Region Protected Area!

up the steps to join the main path. The rest of the morning was spent exploring the back table area – unexpectedly large for anyone who's not been there before – and meandering along the behind the tops of the Twelve Apostles to the Upper Cable Station – having to take a wide detour through the head of Plattekloof Gorge.

The guides stopped frequently to point out flowers, butterflies and colourful endemic sunbirds and sugarbirds, and to remind us of the richness and incredible diversity of this floral kingdom. The descent of the mountain, on the revolving

Once you reach the dam wall of the Woodhead Reservoir you're back on the main paths of Table Mountain.

That famed mountain and its floral kingdom

Table Mountain – part of the Cape Floral Region Protected Area (CFRPA) – is a World Heritage Site that comprises the best reserves in the Cape Floristic Kingdom. It is also one of the most diverse, accessible and important reserves in the Cape Floral Kingdom. So, as you walk through this unbelievable place, ponder on the fact that:

• The Cape Floral Kingdom is one of the oldest plant kingdoms in the world, with some species dating back 60 million years.
• It is the smallest and richest of the world's 6 floral kingdoms and the only one to be completely contained within one country, with nearly 9 600 species crammed into only 0.04 per cent (90 000 square kilometres) of the earth's land surface. To put this into perspective, consider that the Boreal Kingdom covers most of the land in the northern hemisphere. The Cape Floral Kingdom has similar botanical status, but covers only a thousandth of that area!

• The CFRPA occupies less than 4 per cent of the area of southern Africa, yet is home to 40 per cent of the subcontinent's flora of 22 211 species.
• Some 70 per cent of the 9 600 plant species of the CFRPA are endemic – in other words, found nowhere else.
• The diversity of the CFRPA is comparable to many areas of similar size in moist tropics, remarkable for a temperate region. These levels of endemism and concentration of species are found nowhere else in the world. Fynbos, the dominant vegetation type in the CFRPA, has on average more than 3 times the density of different species found in an equivalent area of Brazilian rainforest.

cable car, was a rather Alpine touch to this spectacular hike: we could see across to the V&A Waterfront and Robben Island, along the Twelve Apostles, to Lion's Head, Devil's Peak and over the city bowl. Our bags were waiting for us at the Lower Cable Station,

but I for one would rather have turned around and walked back to the start as I was in no rush to reintegrate into 'normal' life. As Carl Linnaeus commented, having observed the floral riches of the Cape, it simply is 'Heaven on Earth'.

In a nutshell · Hoerikwaggo Tented Classic

BOOKINGS Hoerikwaggo Trails 021-422-2816, hoerikwaggobookings@sanparks.org, www.hoerikwaggotrails.co.za.

START/FINISH Slangkop Trail: Signals Schools / Silvermine; Silvermine Trail: Slangkop Point / Constantia Nek; Orange Kloof Trail, Silvermine Gate / Lower Cable Station.

TRANSFERS You'll need to organise a taxi transfer, or be dropped off at the start.

HIGHLIGHTS The diversity of the trail; the outstanding views and flora; imaginative, tented camps; passionate guides.

LONGEST DAY 21 km.

SHORTEST DAY 9.5 km.

GROUP SIZE Minimum 6, maximum 12.

UP TO IT? This is quite a tough trail, with some steep uphill sections offering little or no shade. A good level of fitness is required, particularly in summer.

DON'T FORGET! Sleeping bag, pillow,

towel, insect repellent, swimming costume, warm and wet-weather clothing. The weather can change rapidly on the mountain, so be sure to go prepared.

LOOK IT UP There is a good outline map on the trail brochure. *A Table Mountain Activity Guide* by Fiona McIntosh (Struik, 2004) covers everything from trail info to history. The best maps are Peter Slingsby's *Table Mountain National Park*, www.themaps.co.za.

WHEN TO GO The trail can be walked year round but spring and autumn are ideal. Summers are hot and dry, and often windy. Winters are cool but there's a good chance of rain.

BEFORE AND AFTER Contact Cape Town Tourism for the vast range of options or visit www.capetown.org.za.

Survival Notes

- Drinking water not available on the trail.
- Tented accommodation.
- Although day 2 on the standard Orange Kloof Trail is 9.5 km long, the emergency descent via Kasteelspoort will add about 1.5 km making a total of 4–5 hours.
- A private company, Slackpacker SA, offers a fully catered, guided and portaged option. Visit www.slackpackersa.co.za.

25

Hoerikwaggo Table Mountain Trail

Western Cape

DISTANCE 18.5 km • **DURATION** 2 days • **DIFFICULTY** 3
TRAIL TYPE Mountain, fynbos, forest **LOGISTICS** Bags driven around
COST RR • **ACCOMMODATION TYPE** Cottages • **AREA** Cape Peninsula

The Hoerikwaggo Table Mountain Trail is the most luxurious and least demanding of the suite of Hoerikwaggo Trails. The views and the scenic beauty of this spectacular short trail are guaranteed to take your breath away, the accommodation is outstanding and superb guides share with you the hidden treasures of the iconic mountain and the Cape Floristic Region World Heritage Site. It's a very manageable trail for any hiker regardless of age or fitness, with plenty of time to enjoy the views and to smell the flowers.

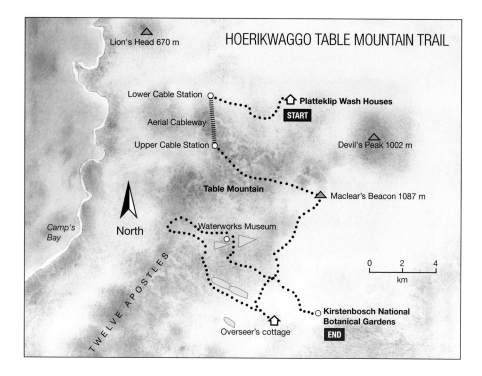

This self-catered trail (with the option for being guided and portaged), showcases the most spectacular section of Table Mountain. Although you must be able to negotiate uneven terrain and steep descents, the pace is slow so the trail is suitable for novice and moderately fit hikers. The standard of guiding is excellent so this is very much an interpretive trail, with the guides regaling you with the history and myths associated with the mountain and pointing out and identifying the magnificent fynbos species, the birds, the reptiles and other small stuff you see along the way – should you choose that option.

The trail starts at the very plush Platteklip Wash Houses trail base at the foot of Table Mountain. (Although there is an option of a 2-day, 1-night trail, I'd thoroughly recommend signing up for the 2-night option and spending the night before the hike at this luxurious spot.) It's only short walk up to the Lower Cable Station where (weather permitting) you are whisked to the top of the mountain by cable car. After you've enjoyed the amazing views from the revolving car and from the viewpoints at the top, the guides lead the way to the Maclear's Beacon, then over to the luxurious Overseer's Cottage for the night. There's time for a short hike on the top of the mountain on the second morning before you descend Nursery Ravine to the Kirstenbosch Botanical Gardens where the trail ends. Given the superb guiding, outstanding scenery and superb overnight accommodation this trail is seriously under-rated. Book on before it takes off – it's the perfect short escape.

► **DAY 1** Wash Houses to Overseer's Cottage (including a cable car ride if the weather permits)

9.5 KM ◆ 5 HR

After a wonderful night at the Wash Houses at the foot of Table Mountain, we were

The view from the top of Table Mountain is among the best in the world, so enjoy it before you move on.

up bright and early to start the trail. The accommodation here is quite unlike any other hikers' hut that I've ever stayed in – in fact it's more in keeping with that of a chic boutique hotel, with en suite bathrooms and a bright, modern interior with a strong African influence.

The guides carried out a short safety briefing then led us up the short, steep hike to the Lower Cable Station. The ride to the top of Table Mountain in the rotating cable car offered an unbelievable 360° view over the city – to the V&A Waterfront, across the City Bowl to Robben Island and to the triangular summit of Devil's Peak. And as we rose above the height of Lion's Head, the gorgeous beaches of Clifton and Camp's Bay came into view – clear evidence that Cape Town is among the most beautiful cities in the world.

Once on top of the mountain, it was a gentle hour-long stroll to the highest point, Maclear's Beacon (1086 m). The senior guide explained that the beacon was constructed in 1844 by the then astronomer royal at the Cape, Sir Thomas Maclear, as part of his efforts to measure the curve of the earth. The views are mind-blowing – we could see all the way to Cape Point as well as down the Twelve Apostles to the blue waters of Hout Bay. The sun was shining, yet we saw no other hikers as we followed the trail through the citrus-like aromas of the indigenous fynbos to our accommodation for the night, the Overseer's Cottage.

We couldn't help but marvel that in a park so close to a major city you felt you had

The accommodation at the Overseer's Cottage on top of the mountain is surprisingly comfy.

Maclear's Beacon, named after the astronomer royal, marks the true summit of Table Mountain at 1 086 m.

the place entirely to yourself. The guides pointed out the main species of protea and erica found on the plateau; we saw colourful sunbirds and sugarbirds and laughed at the lizards that scuttled off the rocks as we approached. But a sudden rustle in the undergrowth had us all on edge. 'Do you often see snakes on the mountain?' we asked the guides. They smiled, 'Hardly ever, they are much more frightened of a big group like this than we are of them!'

Reassured that we were in no immediate danger, we continued down to the cottages. The accommodation was very comfortable, if not quite as spacious as the Wash Houses, but one of the restraints put on the trail developers was that they use only existing buildings or build on previously disturbed sites. We sat out on the rocks, enjoying the late light and the smell of the braai. As darkness fell, the lights of Cape Town twinkled brighter and brighter, producing spectacular night-time views of the city. It was a privilege to sleep up here and we were going to enjoy this evening to the full.

▶ DAY 2 Overseer's Cottage to Kirstenbosch

9 KM ◆ 4.5 HR

The following day, after a leisurely breakfast on what seemed like the top of the world, we explored the back table area before heading down Nursery Ravine to the Kirstenbosch National Botanical Gardens.

A highlight was the magnificent specimens of king protea (*Protea cynaroides*) at the top of the ravine. Nursery Ravine is the easiest and among the most popular routes down the east side of the mountain and the path took us deep into Newlands forest, the shade providing a stark contrast to the previous day's hike when we'd been exposed to the full force of the Cape sun. Although steep and slippery in places, the zigzag path down was not too demanding, and the guides kept us alert, pointing out interesting trees and birds and explaining the history of Kirstenbosch, where the trail ends.

After about an hour we emerged from the forest into the botanical gardens, one of Cape Town's most precious treasures. Cecil John Rhodes cleared much of the indigenous vegetation when he purchased the Groote Schuur estate as his Cape Town home in 1891, and on his death he left the property to the nation. The gardens, which cover an area of 528 ha (including 36 ha of cultivated garden), are a celebration of South African flora, showcasing all groups of indigenous South African plants. Fynbos beds, cycads and rolling lawns intermingle with big trees, streams and ponds, and the well-laid pathways make for easy walking. A great variety of birds inhabit the gardens and the sweeping views from the upper slopes are awesome. Kirstenbosch offers a wonderful 'potted' introduction to the natural flora and wildlife you are likely to see elsewhere on the mountain, and the spot is thoroughly recommended if your knowledge is patchy but you are interested in identifying at least the main species. Free birding checklists are available and the bookshops in the gardens have a large selection of specialist guidebooks.

The trail ends with a descent down Nursery Ravine to the Kirstenbosch National Botanical Gardens.

The trail reached an end at Kirstenbosch but we continued to wander through this tranquil place, enjoying the contrast between the carefully tended beds of the lower reaches and the wildness of the mountain we'd just descended, and realised it was partly these contrasting images that makes this trail so attractive. We had been walking only 2 days yet I felt totally relaxed and at peace. The mountain had refreshed my soul.

Fynbos

The dominant flora of the Table Mountain National Park (and indeed the Cape Floral Kingdom) is fynbos (meaning 'fine bush'), a Mediterranean shrubland flora that consists predominantly of proteas, ericas ('heathers' to Europeans), restios (reeds) and geophytes (bulbs such as lilies). Fynbos grows on the coarse-grained, low-nutrient acidic sands generally characteristic of the region extending from the mountain peaks, down hilly slopes, across coastal plains to the seashore. The region is typified by winter rainfall, constant wind and recurring fires (fynbos plants are renowned for their ability to regenerate after, or even withstand, fire).

Adaptations to these conditions include the extra-thick, waterproof layer on the outer leaf surface of most proteas, which minimises evaporation loss. The silver tree, for example, has a thick layer of hairs that lie flat, protecting the leaf from water loss in hot weather. Ericas have tightly rolled leaves, which also restrict moisture loss, while the 'leaves' of the restios are reduced to papery sheaths. Other species typical of the Cape Floral Kingdom are succulents and geophytes, which store water in their bulbs.

In a nutshell · Hoerikwaggo Table Mountain Trail

BOOKINGS Hoerikwaggo Table Mountain Trail 021-465-8515, hoerikwaggobookings@sanparks.org, www.hoerikwaggotrails.co.za.

START/FINISH The Wash Houses / Kirstenbosch National Botanical Gardens.

TRANSFERS Transfers back to the start can be organised through Cape Town Tourism, 021-487-6800 or 021-487-6899.

HIGHLIGHTS The guided tour of the city; the cable car to the top of Table Mountain; fynbos and indigenous bird life; views; outstanding accommodation and catering.

LONGEST DAY 9.5 km.

SHORTEST DAY 9 km.

GROUP SIZE Minimum 2, maximum 16.

UP TO IT? This is a very straightforward mountain trail, but the paths on the top of the mountain are uneven. The path down is steep and you'll be scrambling at times, so good footwear is important.

DON'T FORGET! Hiking gear, day pack, camera, bird/plant guides and binoculars.

TRAIL NOTES Although self-catered, hikers stay in extremely comfortable renovated cottages with linen provided.

WHEN TO GO Spring (September– November) is wonderful as the weather is at its most predictable and the flowers are at their best. Autumn is also a good time. Summers are hot and dry, and often very windy. The Cape experiences winter rainfall so it can be very wet June–August, but if you're prepared to take the risk of a drenching, these months are cool and pleasant for hiking.

BEFORE AND AFTER For options on where to stay and what to do before and after the trail, contact Cape Town Tourism, www.tourismcapetown.co.za.

LOOK IT UP The best map is the excellent Peter Slingsby's *Table Mountain Map* (Map 1 in the series), which is widely available. *A Table Mountain Activity Guide* by Fiona McIntosh (Struik, 2004) covers everything from detailed trail info and maps to the flora and fauna, and the history and myths associated with the mountain.

Survival Notes

- Drinking water available at least once daily on the trail.
- Luxury accommodation, 4-star, self catered.
- There is a 2-day, 1-night option.
- Guides and portaging are optional. Slackpacker SA offers a fully catered, guided and portaged option on this trail. Visit www.slackpackersa.co.za.

26

Hunter Gatherer Trail

Western Cape

DISTANCE 43 km ◆ **DURATION** 4 days, 2–3-day options ◆ **DIFFICULTY** 2 ◆ **TRAIL TYPE** Beach
LOGISTICS Self-portage of bags ◆ **COST** RR ◆ **ACCOMMODATION TYPE** Tents and rustic hut
AREA Mossel Bay

The Hunter Gatherer Trail is a voyage of discovery, a chance to explore the beaches, dunes, ancient shell middens and fossils on a remote stretch of coast. The sister trail to the world famous Oystercatcher trail, this trail is also guided but the accommodation is more rustic, and hence aimed at families, small groups and those with a sense of adventure who want to wander at their own pace, indulge in a bit of canoeing and fishing, and learn more about the treasures of this rich coastline.

The guided, catered or self-catered trail is centred around 2 rustic but charming base camps in the small villages of Vleesbaai and Boggomsbaai west of Mossel Bay. The daily hiking routes are circular, with 2 nights at each camp, so groups can tailor-make the daily itineraries, with the advice of the guide, to suit their fitness level and interest. The trail slogan 'hunt for signs and gather information' hints that the emphasis is on understanding how the ancient hunter-gatherers lived, how they foraged and survived and their intimate relationship with their environment. As you explore the dunes and beaches your passionate and knowledgeable guide will treat you to some surprising discoveries. The Hunter Gatherer Trail is not only a wonderful, and very affordable, beach walk along a pristine section of our coastline, it's also an example of the way in which irreplaceable palaeontological and archaeological sites can be conserved through education and controlled use.

The trail briefing is on the deck of the Kapokbos, from where you can survey the route of the trail.

► **DAY 1** Vleesbaai Dune Camp to Kapokbos and return

±3 KM ◆ 1 HR

After we'd settled into our tented homes at Vleesbaai we strolled a couple of kilometres down to Kapokbos, a wooden deck on the shore where we got our trail briefing. This stretch of coast is still largely undeveloped and the evidence of past dwellers, from late Stone Age hunter-gatherer nomads referred to as the strandlopers (beachcombers), is well preserved. Walking in the footsteps of the hunter-gatherers with an experienced guide illuminating their legacies and habits was clearly going to be an eye-opener. We were also excited about some of the other treasures we might expect to see along the way: the dramatic rocks and busy rock pools, sea birds including the endangered African black oystercatcher (some of the proceeds from the trail go towards conserving them), dolphins and whales that frequent the waters off the coast, and the beautiful fynbos.

Equipped with maps and checklists we returned to camp, a horseshoe-shaped cluster of safari tents on raised wooden platforms in a clearing in the Vleesbaai dunes. We'd chosen the catered option so our rat-packs awaited: cooler boxes filled with breakfast and lunch packs and the essential dinner ingredients – chops, wors and beer, and a few bottles of decent plonk. Soon we were sitting around the campfire enjoying the smell of the braai and listening to the call of a *whip-poor-will* nightjar.

► **DAY 2** Circular hike from Vleesbaai Dune Camp

15 KM ◆ 5 HR

After preparing our own breakfast, we left the campsite and followed our guide

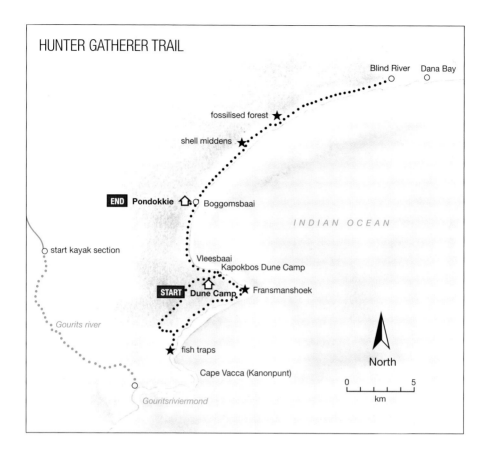

HUNTER GATHERER TRAIL

Blind River

Dana Bay

fossilised forest ★

shell middens ★

END Pondokkie ⌂ Boggomsbaai

INDIAN OCEAN

start kayak section

Vleesbaai
Kapokbos Dune Camp

START Dune Camp ★ Fransmanshoek

Gourits river

★ fish traps

Cape Vacca (Kanonpunt)

Gouritsriviermond

North

0 ——————— 5
km

through the dune and coastal thicket for a while before heading down to the beach. It was a wonderful introduction to the area. Birds flitted from tree to tree and we could hear and smell the sea long before we hit the shore. Our route followed the arc of the bay, along stony beaches, over rocky prom-ontories and along coastal paths flanked by pretty flowers. We were in no rush so stopped often to admire the rock forma-tions and intriguing marine life of the rock pools, to scan the ocean for whales and dol-phins and to enjoy the deserted beaches. We stopped for lunch at a pretty beach just shy of the little information centre at Frans-manshoek, at the western end of the bay.

The French man-o-war, *La Fortune*, was wrecked off this rocky point in 1763 but the sailors all survived. They lived the lives of castaways in this pleasant corner, before walking through wild country to what was then the lonely Dutch East India Company outpost at Swellendam.

Large bones, thought to be the femurs of an elephant, were a surprise discovery on a raised back-shore terrace.

The diverse trail alternates between beach, coastal fynbos and inland dunes.

We tucked into our packed lunches and congratulated the trail organisers for their thoughtfulness. Lunch, like the previous night's dinner and the morning's breakfast, was hearty and filling. The trail is aimed at those on more modest budgets than the slackpackers who sign up for the Oyster-catcher Trail so, although food packs are provided, you cook for yourself and pack up your own lunch. But that's no great sweat as it's so well organised we lacked for nothing.

Soon after Fransmanshoek we headed back up into the dunes, from where, some 80 m above the beach, we could really appreciate the beauty and remoteness of this beautiful stretch of the southern Cape coast. It was a view to die for – behind us were jagged peaks, while rippled dunes tumbled towards the inviting blue waters

Top Tip

Ask plenty of questions at the briefing so you really know what you're looking for. There is so much to see along this coast that even with a guide it's easy to miss little treasures.

of the bay below. Our guide was a fount of information, pointing out and identifying little plovers and sandpipers, grysbok footprints and the spoor of snakes and lizards in the sand, and urging us to look at the colourful little vygies and other tiny blooms that sprouted near the path. 'Look in the shallows over there,' he directed. 'Can you see the rocky structures? These are old Khoi fish traps – the fish would get caught on the outgoing tide.'

The afternoon wanderings back through the dunes were enlivened by yet more bird, buck and lizard sightings and we enjoyed slowing down to the pace of life on the trail. We were walking the same dunes and beaches that the strandlopers had scoured as they eked out a frugal existence from this coastline. However, in true slackpacker style, we were not subject to the vagaries of the natural world – it was time for tea and a snack from the food stores when we got back to camp!

We soon had the fire going and, after a welcome shower, sat out on the deck enjoying cold beers as the evening meal sizzled on the braai.

▶ DAY 3 Vleesbaai to Boggomsbaai

20 KM ◆ 6 HR

We were up bright and early in the morning and after breakfast packed our overnight bags for the short walk to our new 'home', the *pondokkie* above Boggomsbaai where we would be spending the next 2 nights. We took the 5 km walk slowly, enjoying the gentle crashing of the waves and the oyster-catchers that inhabit the coast. The organisers of the trail are passionately involved in trying to protect the habitats of these beautiful but endangered birds, so we had learnt lots about them at the briefing. We were pleased to see signs on the entrances

Pondokkie, the overnight spot on nights 3 and 4, comprises tented accommodation.

to the beach informing visitors of the habits of the birds and warning how beach-users can unwittingly disturb their nests.

Once installed at Pondokkie we headed down a narrow track to the beach again and wandered east along the sand for a couple of kilometres. Our guide led us up into the dunes to see some large shell middens and pointed out flint tools as well as various black and white mussel, oyster and peri-winkles shells that would have constituted the basic diet of the groups that inhabited the coast.

We knew also there were fossils to be found on the raised terraces but were quite unprepared for the extent of the fossilised forests that we soon came to. Careful not to trample or disturb these natural treasures, we studied the great trunks and branches of fossilised trees and flintstone tools. But the highlight was 2 large bones. According to the guide they have been identified by Mel-ani Poupart, who is studying the Pinnacle Point caves as a student of Prof Curtis Mar-ean, of the Institute of Human Origins at the Arizona State University's School of Human Evolution and Social Change, as the femurs

of an elephant. Strange indeed to think such massive mammals once roamed this pretty stretch of seaside. We could imagine our ancestors sitting around a fire up in this raised spot, enjoying a seafood supper; but gnawing on an elephant – that was quite a different matter.

We returned to Pondokkie to start our own fire, then climbed onto a big water reservoir to enjoy the sunset. From this magnificent viewpoint we could see the blue Outeniqua mountains on one side and the shimmering Indian Ocean on the

… and rooms in a rustic cottage behind Boggomsbaai.

other. It had been a fascinating day and we were still discussing our finds long into the evening as we sat around the embers admiring the starry sky.

▶ DAY 4 Canoeing on the Gourits

20 KM • 5 HR (but variable depending on tide and energy!)

Our final day was spent merrily drifting down the tidal Gourits River. No more hiking, simply a glorious day fishing and pottering around in kayaks. As our guide scanned the banks and the sky for bird life, we pulled out a couple of leervis (called garrick further north) and grunter, which supplemented our final meal.

All that remained was to walk back to our cars at Vleesbaai in the morning. It had been a restful and highly educational trail – a wonderful insight into the lives of the forebears and a truly exceptional hike.

In a nutshell · Hunter Gatherer Trail

BOOKINGS Sandpiper Safaris, 044-699-1204, stay@sandpipersafaris.co.za www.oystercatchertrail.co.za.
START/FINISH Vleesbaai / Boggomsbaai near Mossel Bay.
TRANSFERS Transfers back to the start are included while transfers to and from George airport can be organised by Sandpiper Safaris.
HIGHLIGHTS Middens, fossils and unique palaeontological sites; outstanding coastal scenery and landforms; empty swimming beaches and quaint seaside villages; dolphins, and in season, whales; excellent guiding.
LONGEST DAY 20 km.
SHORTEST DAY 3 km.
GROUP SIZE Minimum 4, maximum 8.
UP TO IT? This is a straightforward, flexible trail that is ideal for novice hikers and family groups. The routes are circular from base camps so groups can tailor-make the daily itineraries to suit their fitness level and interest.
DON'T FORGET A small day pack, binoculars, camera, warm and fully waterproof clothing and personal gear. Overnight gear including sleeping bag and pillow.
LOOK IT UP A detailed map of the trail (also available on the website) along with a tide table and a checklist of bird, reptile, mammal and marine species, is given out at the start.
WHEN TO GO The trail can be walked year round except between mid-December to mid-January. July to October is the best time for whale watching from the shores.
BEFORE AND AFTER Sandpiper Cottages at Boggomsbaai, www.sandpipersafaris.co.za.

Survival Notes

- You have to carry your own bags for the short distance between the 2 camps.
- Drinking water is not available on the trail.
- Shorter options available.

Swart Tobie

Western Cape

DISTANCE 75 km ◆ **DURATION** 5 days ◆ **DIFFICULTY** 2/3 ◆ **TRAIL TYPE** Beach
LOGISTICS Part-guided and portered, bags driven around ◆ **COST** R
ACCOMMODATION TYPE Camping, wind shelters and long-drops ◆ **AREA** West coast

The Swart Tobie (black oystercatcher) Trail traverses a remote, mostly inaccessible
stretch of the Cape west coast near the small town of Koekenaap. It's a rustic but
incredibly rewarding journey past fascinating coastal landforms, along beautiful
purple and gold sandy beaches and finally along the banks of the Olifants River:
all of which highlight the best of the marine and riverine environments of the
Western Cape.

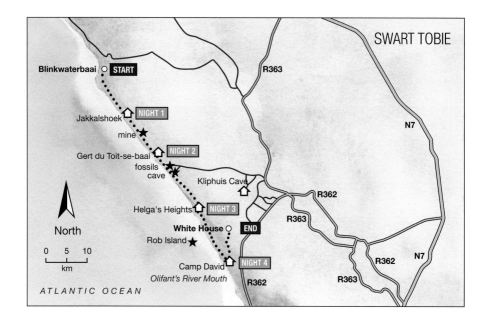

On this trail you're sure to see exquisite flowers and rock pools, be entertained by marine mammals and wonderful bird life, including the ones after which the trail takes its name. While for the most part you hike empty beaches or along sea cliffs, don't go expecting pristine wilderness: the area has been heavily exploited for diamonds and other minerals and there are still working mines and abandoned machinery along the way.

Precious gems

Although diamonds are the main mineral extracted along the coast, various other minerals and metals have commercial value: colourless zircons are a popular substitute for diamonds in jewellery; somewhat perversely, given the origin of its name (from the Latin *rutilus*, red), finely powdered rutile produces a brilliant white pigment that is used in foodstuffs, paper, paints and plastics.

Water and wood are provided at the rustic campsites, but hikers must bring their own tents and everything else they require so this is a trail for those for whom life is about the simple things: sitting around a fire at night, enjoying the sounds of the sea, walking barefoot along deserted beaches and swimming, naked if the fancy takes, in the beautiful bays along the way.

The trail starts at Blinkwaterbaai and finishes some 6 km inland from the Olifants River Mouth. The first 2 and last days are unguided but on days 3 and 4 the trail organiser shares the secrets of the coast with his hikers, guiding them to mysterious fossil formations, to hidden caves and to some fascinating floral and geological sites. This is not a trail for people who need their luxuries. Although your tents and bags are driven around each day and fresh food can be kept until the day it is needed, there is a limited supply of fresh water and no showers, no electricity, no shops along the way, but long-drop loos and only occasional cellphone reception. Then again that is the beauty of the trail: you feel one with nature in this empty, wild place. If you enjoy camping then this is one of the most magnificent coastal trails … anywhere.

▶ NIGHT 1 Settling in

Wynand Wickens, the trail organiser, had a good look at us as we got out of our cars. 'I can judge people's pace as soon as they walk in to my house,' he claimed. 'You lot look pretty fit.' We deposited our clearly labelled cooler bags in his freezer before retiring to our camp, a very comfortable sandstone cave, Kliphuis Boesmansgrotte, at his farm on the Olifants River. Wynand briefed us on what to expect over the next 5 days, then left us to enjoy the sights and sounds (and the camp's luxuries) of the river. As the food cooked on the braai we watched flocks of birds flying in to roost and stars lit up the night sky. The stresses of city life were quickly falling away.

▶ DAY 1 Blinkwaterbaai (or Brand se Baai) to Jakkalshoek

18 KM • 5 ½–6 HR

We woke early to see the early morning mist rising over the river, and after a shower and breakfast hopped into a taxi for the hour-long drive to the trail head. We were doing the Full Monty, hiking from Blinkwater-baai to Jakkalshoek where hikers chose to start is flexible, and dependent on their fitness and time available. Some hikers, particularly those doing weekend trails, prefer the shorter distance from Brand se Baai. In the distance we could see the headland that Wynand had told us was our goal for the day, so we shouldered our day packs and headed south.

The coastline was rugged with great rocky promontories and sandy bays; we had been instructed to follow our noses

Boulder hop or follow the jeep track, the choice of route is yours.

and keep the sea on our right! The only thing to watch out for was incoming tides: there were places where, if we weren't paying attention, we could find escaping the beach difficult. Wynand was insistent that there was no 'best way' as the coast changes markedly with the seasons (it is a high-energy coastal system with beaches being scooped away by winter storm surf and redeposited by summer waves and winds). Sure enough, we soon discovered that walking on the beach at high tide or on the deep mussel beds was hard work. For much of the day we opted to follow jeep tracks just off the beach, although these were sandy in places.

The great thing about a self-guided trail is that you can chose your own route, detouring to peer into rock pools or to collect mussels, walking on the sand or leaving the beach for a cliff path to enjoy the flowers and the views. We left the beach often in fact, fascinated by the number of delicate bird prints and animal tracks – mongooses in particular seem very active along this stretch. Though we knew there were no hills and that the daily distances were not long, it was certainly not going to be a walk in the park. Nor were we walking through pristine wilderness; after a couple of hours we arrived at Brand se Baai and Namaqua

This memorial is to Joseph Andrew Wright who drowned near here in 1964.

Sands, an AngloAmerican mine where rutile, titanium and zircon are extracted. We passed some run-down farmers' huts then stayed on the jeep track admiring the flowers. It was early July and good early rains meant colourful daisies, spectacular purple eland's vy (pig's ear, or cotolydon) and other colourful succulents covered the shrubby veld, stabilising the sandy soil and preventing wind erosion.

We'd been told to look out for middens and sure enough we soon came upon a great raised mound covered with shells – evidence of long-gone strandlopers who scavenged the coast for food ... and the perfect place for us to enjoy our own lunch. Feeling somewhat lethargic after our midday break, we dragged ourselves past more rocky gullies, one bridged by a huge rock, before descending to the beach. I kicked off my shoes for the umpteenth time and enjoyed the feeling of walking barefoot.

The beach, coloured by various minerals, was amazing: deep shades of maroon, pink, purple and black sands punctuated by gnarled outcrops of rock and granite slabs. On our frequent meanderings away from the beach and onto a jeep track we would pass white mounds which, Wynand informed us later, were generally test areas that had been rehabilitated. A couple more little bays and gullies, one of which was so full of foam that when I stood on a rock in the middle I had the impression of being on a glacier, and we saw a telltale flag on the top of a dune announcing the campsite. We walked past a loo with a view to where Wynand had lit the fire and was waiting with our bags.

The campsite was in a great spot – with an awesome view, 2 long-drops in the dunes, a sheltered 'kitchen' with a couple of tables and a protected bathing hole just below. After erecting our tents we scrambled up the dunes for sundowners with views all along coast. The day had not been unduly tiresome but we'd come a long way. Below us were swathes of green mesh indicating areas under rehabilitation. The system works well – Wynand pointed out other areas that had been reclaimed only 2 years previously and were now almost indistinguishable from the untouched areas. Soon after we'd eaten we headed for bed, weary from our exertions and the fresh air, and fell asleep listening to the sounds of the surf.

▶ DAY 2 Jakkalshoek to Gert du Toit-se-baai

18 KM ◆ 6 HR

'Don't rush today,' advised Wynand. 'You have loads of time, so swim and enjoy the rock pools.' And we certainly found plenty of interest in the rocky intertidal zone. The first few kilometres were quite hard work as we trudged along great ridges of mussel shells and leaving the beach quite regularly to scramble over rocky headlands. We stopped for a welcome rest and a swim at another glorious stretch of purple and black sands before spotting a man-made structure on the rocks: a memorial to Joseph Andrew Wright, who drowned off this spot in February 1964. The waves crashed against the rocks, sending up great sprays of water that occasionally carried right to where we stood. It was easy to see how you could meet with an unfortunate end in such a wild place.

After another long stretch of beach we saw a mine ahead and, as instructed, took the dirt road around until we were past the workings. The mine is still active so visitors are not allowed in to the fenced area, including the big hole in the ground from where the diamonds were extracted. From the road we could see plenty of activity and, on the other side of the road, the retainer dam. As we headed back down through the dunes to the beach we saw a timid wild cat only metres away, but it vanished quickly at our approach. We continued, again marvelling at the multicoloured sands, along an incredibly pretty big long beach, where great flocks of gulls and cormorants were sunning themselves.

Sadly humans have left an impact here too, and there was a disturbing amount of rubbish and evidence of old workings creating a rather scraggy appearance. Apparently Coastal Care does an annual clean-up blitz along here and the speculators are supposed to remove all their 'stuff' but we still felt the area was in need of a clean-up. The final section before we spotted Wynand's bakkie was lined with temporary beach shelters and long-drops, this is clearly a favourite fishing spot for locals. Some of the shelters were quite cozy and elaborate, with paths lined with shells, with potted plants, old buoys and other flotsam and jetsam decorating the porches. One even had a swing, which we couldn't resist playing on for a while as we admired a goliath heron

standing elegantly on the edge of a rock pool, its image reflected in the crystal-clear water. We followed the bird's example, peering into gullies full of mussels, redbait and little fish before completing the final stretch of beach to join Wynand with a cold beer.

Camp 2 was quite elaborate compared to the previous one, with a walled braai area and a kitchen covered by shade cloth. We pitched our tents on a flat area near a massive washed-up log before heading for a swim. The rocks were home to a big colony of cormorants so it was rather smelly.

Anyone for a kelp mask?

You might well see old-fashioned hammer mills or kelp drying by the side of the dirt road. The dried, shredded kelp is exported to Japan where it is used in the manufacture of cosmetics, shampoos and other beauty products.

That did not deter us from gathering some mussels to put on the fire – bird and human alike must eat. If you have a mussel permit, and, in season, a crayfish permit, you can harvest molluscs or crays every day and virtually live off the sea! Sadly, it was not crayfish season (mid-November to end of year daily, January to April weekends and public holidays only) but the number of empty carapaces on the beaches certainly indicated there was no shortage of crays out there.

▶ **DAY 3** Gert du Toit-se-baai to Helga's Heights

18.7 KM • 7 HR

We'd been warned that day 3 was the most strenuous of the hike – but that our efforts

The beaches along the trail are coloured light and dark by minerals such as titanium and kaolin.

would be rewarded. 'The trail is like a piece of music, starting quietly and building to a crescendo,' Wynand had eloquently described it at the initial briefing. He would be guiding us for the next couple of days so we set off expectantly along the jeep track. After a couple of kilometres we followed him down to a big bay beach. At the end of the beach was a wonderful gully where we had our first swim of the day, then continued over rocks and sandstone slabs.

'Look at the layers in the eroded cliffs,' said Wynand. 'These are windows in time; you can see how the environment has changed over the past few million years. The redder layers indicate dry desert conditions, while the paler and white layers were laid down when this land was under water.' A former diamond diver, Wynand knows this coastline like the back of his hand. 'This is millionaire's gully I once pulled out 720 carats here in 2 days. I was rolling in it with a salary plus 10 per cent of the diamond's value. It was hard, dangerous work, but those were happy days.'

The geology of the coast had changed. By the time we reached Ryk Bay we were walking over conglomerate and were surprised to see oyster shells embedded in the matrix – evidence of a warmer climate in the past. It was prospector Hans Merensky who discovered that the fossil oyster layer coincided with the diamond deposits along the west coast, having been brought down by the Orange River when its course was much further south.

We stopped for another break to swim and explore big rock pools and the colourful pebbles washed up by the waves. We identified red jasper, delicate, flecked pink and grey granites, some smooth black rocks we thought might be obsidian and the ubiquitous white quartz. 'There's plenty of quartzite along the coast, and Trans Hex mining company says you must leave the diamonds but you can take this home if you wish,' teased Wynand, pointing to a boulder the size of a small car. The scenery just got better and better, the colourful cliffs were riddled with caves and overhangs while out to sea we saw whales blowing, a big colony of cormorants, then a flurry of activity as gulls and gannets dived into a big shoal of sardines.

By the time we stopped for tea in the shade of a big cave we had covered only about 5 km. The overnight camp was still a long way, probably some 15 km off in the distance, but the coast was so beautiful we didn't want to miss out on anything.

We left the beach and climbed up to Duiwegat. The viewpoint over wave-eroded potholes and swirling waters still has a bucket winch down into the gully below, which the diamond extractors used to bring up their booty. We spotted other abandoned pipes and machinery. Wynand elaborated on the history of mining in the area and regaled us with more stories of his diver days, then it was back to the beach at Geelwal Strand. This, apparently, is the start of the succulent Karoo biome and a big vegetated wall was the backdrop to the next section of long beach. We climbed to the cliff top a couple of times to negotiate rocky promontories, stopping often to admire the flowers.

Wynand pointed out distinctive leaves of the soutslaai (salt salad), the colourful yellow botterblom (butter flower). 'The stem looks like butter and tastes quite good – try it. And if you squeeze the juice out of the leaves and leave it on overnight, it will take the hair off your legs!' Next he pointed out the penny bush, the leaves of which look like old British pennies, opening up to reveal a pretty yellow flower in the middle. And of course there were Namaqua daisies everywhere. 'They are pioneer plants,' Wynand explained, 'and the tourists' obsession with the colourful daisies has caused unnecessary destruction. Money-orientated farmers have burnt or otherwise disturbed their fields to ensure the daisies will come through and please the undiscerning visitors.'

We headed down to the beach again for lunch, passing a blowhole that is always good for an admiring stop. Again we were in for a surprise. A black putty-like substance oozed from the cliff face and Wynand pointed out large sections of soft white kaolin.

We climbed again, noting some unusual tubular features at the top of the cliff: our guide gave us the local version, that they were fossilised mangrove forests, sitting high and dry on the 50 m cliff top. Later sleuthing revealed the truth: they are the tunnels of ancient termite nests. He was more accurate in the dating: 'They have survived 100 million years or more, since the Karoo dinosaurs died out.' The high, narrow traverse past the mangroves and the steep ridge down to the beach had our hearts beating a bit faster – we'd been warned that this was not a good route for anyone with vertigo – so we were eager for another swim by the time we arrived at Scratch Patch, a beach full of exquisite pebbles. Wynand was now forced to chivvy us along. We'd added a beautiful green olivine stone to our list of desirable gemstones and could have rummaged for hours. But we had a date with our luggage delivery to keep so reluctantly climbed up to the brick built shelter at Helga's Heights.

In summer groups can camp on the extensive beach, but in winter the tide comes almost up to the cliff edge so the raised campsite is the only option. Feeling lazy, we chose to sleep in the shelter looking at the stars and listening to what was left of the corrugated-iron roof flapping in the wind!

A big cave resembling an old-fashioned bread oven is just one of the geological wonders on the trail.

▶ DAY 4 Helga's Heights to Olifants River Mouth

21 KM • 7 HR

Wynand arrived early to guide us again on day 4 and set we off along the cliff path, passing more fossilised mangroves. Again the views were spectacular, the sea stacks reminiscent of the scenery on Australia's famous Great Ocean Road along the south coast of Victoria. There was more evidence of diamond workings, which though an eyesore, gave us insights into the way of life in the area. We passed the Marine Protected Area of Mossel Bay, then paused on top of a big quarzite outcrop and from where we could see a memorial to another 3 people who had drowned here.

A rare bird

The swart tobie, or African black oystercatcher (*Haematopus moquini*), breeds on rocky coasts and in-shore islands of southern Africa. Although commonly sighted on this trail, the bird is endangered with a global population of less than 5 000 adult birds. They are distinguishable by their bright red legs and bill and entirely black plumage.

Robinson Crusoe's hut at Skilpadbaai was our first tea stop; we peered longingly at the fat mussels in the rock pools and spotted the prints of a brown hyena which had clearly been scavenging along the bay. A great spout of water alerted us to the presence of another blowhole – the erosive power of the waves has produced some spectacular landforms.

One of these was our next port of call; Voelklip (Bird Island) a sea stack covered in white guano. It didn't take much imagi-

nation to work out why the next formation was nicknamed 'the woman'. As the pressure of the waves forced the water up through a narrow gully in the cliff it trickled down back into the sea. 'A woman peeing,' grinned Wynand. As promised we were nearing the crescendo. We stopped to admire a fossilised tortoise and swim in the clear water of Solitaire Bay, and quickly identified a rock formation from the cryptic clue: 'Think of a Beatles' song.' There was no doubting the shape of a yellow submarine: it even had the periscope.

Whales were blowing off Bethel beach as we stopped to inspect some ill-advised and abandoned diamond workings and noted again that the rock type had changed – we were now scrambling over pink and grey mica schists, which often flaked away as we scrambled over.

Wynand pointed out the face of an old man in the cliff face, then disappeared into a hidden crack in the rock. It was like being in an Indiana Jones movie: we followed him through the narrow canyon then emerged into a new world of shimmering rock pools full of mussels, limpets and colourful anemones.

Bakoond, a big cave with a sandy base that resembled an old-fashioned bread oven, was the next geological wonder. We scrambled down through the cave to a tunnel that penetrated deep into the folded rock, then swam in the sheltered gully on the ocean side. It really was an incredible stretch of coast and we appreciated why we were being guided.

As we returned to the beach in front of Rob Island several hundred resting cormorants took flight. There were thousands of seals on the rocks and in the water around the island, barking noisily. We passed more middens and another tortoise fossil, each time stopping to look and take photos and

The end of the trail is celebrated with a braai prepared by your hosts at the Kliphuis Cave.

delay the journey. By now we were getting somewhat blasé, there was just so much of interest it was hard to take it all in!

We climbed again above the gorgeous sands of Luck-se-baai, following a path through the colourful succulents and yum-yums (clover) before returning to the beach for the final, long stretch to the river mouth. Our bags were heavy with the weight of collected treasures – our favourite olivine, jasper and quartz pebbles that we could not throw back into the sea – yet we could not take our eyes off the wet sand in the hope off finding another shiny wonder.

So far the oystercatchers had been conspicuous by their absence, but as we reached the wide wave-cut platform approaching the river mouth, we spied 5 pairs foraging on the rocks. As we rounded the bend and found the path up the northern side of the Olifants River, the change in scenery was remarkable. The river lapped gently against the vegetated banks, grey herons stood in the shallows and across the river we could see the villages of Strandfontein and Ebenhaezer. It was only a couple of kilometres to the overnight camp, jokingly named Camp David (the trail ends at The White House). The campsite was flat and spacious, but moving back into the occupied world after 4 days in the wilderness was a shock.

▶ DAY 5 Camp David to The White House

6 KM ◆ 2 HR

Our final day was a gentle stroll from Camp David to our rendezvous point at a derelict white house from where we would be transferred back to base camp. The riverbank path was easy so we took our time and admired the birds and the wide, gently flowing river. After a shower and lunch back at the Kliphuis Cave we headed into Lutzville for a wine tasting at the local cellars, then again back to Kliphuis for an evening braai, courtesy of Wynand and his wife Ronel. We slept soundly, lulled by the gentle lapping of the water. The Swart Tobie trail is an undiscovered gem. If you are reasonably fit and don't mind roughing it a bit, this one is an absolute must.

In a nutshell · Swart Tobie

BOOKINGS Jacana Marketing & Reservations, 0861-JACANA (0861-52-2262) or 011-656-0606, bookings@jacanacollection.co.za, www.jacanacollection.co.za or 027-217-1790, swarttobie@kingsley.co.za.

START/FINISH Just outside Koekenaap in the Western Cape.

HIGHLIGHTS The incredible geology of the coastline; the purple beaches and wonderful pebbles; the fossilised swamp forests and tortoises; the wild flowers; the indigenous bird life and marine mammals; views; the sense of wilderness; the well-equipped cave where you spend the first and last nights.

LONGEST DAY 21 km.

SHORTEST DAY 6 km.

GROUP SIZE Minimum 2, maximum 20.

UP TO IT? You need to be reasonably fit for this hike as the distances are quite long and walking on sand is quite tiring. If low tide falls over midday the trail can be regarded as moderate, but high tide at midday makes it more strenuous. Nonetheless, apart from day 3, which is moderately challenging and might present problems for those with serious fears of heights, it's a straightforward beach and coastal walk on which you choose your own route according to the tides and your interests.

DON'T FORGET! Swimming costume, mask and snorkel, camera, bird/plant guides, tide table, mosquito repellent and binoculars. Open shoes or sandals are ideal footwear. A mussel permit and, in season, crayfish permit. You could harvest your own food every day! On the camping front bring everything you need (other than firewood and water), including a tarpaulin to protect supplies from the damp overnight sea air, firelighters and toilet paper. Pack cleverly by putting your daily rations of food and drinks into separate packs, which the trail organiser will keep in a deep-freeze and bring out to you on the appropriate evening. If you run out of anything, or fancy ending the day with a cold beer, you can also put in an order for supplies.

WHEN TO GO Spring (August–October) is wonderful as whales are usually seen in abundance and the flowers are at their best. Autumn (March–May) is also a good time. Summers (November–February) are often windy, but if you have a crayfish permit you might fancy these months, while winters (June and July) can be wet and cold.

BEFORE AND AFTER The cave can be booked by those wishing to stay longer in the area.

Survival Notes

- No drinking water available en route.
- Hikers stay in rustic campsites with long-drops and basic wind shelters.
- Days 3 and 4 are guided so you don't miss the geological attractions and the fossils.

28

Cape of Good Hope Hiking Trail

Western Cape

DISTANCE 33.8 km ◆ **DURATION** 2 days ◆ **DIFFICULTY** 3 ◆ **TRAIL TYPE** Hills, fynbos flats, beach
LOGISTICS Bags transported on request ◆ **COST** R ◆ **ACCOMMODATION TYPE** Hiking huts
AREA Cape Peninsula

This superb trail is one of the Cape's best-kept secrets on which hikers enjoy the best of the Cape Peninsula: dramatic and changing scenery; colourful flowers; herds of bontebok, eland and other game; outstanding beaches. And you get the reserve all to yourself once all the day-trippers have left. Although much of the literature will tell you that the Atlantic and Indian oceans meet at this point, it's not strictly true. But hey, let's not split currents – the ocean and the lighthouses, the funicular and the walk along the cliff tops to the Cape of Good Hope are impressive enough without that distinction.

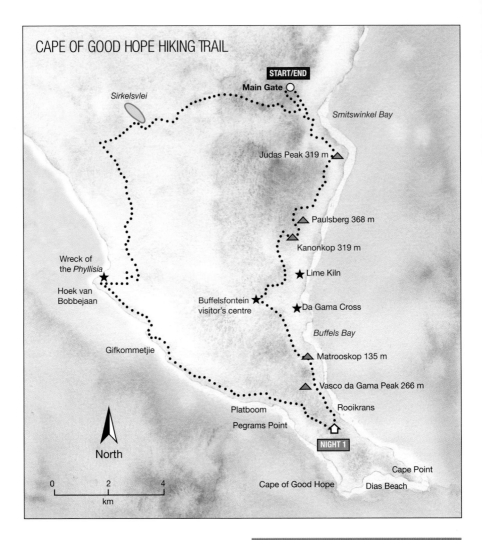

CAPE OF GOOD HOPE HIKING TRAIL

START/END
Main Gate
Sirkelsvlei
Smitswinkel Bay
Judas Peak 319 m
Paulsberg 368 m
Kanonkop 319 m
Wreck of the *Phyllisia*
Lime Kiln
Hoek van Bobbejaan
Buffelsfontein visitor's centre
Da Gama Cross
Buffels Bay
Gifkommetjie
Matrooskop 135 m
Vasco da Gama Peak 266 m
Platboom
Rooikrans
Pegrams Point
NIGHT 1
North
Cape Point
0   2   4
km
Cape of Good Hope
Dias Beach

This circular, overnight trail starts at the entrance gate of the Cape of Good Hope section of the Table Mountain National Park and winds its way around the dramatic cliffs and wild beaches of the False Bay coast to the overnight huts high on the slopes of Vasco da Gama Peak near Cape Point. Day 2 completes the circle with the trail crossing over to the long, sweeping beaches and down the flat fynbos-covered plains of the Atlantic coast back to the gate.

It's a beautiful trail at any time of year, but at its finest in spring when the plains are covered by a mass of colourful blooms.

Top Tip

Factor in a few diversions. Pack a swimming costume and, on day 1, stop at the tidal pool or Buffels Bay for a swim. If you're really feeling energetic climb down to the gorgeous Dias beach between Cape Point and Cape of Good Hope (not the same place). And don't miss a visit to the lighthouses. Carry plenty of water, too, as it can get very hot and there are few opportunities to fill your water bottles.

Sightings of Cape mountain zebra are a special treat, but you're most certain to see ostrich, bontebok and other antelope, dassie (rock hyrax), baboons and sea birds. If you're on the trail any time between July and December, there's an excellent chance of seeing whales and there are marked whale-watching viewpoints, with information boards. Although it's not particularly mountainous or long, don't underestimate this trail. The path is undulating and often rugged underfoot so a good pair of boots and a fair level of fitness are recommended.

It's bit of a detour, but you really should make time to visit the lighthouses at Cape Point.

▶ DAY 1 Cape of Good Hope entrance to Vasco da Gama Peak

13 KM ◆ 6 HR

After parking the car just inside the reserve's entrance gate, we bought wood and arranged for our overnight bags to be delivered to the overnight hut, then headed out along the road to the start of the trail. (You *can* carry your own bags – so if you want to save yourself a few bucks, have masochistic tendencies or enjoy warm beer, go right ahead!) Soon we could see the clear, turquoise water of Smitswinkel Bay far below us. We stopped at the viewpoint for what is one of my favourite outlooks in the world, the view over False Bay and all the way down the Peninsula, then followed the clearly marked trail towards the rocky, fynbos peaks that jutted into the blue sky.

The trail took us round the back of Judas Peak and De Boer, but we also took a detour to climb Paulsberg, the highest peak in the area at 367 m. From there we could see the great cliffs on the seaward sides of the mountains dropping precipitously into the sea. The old cannon on top of Kanonkop made for a good spot to take a break. In the days when the British occupied the Cape it was used to signal Simon's Town of the arrival of ships in False Bay, but it looks as if it could have had a more menacing intent. Not far beyond the cannon the path splits with the 'official' route to the right leading to the Buffelsfontein visitors' centre. We, however, decided to take the road less travelled and headed down towards the sea for a dip.

Sharing the space

The Cape of Good Hope section of the Table Mountain National Park is extremely popular with day visitors (second only in number to Kruger Park). They come to visit one of the most accessible parts of the Cape Floristic Region Protected Area – a World Heritage Site – to see the celebrated fynbos, the plains game and to walk to one of South Africa's most iconic spots: Cape Point. The reserve is also frequented by local beach lovers, fishers, surfers and free divers (particularly during the crayfish season) but the stunningly beautiful overnight hiking trail is surprisingly underutilised, so it's usually easy to book a place.

On day 2, try to imagine these rocks as the base of huge mountains that once arched right across False Bay to the Hottentots Holland, between 100 and 60 million years ago.

The path led down a small kloof to the car park at Booi se Skerm. If you have time, a good detour from here is to head north (i.e. with the sea on your right) to Venus Pool, a great swimming spot on a rocky ledge, but we continued along the trail to Bordjiesrif for a swim in the tidal pool. If you want to swim in the sea, the next bay, Buffels Bay, is also a good spot and in season you'll often see divers trying to catch crayfish in the kelp.

From Buffels Bay we took the narrow path leading along the coast enjoying the smell of the sea and the views over False Bay to a grassy area known as The Meadows where we were surprised to find a herd of eland grazing. I somehow hadn't expected to find big antelope here but apparently

The wreck of the *Phyllisia* which ran aground on the Atlantic coast in 1968.

Dassies

The dassie, or rock hyrax, is probably the most frequently sighted mammal on the rocky areas of the Peninsula, particularly around the lookouts at Cape Point and around the Upper Cable Station where they scavenge for food. (Visitors are requested not to encourage this behaviour by feeding them.) The small, tailless dassies live in colonies and never venture far from their rock shelters. Males tend to occupy high vantage points and give a harsh warning call when danger threatens. Unfortunately for dassies, they are the Verreauxs' (black) eagle's favourite food so they have to be particularly wary in autumn when black eagles are rearing chicks. Dassies usually urinate on the same spot and the excretion evaporates to a hard, glassy substance, which the Khoi used to collect for medicinal purposes.

hikers often see them. The path then climbed up to rejoin the main trail, so we enjoyed the raised vantage point of the fynbos-covered cliff tops before the final scramble up over the weathered ancient rocks from Rooikrans to the huts. The red sandstone ledges are a popular whale-watching and fishing spot (for yellowtail mainly) and even this early in the day there were plenty of anglers trying their luck.

It was early afternoon when we arrived at the overnight huts so we pushed on for a couple more kilometres across the slopes of Vasco da Gama Peak to Cape Point, stopping for a welcome drink at the Two Oceans Restaurant. The baboons were up to their tricks in the car park, pulling off windscreen wipers and otherwise vandalising cars – all the time being chased by 'minders'.

We ambled up to the old lighthouse (built in 1860 but now replaced by a stronger one lower down that is more easily visible at sea), a dramatic place where the cliffs fall away, the sea looks menacing and the waves crash against the rocky shore as if to remind you of its treacherous waters that gave the place its first European name, the Cape of Storms. Despite our weary legs, we walked down to the lower lighthouse – an even more photogenic spot – and then hiked back to the overnight cottages.

Although the distance is short, the terrain on day 1 is challenging so stop often to enjoy the view.

We'd booked the nicest of the 3 huts, the 6-bedded Erica; after showering we lit a fire and sat out as the convoy of departing cars snaked towards the gate. It's a privilege to overnight here – the scenery is at its most impressive in the late golden light and we sipped cold wine from our high vantage point as the sun melted into the sea, a brilliant ball of orange that seemed to set the ocean alight.

Local is lekker

Cape Town's Wild Card, which costs R75, is available exclusively to Capetonians and offers affordable limited entry to the Table Mountain National Park's pay points at the Cape of Good Hope, Boulders Penguin Colony, Silvermine and Tokai, as well as the picnic site at Newlands, Perdekloof and Oudekraal. Wild Cards are available at Cape Nature and Sanparks offices or through www.wildcard.co.za.

The clouds turned a vibrant pink and then faded as night rolled in. The lights around False Bay twinkled in the distance, but we felt as if we were in the wilderness: there was no noise save for the crashing waves, no traffic, no other voices as we braaied under a sky brilliantly lit by stars.

▶ **DAY 2** Vasco da Gama Peak to the reserve entrance

20.5 KM ◆ 10 HR

On day 2 we woke to the sound of baboons on the roof. We had slept well – the rooms are spacious and quite luxurious, with bunks and big, thick mattresses, hot showers, gas stoves and essential cooking and decent tableware.

Sunrise over False Bay was as impressive as always and we looked down the Peninsula at the familiar profiles of Judas Peak, Paulsberg and Kanonkop, which we passed the day before.

If you didn't visit Cape Point on your first day you really should factor in some extra time to hike the long way round on day 2 – the views from Cape Point and along the cliffs and boardwalks above Dias Beach to the Cape of Good Hope are very impressive. However, it does add considerably to the difficulty of the trail so attempt it only if you're fit, start early and take plenty of water. Otherwise follow the yellow footprints from the huts down and over the tarred road in the direction of Pegram's Point.

Once on the Altantic coast we stopped to swim and watch surfers in the chilly water of Platboom Bay, then refilled our water bottles and continued along the shoreline past the bobbing heads of the dense kelp. We passed a couple of small islands, then followed the yellow marked poles past Bloubergstrand and Gifkommetjie to Hoek van Bobbejaan where there are the remains of old Khoisan middens. On the beach you can still see the wreck of the *Phyllisia*, which ran aground here in 1968. The trail leaves the coast at this point and cuts through a

The top of Kanonkop is a good spot for a breather.

restricted area that only overnight hikers are allowed to traverse, so our eyes were now on the fynbos.

Again the path split and we headed east towards Sirkelsvlei and the gate. A family group of white-faced bontebok lifted their

Beleaguered baboons

Large baboons are regularly found in troops on rocky cliffs around the southern Peninsula and around parked vehicles at Cape Point where they have become a serious nuisance. There used to be a sizeable population but their mortality rate is very high, especially for adult males: with their intimidating size and dog-like bark, they are often shot or become victims of power struggles between the males in the troops. In an attempt to educate the general public and dispel some negative perceptions about the baboons, Baboon Matters trains and equips baboon monitors (who patrol the primates' territory and try to minimise their nuisance value)

and offers fascinating guided trips to see the animals in their natural habitat. For more information visit www.baboonmatters.org.za

heads, clearly unconcerned by the presence of hikers, then we strolled gently through a damp area dominated by reeds before stopping at Rooihoogte to look back on our route. We could see the faint path around the massed peaks of the False Bay coast that we'd followed on day 1, all the way down to the lighthouse and over the beaches of the Atlantic coast and we sat reminiscing on the varied experiences that we'd had in such a short time. What a memorable trail – and one that you can easily do in a weekend and return home refreshed and ready to start a new week!

In a nutshell · Cape of Good Hope Hiking Trail

BOOKINGS Table Mountain National Park Buffelsfontein Visitors' Centre 021-780-9204, www.sanparks.org/parks/table_mountain/tourism/overnight_hikes.php.

START/FINISH Entrance gate to the Cape of Good Hope section of the Table Mountain National Park.

HIGHLIGHTS Fynbos and plains game; the cliffs and bay between Cape of Good Hope and Cape Point; great overnight huts; mountain scenery on day 2.

LONGEST DAY 20.5 km.

SHORTEST DAY 13.3 km.

GROUP SIZE Minimum 1, maximum 18.

UP TO IT? Anyone can do this trail but the fitter you are the more you'll enjoy it. Day 2 is flat, but there are some steeper sections on day 1, where easy scrambling is required.

DON'T FORGET! Your Wild Card if you have one (see page 16). Sleeping bags, warm and fully waterproof clothing (bring a backpack cover in winter), binoculars (particularly in whale season), a guide to the flowers and personal gear. The water is cold and it can be rough, but the beaches are inviting so pack a swimming costume. Braai grids, a 3-ring gas stove, cutlery and crockery are provided at the hut, and firewood (which is actually delivered to the hut!) can be purchased at the entrance gate.

LOOK IT UP Good maps showing the trail are the *National Geographic Adventure Map of Table Mountain* and Peter Slingsby's *Map of Cape Point* (Map 5 in the Table Mountain series).

WHEN TO GO The trail can be walked year round but it can get very hot in summer. The Cape experiences winter rainfall and it can be very cold and wet at this time, so go prepared.

BEFORE AND AFTER Cape Town Tourism will advise on accommodation and other activities, 021-487-6800, www.capetown.travel

Survival Notes

- Very limited drinking water available on the trail.
- Hutted accommodation.
- Souvenir shop and restaurant on route.
- Keep food away from baboons, and give them a wide berth.

29

Whale Trail

Western Cape

 DISTANCE 55 km ◆ **DURATION** 5 days ◆ **DIFFICULTY** 3 ◆ **TRAIL TYPE** Hills, fynbos flats, coastal path, beach ◆ **LOGISTICS** Bags transported on request ◆ **COST** RR **ACCOMMODATION TYPE** Cape-style cottages ◆ **AREA** Southern Cape, De Hoop

Although the Whale Trail winds its way through some very rugged scenery, don't for a minute think this trail means roughing it. You stay in very comfortable, self-catering cottages and A-frames with flush loos, hot showers, solar lighting and spacious kitchens and living areas. If you're a seasoned trekker looking for a bit of comfort and time out from heavy-duty backpacking, or an occasional hiker who wants a gentle introduction to long-distance trails, then this is as good as it gets.

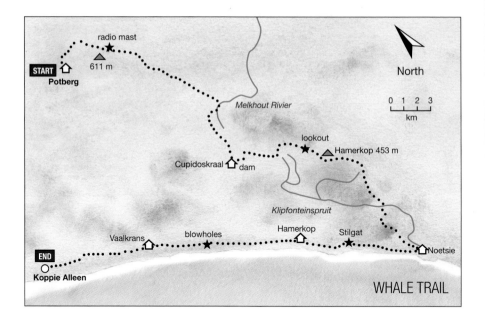

radio mast

START Potberg

611 m

North

0 1 2 3 km

Melkhout Rivier

lookout

Hamerkop 453 m

Cupidoskraal dam

Klipfonteinspruit

Vaalkrans

blowholes

Hamerkop

Stilgat

END

Koppie Alleen

Noetsie

WHALE TRAIL

Whales are only one of the attractions on this magnificent trail in CapeNature's flagship reserve, the De Hoop Nature Reserve in the Overberg region. To see the whales you'll have to do the trail between June and December, but it's a wonderful hike at any time of year. The route winds its way through a variety of habitats – rugged sandstone and limestone hills and coastal thicket – and along a wild, dramatic stretch of coastline bordering a marine reserve.

The trail leads through the eastern section of the De Hoop reserve, a pristine, ecologically fascinating area that is otherwise rarely accessible to the general public. It's rich in endemic flora and fauna – De Hoop is 1 of the 8 protected areas that comprise the Cape Floristic Region World Heritage Site – so do your homework and read up on what to look out for in the way of unusual and striking plants, birds and animals and you'll enjoy the experience even more. Even without a guide you'll come away enriched, refreshed and inspired by the mind-blowing diversity here. There are more rare and endangered species of fauna and flora here than anywhere else of comparable size in the country.

▶ **DAY 1** Potberg to Cupidoskraal

15 KM ◆ 7–8 HR

The trail starts from a lovely old farmhouse, the Potberg homestead and hiking hut, where you will have overnighted. Black boxes are provided for you to pack your belongings into (since you pay a box, pack carefully) and these are then transported to the next camp. Then you head directly for the summit of Potberg hill, which stands sentinel over the trail. Take it easy on this first stretch – it's quite a haul up to the top and there's no shade so slow down and smell the flowers. The hill is an isolated outlier of Table Mountain Sandstone amid a floral sea of limestone and strandveld fynbos, and harbours some rare species.

This fynbos is unbelievably special, and some of the species here are found nowhere else. Keep your eyes peeled for vultures swirling overhead, as the Potberg cliffs are the refuge of the last breeding colony of 150

The beautifully located, well-equipped overnight huts are for many people the highlight of the trail.

Cape vultures in the Western Cape. The view from the clifftop is just reward for your efforts. You can see across the reserve to the sea. To the west lie sweeping dunes beyond which is Cape Agulhas, the southernmost tip of Africa. To the north the Breede River winds its way through rolling wheat fields, and beyond that tower the jagged peaks and ridges of the Langeberg mountains.

Pat yourself on the back – you're now 611 m above sea level and have broken the back of the day's hike. It's not quite down-hill all the way – but almost! We lingered for a long while taking in this view, spotting familiar peaks and looking for the route of the trail ahead. It's not often you get such an excellent vantage, so we chose to enjoy it to the full. Eventually we headed down through more glorious, dense fyn-bos along the watershed above Grootkloof to the Melkhout River where we swam and had lunch.

The map indicated we had only 1 more short climb, so we strolled along enjoying the peace and quiet and watching out for game. Others in our party had seen klip-

springer on their previous outing on the trail, but we weren't so lucky. Again the hut, on the edge of trees, is superb, with great views, plenty of space and – what a treat! – outdoor showers. About half a kay further along the trail, a dam where you can swim – oh that all hikers' huts were so luxurious!

▶ **DAY 2** Cupidoskraal to Noetsie

14.7 KM ◆ 7–8 HR

We were in no rush to get started on day 2, so we stopped at the dam for a morning swim before heading off up through the fynbos-covered hills again. The trail follows the crest of the range, through aromatic buchu and colourful heath. The vegetation had subtly changed. We were now on the limestone knolls that characterise the Agulhas Plain (a former sea bed) that has only thin, poorly developed soils. Proteas dominate here and our eyes were caught by bright patches of colour such as that of the spectacular red fire lily. The botanist in our midst was keen to impress – apparently De Hoop harbours 70 endemic limestone fynbos species and is 1 of only 2 nature reserves where this vegetation type is conserved. Mmm, as I said, it pays to do your homework!

The rains had been particularly good in spring and a blanket of vivid colour spread out before us. In fact, the display of spring wild flowers at De Hoop has to be seen to be believed. We stopped to admire butterflies, sunbirds and sugarbirds flitting from plant to plant, gazed up at buzzards, saw tortoises labouring past and rock lizards sunning themselves. Keep your eyes peeled for Cape mountain zebra as you descend to the coastal plain. They're nu-merous in the reserve, particularly in these rocky areas, but that wasn't always the case. In fact, their presence here is something of a conservation success story: they were on the brink of extinction in the 1920s but new populations were introduced from the Eastern Cape in the 1960s and the herds have thrived here – but they are still critically endangered as a species.

By early afternoon we had hit the coastal plain and were looking forward to reaching the overnight hut at Noetsie. En route we passed through an area that had recently burnt, where only tok-tokkie beetles scuttled along the undulating path. A fellow hiker observed that it was a little like walking through a painted landscape: the black skeletons of trees in the grey veld had a haunting beauty.

Fynbos is a fire-dependent ecosystem so controlled burns every 12 to 15 years are vital for its regeneration. It's amazing to see the difference in the vegetation of recently burnt areas. Once the bushier scrubs have been reduced to cinders and skeletons, the geophytes (bulbous plants) thrive, often covering the veld in a blaze of new colour and antelope take advantage of the grazing opportunities provided by the young plants.

At last we saw some of the mammals for which De Hoop is famous – the bontebok eyeing us was easily recognisable from the large white stripe down its face. The sighting of this beautiful animal put a new spring in our step and before we knew it we were at Noetsie, 2 A-framed, thatched huts or *kapstylhuisies* (in the style used by local farmers for their holiday homes) that sit on the edge of the bay.

They're certainly lovely to look at, but the limitations of the set-up – the only hut without an indoor braai area – were exposed once the skies opened. If you emerge

Finding favour

To single out any of the trails in this book as my favourite would be invidious. Nevertheless I have to say that, in terms of the variety of attractions it offers, the Whale Trail would be a strong contender for my number 1. It's unguided and you self-cater, but I have to declare a penchant for preparing my own food, and for going at my own pace. And just in case you think this implies that you might be roughing it, then rest assured that nothing could be further from the truth.

You get the luxury of walking without a pack through a World Heritage Site that showcases some of the finest scenery that South Africa has to offer. And if you time it right you'll see whales, dense fynbos, a colourful carpet of wild flowers, rare birds such as blue cranes and Cape vultures, and magnificent game such as the endangered Cape mountain zebra, bontebok and eland. Quite simply, it's a winner.

The views on the descent from Potberg – an isolated Table Mountain Sandstone outcrop – are spectacular.

from the sleeping and kitchen area to go to the loo or the braai, you will get drenched!

► **DAY 3** Noetsie to Hamerkop

7.8 KM • 3 HR

It rained on and off for most of day 3, but we made a plan, sheltering in the many overhangs and caves in the cliffs and watching the grey clouds moving in. At every break we sprinted to the next refuge! But when the rain finally stopped we enjoyed a glorious walk through coastal fynbos and along the beach, and we were enchanted by the colourful life in the tidal pools. We explored the caves and protrusions in the cliffs – weird formations sculpted by the waves and the wind. The wave-cut platform in the grey limestone had big, circular depressions, giving it the appearance of Chinese paddy fields.

Despite a stop to scramble down a chain ladder to explore Stilgat cave and snorkel and laze in the rock pools, we were soon on back on the beach with our overnight spot in sight. Hamerkop, only a stone's throw from the beach, was my favourite hut on the trail and we sat out on the ter-

race with our binoculars, watching whales blowing and breaching out at sea. De Hoop is renowned as one of the world's most important nursery areas for southern right whales and there they were, a mass of great grey behemoths floating just off the beach.

► **DAY 4** Hamerkop to Vaalkrans

10.5 KM • 5–6 HR

A big eland bull stared down at us as we walked along the beach between Hamerkop and Lekkerwater, its presence quite unnerving in this environment defined by

Grab your binos and watch the whales from the deck at Hamerkop.

Whale Trail **239**

oystercatchers, cormorants, gulls and shell middens. We envied the inhabitants of Lekkerwater Lodge, sited on sloping ground above the beach and beyond the cliff tops: its location is incredible, but only hikers on the Whale Trail can pass by (and they're warned to give a wide berth and respect the privacy of the guests), so if you book the lodge you effectively have this whole stretch of glorious beach to yourself.

De Hoop – a World Heritage Site

The Whale Trail is 1 of 5 slackpacking trails in South Africa that run through the Cape Floristic Region Protected Areas (CFRPA), declared a World Heritage Site in 2004; the others being the 2 Hoerikwaggo portaged trails, the Eden to Addo hike, and the Cape Point Hiking Trail. Another 2 featured in this book – the Amphitheatre Heritage Hike and the Giant's Cup Hikeathon – run through the uKhahlamba-Drakensberg World Heritage Site. The Kosi Bay Trail runs through the iSimangaliso Park World Heritage Site.

The fynbos biome, covers most of the Western Cape, some of the Eastern Cape and a small part of the Northern Cape. But, rather confusingly, the World Heritage Site inscription does not refer to the whole biome (also known as the Cape Floral Kingdom), but rather to 8 separate, but representative sites chosen because of their diversity and natural beauty (the others are the Cederberg Wilderness Area, Groot Winterhoek Wilderness Area, Boland Mountain Complex, Boosmansbos Wilderness Area, Swartberg Complex, Baviaanskloof and Table Mountain National Park). All told they total 500 000 ha, or about 6 per cent of the fynbos biome. But they are the gems that showcase the highly distinctive flora, exceptional richness of species and the incredibly high degree of endemism.

In case you need any more convincing that the Whale Trail is kinda special, here are interesting facts you can throw into any conversation about your hike! Some 70 per cent of the plants found in the CFRPA occur nowhere else in the world. Lose these populations and the species is wiped out forever. The combination of plant diversity and its vulnerability has earned the Cape Floral Kingdom the elevated title of global biodiversity 'hotspot'. The CFRPA is recognised as being unique and irreplaceable, a natural phenomenon of outstanding universal value to humanity that needs to be conserved. So De Hoop, as part of it, joins the list of those all-time great places – the Pyramids, Victoria Falls, Great Barrier Reef, Taj Mahal – that are recognised as being spectacular, mind-blowing.

So when you lace up your boots and head out up the trail to Potberg, take a moment to reflect on where you are. Even if the bushy shrubs at first look boring and grey, squat down and look at the amazing number of different plants, the little succulents and delicate, brightly coloured flowers; the ants, insects and rodents that dart around; the extraordinary birds that flit from bush to bush.

Take a deep breath and inhale the scent of the fynbos, the citrus aromas or the distinctive smell of the buchu you've just brushed past and you'll begin to understand that De Hoop is an extra special place.

The trail then took us away from the beach into the coastal fringe, through a stretch of dunes, in places vegetated and others bare sandy tracts where crisscrossing tracks had us guessing at all the little antelope, mice, reptiles and birds that must inhabit this part of the reserve. The overnight cottage at Vaalkrans was once again a joy, its location right on the top of spectacular limestone cliffs providing the ideal vantage point from which to admire the coast, with its rocky shore, intertidal pools, projecting reefs and the frolicking whales just beyond.

The eroded limestone cliffs and tidal pools make for fascinating exploration.

▶ **DAY 5** Vaalkrans to Koppie Alleen

7 KM ♦ 3HR

It was with regret that we set off on the trail on the morning of day 5 – our magnificent journey was heading to its conclusion while we would have all happily stayed longer in this beautiful place. The sun was now cheerfully out, the tide was low and the sea was calm, so we slipped off our shoes and walked in the shallows, stopping frequently to swim and enjoy our final day. Many of the rock pools are deep, enclosed turquoise gullies fringed by fern-like seaweed – little refuges in a heavily contested biological zone. The clear water was inviting, if chilly, so we lingered a little, wallowing in the appropriately named Hippo Pools.

We passed shell middens that told of cultures long gone, and wondered what of our own lifestyle future generations might marvel over. Finally, the end was nigh. Just 2 attractive beaches linked by a boardwalk were all that remained – and they had daytrippers on them. It was quite a shock after 4 days without seeing other people and we were reminded of what a privilege it was to walk such a trail. We walked a little further from the end point and on to the impressive dunes of Long Beach to take a last look at the sea and wave goodbye to the whales. Then reluctantly we headed past the cottages at Koppie Alleen to where a shuttle bus waited to take us back to our cars. We agreed that the optimistic Afrikaans *totsiens* is a far better farewell than the final-sounding 'goodbye', because in our hearts it really was a case of until next time, soon!

Top Tip

This is an extremely popular trail so you need to book well in advance. Take time to investigate the rock pools (aim to be there about an hour before low tide) and the weird coastal formations. The more you look, the more incredible things you will see. You can take your own cooler box (which you pay to have transported) and request that meat is kept frozen and delivered (along with any ice you have ordered) to each hut, so freeze enough meat for days 2 to 5.

In a nutshell · Whale Trail

BOOKINGS Cape Nature Reservations, 021-659-3500, bookings@capenature.co.za, www.capenature.co.za.

START/FINISH Potberg Environmental Centre / Koppie Alleen.

TRANSFERS There is a shuttle bus transfer at noon from Koppie Alleen, where the trail ends, back to the car park near the Potberg hut where you left your car.

HIGHLIGHTS The variety of different landforms and biomes; fragrant fynbos; outstanding scenery; empty beaches; rock pools and marine life; whales.

LONGEST DAY 15 km.

SHORTEST DAY 7 km.

GROUP SIZE Bookings taken only for 2 groups of 6 or 1 group of 12 hikers to fill each cottage.

UP TO IT? Although there is a steep uphill on day 1, if you take it easy and time the beach sections so you walk at low tide, the trail is not unduly strenuous. Children over 8 years old can sign up.

DON'T FORGET! Binos, a bird book, flower book and a marine identification guide. Carry a swimming costume and kikoi. Your personal gear will need to be transferred into boxes so pack carefully and as a group – each large cooler box or bag will cost you R300 to be transported from hut to hut. Braai grills, wood, candles, a kettle, cutlery and crockery are provided but it's worth carrying items such as a small stove.

LOOK IT UP Fabulous, annotated maps of the trail are issued on booking and a great little booklet on De Hoop is available at the reserve. A useful guidebook is *The Cape Floral Region* in the Southbound Guides series.

WHEN TO GO The trail can be walked year-round but the whales are usually seen only from May/June to December. The flowers are at their best July–September. De Hoop has a mild, Mediterranean climate, with rain falling throughout the year and peaking in March. During the summer months insects can be pests.

BEFORE AND AFTER The De Hoop Collection manages a number of lovely rondavels, luxury cottages and camping sites in the reserve, 0861-33-4667, info@dehoopcollection.co.za, www.dehoopcollection.co.za.

Survival Notes

- There's no drinkng water (except on day 1), so carry at least 2 *l* a person.
- Horseflies and mosquitoes can be a menace in the summer, so don't skimp on the insect repellent.
- Order ice, to be transported with your daily rations, and live like a trail king or queen.

30

Tsitsikamma Trail

Eastern Cape

DISTANCE 61 km ◆ **DURATION** 6 days ◆ **DIFFICULTY** 5 ◆ **TRAIL TYPE** Mountain, forest, fynbos **LOGISTICS** Bags ferried between huts ◆ **COST** R ◆ **ACCOMMODATION TYPE** Rustic but comfortable hiking huts ◆ **AREA** Garden Route

This trail through the Tsitsikamma mountains, running parallel to but inland of the Otter Trail, needs no introduction to most hikers. But, unlike its overbooked sister, if you hit the Tsitsikamma outside peak season you'll never be part of a crowd. In fact you might even be lucky enough to have the trail to yourself. It's a wonderful journey through a magical fairyland of indigenous forests, misty mountain peaks and deep, dramatic river gorges that will take your breath away – in more ways than one.

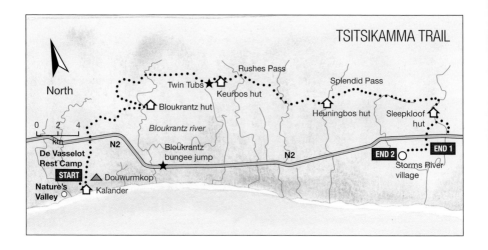

The Tsitsikamma Trail, from Nature's Valley to Storms River, is the most challenging featured in this book. So, while you don't need to carry more than a day pack, take heed – this is no hike for slackers. Instead, it's a true mountain outing with some long days and steep sections, where you need to be self-sufficient and prepared for inclement weather. It's unguided, but very well marked, and you self-cater and sleep in the recently upgraded and comfortable – if basic – trail huts. You go at your own pace, enjoying splendid mountain views and some of the last refuges of indigenous forest in these mountains, stopping to smell the flowers or skinny dip if you feel so inclined and lying out at night under starlit skis.

The recently upgraded huts on the Tsitsikamma Trail are clean and comfortable.

But what is new and exciting on this well-loved backpacking trail – and why it's included here – is that you can now have your bags driven from hut to hut. And even better (and I think this is unique on the trails I've come across) you can pack your food and booze into containers that are refrigerated (or even frozen) until the night you wish them to be delivered to your overnight spot. So, even on the last night, you can have fresh meat and veg and an ice-cold sundowner. What a treat!

Lest you think catering is my soul judge of a trail's merits, let me assure you the scenery on this one is simply mind-blowing too. You trek through extensive indigenous Afro-montane forest and lush mountain fynbos, up to high saddles between towering peaks and through ancient gorges where rushing rivers have gouged out the rock to create perfect fern-fringed swimming holes. The word *tsitsikamma* translates to something like 'place of many waters'. The creative power of these waters moulding and eroding the landscape is very much a feature of the trail. This is an enchanted world where echoes of past giants such as elephant and buffalo can still be felt and where remaining giants, including some of the finest specimens of South Africa's national tree, the Outeniqua yellowwood, stand sentinel over you as you clamber over their outstretched roots. If mountains and forests make your spirit soar, you'll be flying on the Tsitsikamma.

▶ DAY 1 De Vasselot to Kalander

3.6 KM ◆ 1½ HR

A fish eagle called as we parked at the De Vasselot Rest Camp in Nature's Valley, then flew over as if by way of welcome. I knew then this was going to be a special trail. The hike to the Kalander hut was short and sweet, a gentle introduction to the lush Tsitsikamma region, first on a boardwalk, then through the tall, dry indigenous forest on the eastern bank of the Groot River lagoon. We couldn't resist a quick detour to the beach. Oh, what a beach. It's among my all-time favourite places, a long stretch of golden sand flanked by greenery and, at its eastern end, dramatic cliffs. But as we played in the waves an awful thought flashed through my head: tomorrow's trail must lead up those cliffs. Still, today we play, tomorrow is another day!

We met a group coming off the Otter Trail, tiny figures dwarfed by their big packs. They laughed when we told them we were on the Tsitskamma Trail. 'What? With those little packs!' So we let them into the secret. Somehow, I think their next trail will be slackpacking!

▶ DAY 2 Kalander to Bloukrantz

13.5KM ◆ 6–7 HR

We rose early and enjoyed another swim before breakfasting in the lapa. Kalander, nestled in the dune forest at the base of the spectacular Douwurmkop (apparently, the name – meaning 'glow worm' – originates from sightings of fireflies here, but we saw

There is no shortage of pools in which to bathe on this trail through the 'place of many waters'.

no nocturnal light shows), is typical of the well-equipped huts on the Tsitsikamma Trail. It has 4 rooms, each with 6 beds, a braai area (complete with braai grids, tongs, kettle, pan and iron pots) and a covered lapa so even when it rains (which it does, not infrequently) even a big group can stay warm and dry. There are flush loos, and you can even have hot showers by adding hot water from the optional shower bucket to the main cold-water system.

Our fears of the previous day were realised as soon as we hit the trail – what a rude start! If ever I felt justified in taking the slackpacking option, this was it … The path headed straight up a steep, slippery slope and we were relieved not to be carrying 5 days' worth of provisions on our backs.

We detoured up an obvious path leading off to the left, which took us to a ridge and viewpoint at the top of the Monkey's Back (or the Pig's Head, as it's sometimes shown on maps) from where we enjoyed the awe-

The trail takes you deep into the forest, through dense clusters of ferns.

Meet the locals

Each of the overnight huts on the trail has a resident large-spotted genet, which you might spot in the evening or early morning. The genet is a small and beautiful animal belonging to the largest carnivore family, the Viverridae, and most closely related to the mongooses. It has both spots and stripes on its short coat and a black-ringed fluffy tail of equal length to its body.

Large-spotted genets live in the wetter regions where trees are plentiful and will never be found far from water. They are very agile predators and feed on a wide variety of prey, including rodents, reptiles, frogs, birds, fish and the fruits and nectar of forest trees.

some views back over Nature's Valley and the cliffs at the end of the Otter Trail, before heading on up the escarpment through the forest. The trail eased off as we hit a glorious open section of fynbos and saw the towering blue ridges of the Tsitsikamma mountains for the first time. The next few kilometres alternated between fynbos and forest, and we revelled in the fynbos flowers, the bright pincushions and other regal protea and the pink and purple ericas that reminded me of my birthplace in Scotland's Pentland Hills.

The forest was alive with birds: cuckoo shrikes and flycatchers, turacos (louries) and white-eyes and other little canopy-dwellers flitting from branch to branch; and the dank smell of the forest replaced the salty sea air. We climbed up and up, through stands of yellowwoods and dense clumps of ferns until we heard the welcome sound of falling water. A steep downhill and we were at dark tannin-stained pools, into which we gratefully flung ourselves to cool off.

Commercial forestry has been practised in this area since the mid-19th century when the incredible road engineering feats of Thomas Bain opened up these mountains; the final section of the day 2 trail heads through plantations that replaced much of the indigenous forest. It was much less scenic than the earlier stretch as recent felling of pines had taken place, but it at least afforded great views. You're soon through the cleared section and hiking above a dramatic rocky gorge before being reunited with your overnight bags at the stunningly located Bloukrantz hut, right on the edge of the cliffs.

After admiring the view from the terrace over the blue gorges (from which the hut takes its name) towards Peak Formosa that lords over the other Tsitsikamma peaks, we headed down to some pools we'd spot-

The view from the terrace of the Bloukrantz hut is across the deep gorge and over the blue mountains.

ted in the gorge below. The walk had been stiff – this is very much a mountain lover's trail – and as we sipped our sundowners from our improvised bath we toasted the trail co-ordinator and MTO Ecotourism manager, Graeme Pienaar, and his team who had kindly refrigerated our beers and transported them to this out-of-the-way place. We had been told to watch out for a large-spotted genet couple and male bush pig, which are apparently regular overnight visitors, but the exertions of the day saw us early to bed and any would-be camp raiders were back in their lairs by the time we rose the next morning.

▶ DAY 3 Bloukrantz to Keurbos

13.7 KM ◆ 6–7 HR

The path took us deep into the Tsitsikamma mountains and forested gorges, a wetter and more remote world where a true sense of isolation began to take hold. After a couple of kilometres we entered an eerie and enchanted patch of indigenous forest called Buffelsbos, where the last buffalo of the Tsitsikamma was shot and killed in the late-19th century. It was strange to think that big game once inhabited these high mountains. We crossed the Bloukranz River at Waterwitelsgat, a magical and very scenic river crossing that was perfect for swimming and chilling.

For the rest of the day the trail took us over flat terrain, through flower-rich fynbos and patches of relic forest. Around 10 million years ago all of Africa was covered in dense forest, from the temperate to the tropical zones. But since then the continent has been warming up and drying out, and as the forests have receded grasslands and savanna have largely replaced them. The Cape Folded Mountains are one of the last holdouts of temperate Afro-montane forest, the deeper valleys and gorges on the wetter, cooler southern slopes harbouring what are known as relic forests. Over the past 2 centuries extensive burning and cutting have reduced them in many places and weakened their internal dynamics by taking out most big trees, as well as slicing them into increasingly smaller patches.

We stopped to splash at the water points just after leaving Benebos, then for a proper dip just before reaching the Keurbos hut in the 'twin tubs' rock pools resembling natural jacuzzis. The hut has a brilliant setting on the fringe of a relic patch of indigenous forest, surrounded by red and white alder, and as we arrived we heard the plaintive call of a narina trogon. Graeme suggested that the name of the hut comes from the proximity of the keurboom trees, a short-lived pioneer species that forms a natural buffer against fire – hence the name, *keur* or fire-stopping. Others believe keur in this context means 'choice' or 'pick of the bunch', a reference to the beautiful pink and purple flowers sported by this member of the pea family.

▶ DAY 4 Keurbos to Heuningbos

13.4KM ◆ 6–7HR

Day 4 passes through very diverse habitat types and has a number of exciting river crossings. It's downhill all the way to start with – nearly 2km of gradual descent from the Keurbos hut through very tall fynbos to the Lottering River – but what goes down must come up. Soon we were climbing not too steeply but steadily to Rushes Pass, pausing regularly to appreciate the majestic views. Once over the saddle, large pockets of indigenous forest became visible in remote mountain regions approaching the Elandsbos River. The path then descended for a similar distance to follow the western bank of the Elandsbos stream for about a kilometre before reaching the newly constructed swing bridge – quite a hairy way to cross the river, particularly after heavy rain.

Then it was into the Heuningbos forest, under a dense canopy and back among the ferns. It felt as if we were entering a secret, hidden place, far removed from the expansive open sections of the trail. The final part of the day's hike crossed the Kleinbos River before reaching the Heuningbos hut – a great location in the open, surrounded by magnificent watsonias, albeit with rather too many dead pines around. There's a very pleasant natural swimming pool just in front of the hut, which is also great for sunning and picnicking on the rocks, but it's also worth scrambling down to a lower pool above a waterfall, a natural flow-rim pool with a stunning view.

In the beginning

The Tsitsikamma Trail was the first hiking trail in South Africa accredited by the South African Hiking Trail Owners Association (SAHTOA) as a trail that is …

- in a pristine environment
- with standard to luxury accommodation
- with a moderate-to-difficult grading
- with excellent trail facilities.

SAHTOA is a non-profit organisation established to represent hiking-trail owners and all related interested and affected role-players. Its focus is to promote a healthy, sustainable dynamic and growing hiking industry in southern Africa, with the final aim of establishing a uniformly focused hiking industry as part of the tourism industry, with internationally accepted norms and standards in respect of trails and related facilities. For more information visit www.trailinfo.co.za

Waterfalls tumbling into inviting pools and forested glades make this an enchanting trail.

For much of the trail you are under the canopy of the great giants of the forest.

▶ DAY 5 Heuningbos to Sleepkloof

14 KM ◆ 7 HR

After being woken by baboons in the morning, we lingered, swimming and enjoying the warm sun. Another pool in a tranquil dell of ferns only 400 m from the hut proved a second distraction but eventually we hit the trail in earnest. After winding through Tweedebos, we climbed to Splendid Pass (splendid indeed, but actually named after a striking proteacaea found on its slopes, *Mimetes splendidus*), through recently burnt fynbos now ablaze with vivid watsonias. We were deep in the mountains, surrounded by splendid peaks, so we stopped and rested awhile, appreciating the solitude of the place that only a privileged few get the chance to savour.

Just over the crest we entered an area of fynbos untouched by fires that ravaged the region in 2005. It was wonderful to be back in well-established fynbos again, though we could see it was no easy path ahead. The trail headed down to the next forested stream and then up again the other side, and it wasn't long before we were down in the wet indigenous Mostertsbos –

a cool, shaded environment that provided relief from the blazing sun of the open mountain slopes.

These isolated forest pockets are generally sparser in species composition than the larger forests of the plateau you pass through on the second and final days of the trail, and comprise mainly of rooiels, witels, forest elder (*Nuxia* sp), stinkwood and both Outeniqua and real yellowwoods, along with fascinating smaller organisms living beneath the canopies of these giants.

We admired the wonderful ferns and kept hiking through the forest till we crossed the main watercourse, the Witteklip River, which marked the day's halfway point. Again it was the ferns and tree ferns that impressed us. Great, towering plants dwarfed us and blocked out the light: *Gleichenia*, coarse ferns, maidenhair ferns and tree ferns that had inhabited these forests since time immemorial. Sacred old souls that lorded over the toadstools and lichens of this damp, dark world.

After another dip we began the long climb through dense fynbos to Nademaalsnek, between Storms River Peak and Heidekop. The view from the top of the pass over to the spectacular Storms

Top Tip

This is a trip worth getting fit for. Take time to enjoy the forest and the wonderful rock pools on the way and, if you can, stay on and explore the coastal part of the Tsitsikamma National Park – or complete the circle by doing the Otter Trail! If you're photographing with film, remember that you'll be in forest much of the way – and it's often dark and overcast, so you'll need a fast film rated at 200 or 400 ISO.

The mountain sections lead through exquisite fynbos and over high mountain passes.

River gorge was just reward for our efforts and we caught sight of our overnight hut at Sleepkloof. This put new life into our weary legs and we fairly cantered down the ridge. Signs led to a swimming hole in the indigenous forest some 2.2 km from the hut, but we hurried on in the knowledge that the pools and waterfall at the hut itself would more than suffice.

Sleepkloof hut nestles on the slopes of a densely forested gorge, where wood was dragged out and hauled down the kloof during the woodcutter era, so we toasted our last night on the trail as the sky turned pink and the peaks and ridges were silhouetted against the night sky. By the same time the next day we would be far from these magnificent and magical mountains.

▶ DAY 6 Sleepkloof to Storms River Bridge

3.2 KM ◆ 1 HR

It was hard to tear ourselves away from the trail, back to work and to civilisation, so we took our time packing up and eating the last

of our trail food. A resident troop of vervet monkeys moved closer and closer as we procrastinated – they were clearly waiting for us to leave, optimistic that there might be scraps they could forage. We'd chosen to finish at Storms River Village rather than the closer Storms River Bridge trail head, but it was still only a short easy walk back to the car. Both routes follow a rocky track through dense pioneer forest vegetation for the first kilometre before splitting, with the route to the bridge a very easy 2 km descent through pioneer species and tall fynbos.

The alternative on day 6 is either Sleepkloof–Storms River Bridge, which is 3.2 km (1 hr) or Sleepkloof–Storms River Village, which is 5.5 km (2 hr).

The hardy hiker

The trail is well marked and a wonderful hike even if you opt not to have your pack driven around. There are obviously the same shorter options as on the slackpacking trail.

The slightly longer walk to the village led into the tall, indigenous Plaatbos forest (where you'll find the Garden of Eden), eventually emerging on the 4×4 track at the top of the old Storms River Pass. The hiking gods had smiled on us. We had had good weather for all 6 days and both the quality of the accommodation and the spectacular scenery had convinced us all that the Tsitsikamma Trail was one of the country's best.

In a nutshell · Tsitsikamma Trail

BOOKINGS MTO Ecotourism, Lottering Forest Station 042-281-1712, gpi@mto.co.za, www.mtoecotourism. co.za/tsitsikamma.htm.
START/FINISH De Vasselot Rest Camp (Nature's Valley) / Paul Sauer Bridge (or Storms River Village).
TRANSFERS Transfers back to the start can be organised through Tube 'n Axe Backpackers in Storms River Village 042-281-1757, or through Hikers Haven in Nature's Valley 044-531-6805.
HIGHLIGHTS Mountain views; indigenous forest; bird life; ferns and mosses; mountain fynbos; gorges and rivers; Nature's Valley; great overnight huts.
LONGEST DAY 13.9 km.
SHORTEST DAY 3.2 km.
GROUP SIZE Minimum 2, maximum 24.
UP TO IT? This is a strenuous mountain trail that demands a good level of fitness. Slackers need not apply.
DON'T FORGET! Sturdy hiking boots. Everything you need for a self-sufficient hike. Firewood is provided. Make sure first-aid supplies and emergency rations are carried by some members of the party. Safety precautions with regard to heavy rainfall and river crossings are conveyed to hikers when they register.
LOOK IT UP A fabulously detailed map of the Tsitsikamma Trail (compiled by MTO Forestry (Pty) Ltd) is issued to hikers doing the trail. Many of the forest giants are labelled with their tree names.
WHEN TO GO Most rain falls in April/May and October/November, so unless you fancy a slippery slide these months should be avoided! The mountains are often misty in winter so take heed of the map's warning: 'Consider turning back if there is a problem. Don't be heroic, the elements are merciless!'
BEFORE AND AFTER Nature's Valley: Kalander Hut; De Vasselot has chalets and camping available. Storms River: At the Woods, in Storms River Village, is a friendly guesthouse with stunning views back to the mountains whence you've come 042-281-1446 info@atthewoods. co.za, www.atthewoods.co.za.

Survival Notes

- Drinking water available at regular intervals on the trail.
- You are in the high mountains here so go prepared for inclement weather.
- Good gear is a must.
- 2- to 4-day options available.

31

Drifters Wild Coast Trail

Eastern Cape

DISTANCE 59 km ◆ **DURATION** 6 days ◆ **DIFFICULTY** 3 ◆ **TRAIL TYPE** Sand and rocky beaches, grassy hills, cliffs and gorges ◆ **ACCOMMODATION TYPE** Well-appointed safari tents **LOGISTICS** Guided or unguided, porters can he hired to transport bags ◆ **COST** RRR (or RRRR for the fully catered 3-day option) ◆ **AREA** Wild Coast

The Drifters trail takes hikers along some of the best-known landmarks of the northern Wild Coast including Waterfall Bluff and Cathedral Rock. The trail is run in conjunction with the local communities, with hikers self-catering and staying in comfortable tented camps. It's a magnificent journey through beautiful, unspoilt wilderness far removed from the trappings of civilisation. There is little other tourist accommodation along the way so, apart from the occassional Coastal Care worker cleaning the mainly jetsam off the beaches, you'll have the entire area to yourselves. If crashing waves, endless horizons and dramatic landscapes are your soul food, tuck right in.

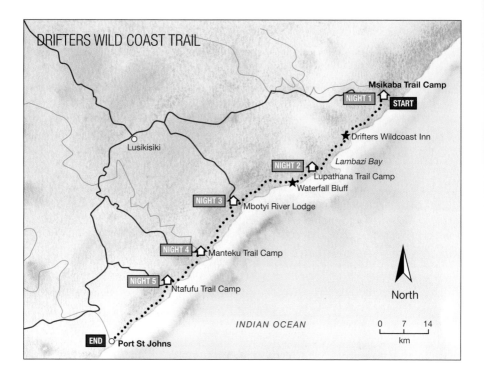

DRIFTERS WILD COAST TRAIL

Msikaba Trail Camp
NIGHT 1   START

Drifters Wildcoast Inn

Lusikisiki

Lambazi Bay
NIGHT 2
Lupathana Trail Camp
Waterfall Bluff

NIGHT 3
Mbotyi River Lodge

NIGHT 4   Manteku Trail Camp

NIGHT 5
Ntafufu Trail Camp

North

INDIAN OCEAN   0   7   14
                              km

END   Port St Johns

This trail, from Msikaba to Port St Johns, is an absolute gem. You can hike the full distance unguided and catering for yourself, or opt for a luxury 3-day, fully catered, portaged and guided package. Either way this truly magnificent hike along a pristine stretch of coastline is guaranteed to blow you away. The natural landscape is sensational, with waterfalls plummeting straight into the sea, while other highlights include deep, freshwater pools in which to swim, exquisite beaches and rock pools, sightings of dolphins and whales and entertaining local kids. The tented camps, nestled in coastal forest, have spacious en suite 2-bed safari tents and a generous living and kitchen area that's more in keeping with a bush camp. You need to carry your own food and bedding, but a stove, fridge, lighting and everything you need to cook and eat with are provided so you can travel a little lighter. Distances are not too taxing and porters and guides can be hired, which make the trail suitable for inexperienced, moderately fit hikers.

On your bike

With its exciting narrow tracks, awesome views and sense of wilderness, the Wild Coast is one of the country's best mountain biking playgrounds. Cyclists take advantage of the Drifters infrastructure and portage system between the huts. However, instead of following the hiking trail along the coast, riding trails are diverted much more to avoid obstacles and to get more miles in the saddle.

▶ NIGHT 1 Settling in

We took advantage of the Drifters transfer service from Port St Johns to Msikaba, buying last-minute food in town before we left. Msikaba, the first overnight camp, enjoys an idyllic setting, with a wonderful beach, river estuary and upper gorge and even a quaint little off-shore island. In fact it's all so perfect that we wished we didn't have to move on in the morning! Once we'd dumped our bags we took a stroll across the estuary to the Mkambati reserve, one of the best-kept secrets of the Eastern Cape.

The grassy plains of the reserve are home to large numbers of antelope including a big herd of eland ... but we had little time for game viewing. Instead we hiked a short way up-river to a beautiful waterfall. This was in part a botanical mission – a quest to find the Pondo coconut *Jubaeopsis caffra*, a rare species of palm that is endemic to the Msikaba and Mtentu river valleys. And it was not long before we spotted one of the miniature palms on the bank on the other side of the river. This is a truly magical place.

Exploration done, we retired to Msikaba camp and were impressed by the quality of the trail accommodation. The lodge, hidden

The crashing of waves against the rock platform at Luphatana is very dramatic, wear a raincoat if venturing out.

Pondo hot spot

The Msikaba River valley is part of one of the world's most important botanical hotspots, the Pondoland Centre of Endemism, which hosts close to 200 endemic or near-endemic plant species. It's also a twitcher's paradise. A colony of Cape vultures breeds on the sheer cliffs of the gorge while a natural amphitheatre of towering evergreen forest is inhabited by a spectacular variety of birds including trumpeter hornbill, rameron pigeon, black-bellied starling, forest weaver and, in winter, small parties of raucous Cape parrots.

in a grove of milkwood trees overlooking the tranquil Msikaba lagoon, consists of 12 en suite tents with a spacious, open-plan wooden building housing the kitchen, lounge and dining area. It's barefoot luxury indeed and the kitchen is well equipped with fridges, plenty of pans, sharp knives, glasses, crockery – in fact everything you'd need to knock up any meal you fancy. We dined in style on the open deck listening to the rustling of the trees and enjoying the starlit sky as we dreamed of the balmy days ahead.

▶ DAY 1 Msikaba to Luphathana

16 KM ◆ 6–8 HR

We woke early and enjoyed an early morning swim before taking coffee on the deck. This was the longest day of the hike so we knew we should get going, but it was such a stunning place we lingered, photographing the island and the glorious beach. It was a fairly easy walk along the coast, sometimes on the beach but largely along grassy paths, to the half-way point, the beautifully located Drifters Port Grosvenor Inn at Luphathana (a lovely retreat which casual visitors can book into on a fully catered basis). After a quick look around we headed back to the coast to check out the site of the wreck of the *Grosvenor*, one of numerous wrecks that litter the Wild Coast. A merchantman in the fleet of the East India Company, the *Grosvenor* came to a tragic end on 4 August 1782, when she ran aground and sunk on a dark and stormy night while on a return voyage from India. Rumours that the ship had been carrying a fortune in bullion or other treasure resulted in a number of costly (and some extremely zany) recovery schemes, but only a couple of cannons and several coins have ever been recovered.

The afternoon was much of the same, a stunning hike along the beach and coastal footpaths until, just north of Luphathana, we suddenly came upon a dramatic show of waves crashing violently onto the hard rock platform and spraying high into the air. Donning our waterproofs, we walked out along the flat sandstone barrier as far as we dared and stood watching the action

A Pondo family's wealth takes a walk on the beach.

and listening to the thump of the water for a while before making our way across the estuary to Luphathana camp.

The little hideaway in the coastal red milkwood forest is beautiful, with shells lining the paths, well-tended little gardens and numerous other little displays of the love that the camp manager has for her little piece of paradise. Again we were very impressed by the beautiful tents and well designed communal buildings, which offered such comfort, yet blended into the surroundings. Drifters has gone to great lengths to develop sustainable, eco-friendly camps and our camp manager was delighted to explain the interesting innovations, which included wind-powered turbines to pump water and generate electricity.

▶ DAY 2 Luphatana to Mbotyi

14 KM ◆ 6–7 HR

The trail took us along the extensive table of resistant rock – most of the dramatic landforms here are a result of the extremely hard, dark-coloured dolerite or shale – for another spectacular hydrophonic display before we continued south. The terrain changes here and you walk more inland in order to cross the deeply incised, densely vegetated gorges. We passed the Top Hat and 2 of the Wild Coast's most iconic sites, Waterfall Bluff, where the Mlambomkuklu River tumbles some 100 m over a sandstone cliff straight into the sea, and the impressive sea stack of Cathedral Rock complete with spires, arches and flying buttresses.

Several smaller rivers have carved steps and deep pools into the sandstone here so we stopped often to swim and enjoy natural showers in the cold water of the falls before continuing through the rolling grassland to Mbotyi. After a final section on the beach we saw the wooden chalets

The only outsiders who get to see the rugged and wild coastline near Manteku are hikers.

Mbotyi River Lodge provides a slice of luxury on the third night of the hike.

of Mbotyi River Lodge on the bluff above the lagoon and headed up the track to our home for the night and were welcomed by the smiling staff.

If you've never stayed at Mbotyi River Lodge you've missed out. The resort is a real Wild Coast institution – a favourite of fisherfolk and families who come down to enjoy its wonderful beach and lagoon. The place really comes to life during the annual sardine run in June/July when divers from all over the world descend to witness the spectacular marine phenomenon. The wooden chalets, each with its own terrace, are set high over the lagoon and beach with stunning views, and the enlightened management has joined forces with the local community to provide a range of locally guided hiking, horse-riding, canoeing and cultural tours. And as for the meals – the Wild Coast hotels are all renowned for their food so be prepared – even breakfast nearly defeated me! For the more budget conscious, there's a secure community-run campsite with bungalows behind the hotel.

▶ DAY 3 Mbotyi to Manteku

10 KM ◆ 5 HR

From Mbotyi there was a short section along a steep slope before we headed back to the beach. Walking on the sand was the only option as grassy plains that had been a feature of the previous days were now replaced by densely vegetated hills. We stopped often to swim, to photograph cattle chewing the cud and to enjoy the pristine wilderness and black sand beaches. The trail then climbed the humped-up hills, gaining height as it undulated up and down until we began the steep descent from the grassy peak of Mgoma to Manteku, which was visible from high on the cliffs.

The cushy option

Drifters also offers a 3-day fully catered, luxury hike or mountain-bike trail from Msikaba to Mboyti where linen is provided and your luggage is transported from camp to camp.

Most nights on the trail are spent in two-bed tented chalets such as these at Ntafufu.

It was a short walk across the sandy estuary to the camp, which enjoys a superb site just back from the beach. That night we sat out admiring the views of the rolling hills and the vast expanse of sand that stretches all the way to the sea. There wasn't a single light visible and we felt totally at peace in this beautiful wilderness. Slackpacking is such a wonderful way to de-stress!

▶ DAY 4 Manteku to Ntafufu

9 KM ◆ 4–5 HR

The scenery after Manteku is much more like the southern section of the Wild Coast, with gently rolling green hills and rocky promontories separated by river valleys. The gorgeous beaches were empty and, since it was a short day, we took it slowly stopping often to look at shells, to swim and to sit on the edge of the water taking in the views. We waded a couple of rivers – always good entertainment – before hitting the long beach that led to the camp. Ntafufu is set back a bit from the coast and getting to the camp involved crossing a river. At low tide

it is easily waded, while at high tide hikers are paddled across in canoes by the camp staff. A short hike up through the coastal forest took us to the camp itself, high up on a bluff; after dumping our bags we sat out on the wooden decks enjoying the views back along the trail.

▶ DAY 5 Ntafufu to Port St Johns

11.5 KM ◆ 5–6 HR

From Ntafufu we followed coastal paths around the rolling bluffs, past bright red

When you carry a full backpack on a trail there is seldom time for a bit of frivolity.

aloes, grazing goats and lone fishers. It's a gorgeous section of the coast, with awesome views and plenty of sightings of dolphins (and, in season, humpback whales) from the high vantages. At Poenskop headland we left the cliffs, taking a steep descent to Agate Terrace. From there it was a long final pull on soft sand until we reached the estuary of the Mzimvubu River. We rounded the point and boarded the ferry for the short ride to the other bank, and the well-known colourful town of Port St Johns. A short walk took us to the Outspan Inn where we were welcomed in as long lost friends – a perfect end to a wonderful wilderness trail.

In a nutshell · Drifters Wild Coast Trail

BOOKINGS Drifters 011-888-1160, drifters@drifters.co.za, www.drifters.co.za

START/FINISH Msikaba / Port St Johns

TRANSFERS Transfers from Port St Johns to the start of the trail at Msikaba are available at 14.00 day 1.

HIGHLIGHTS The incredible scenery of the Wild Coast; dramatic landforms such as Waterfall Bluff; dolphins; the sense of wilderness; the outstanding and well-equipped overnight camps.

LONGEST DAY 16 km.

SHORTEST DAY 8.9 km.

GROUP SIZE Minimum 2, maximum 24.

UP TO IT? This is a very straightforward coastal trail largely along beaches and undulating terrain. Daily distances are moderate, guides can be hired and bags can be portaged so the trail is suitable for inexperienced hikers and family groups.

DON'T FORGET! Sleeping bag, food and drink for the duration of the trail, hiking gear, backpack or day pack (depending if you hire porters), camera, bird/plant guides, binoculars, small medical kit.

WHEN TO GO The trail is open year round and each season has its own attractions. Whales are often seen off the coast between July and December (mainly humpback but also Bryde's).

BEFORE AND AFTER Contact Port St Johns Tourism for accommodation and activities. Good options include Drifters Wild Coast Inn, Mbotyi River Lodge and the Outspan Inn.

LOOK IT UP Peter Slingsby's *Wild Coast Map* and *Mkambati and the Wild Coast*, by Div de Villiers and John Costello (published by Wilderness Safaris, 2006) are excellent references.

Survival Notes

- Luxury guided option available.
- Drinking water available at least once daily on the trail.
- Tented accommodation; self catered.
- Spaza shops on first and last days.

32

Mosslands Two River Trail

Eastern Cape

DISTANCE 30.5 km ✦ **DURATION** 2 days ✦ **DIFFICULTY** 2 ✦ **TRAIL TYPE** Farmland, bushveld, hilly ✦ **LOGISTICS** Bags driven around ✦ **COST** R ✦ **ACCOMMODATION TYPE** Self-catering cottages ✦ **AREA** Grahamstown

This scenic trail on the Mosslands farm just out of Grahamstown in the Eastern Cape is a great weekend escape and the valley bushveld you hike through comprises flora you rarely see in the highveld or in the Cape. The trail winds along, and repeatedly crosses, the Kariega and Assegai rivers so it's the perfect trail for families or those wanting to take it easy, to listen to the birds and to stop often for a refreshing dip.

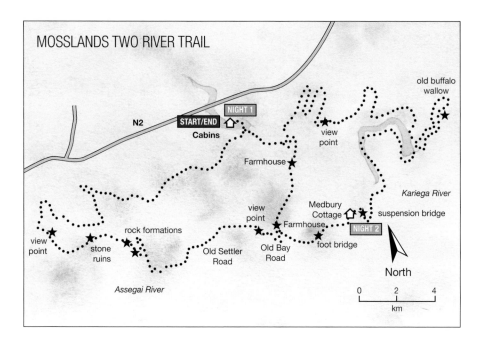

MOSSLANDS TWO RIVER TRAIL

N2

START/END
Cabins

NIGHT 1

old buffalo
wallow

view
point

Farmhouse

Kariega River

view
point

rock formations

view
point

stone
ruins

Old Settler
Road

Old Bay
Road

Medbury
Cottage

foot bridge

suspension bridge

NIGHT 2

North

Assegai River

0   2   4

km

The 30.5 km circular trail takes hikers across the undulating hills and river valleys of a working dairy and citrus farm, which has been consolidated from grants of land allocated to British settlers in the 1820s. For much of the trail you meander under

Day 2 starts with a wobbly journey on a suspension bridge over the Kariega River.

the canopy of indigenous trees – gnarled yellowwoods and milkwoods – and among dense mosses and lichens, stopping to swim in dark tannin-stained pools. Once in the open veld you'll put up with squawking francolin, hares, bontebok and other antelope as you stroll along. And your overnight accommodation is an indulgence. Opt to spend the night before the start of the trail at lovely cabins, or spend just one night halfway at the recently restored Medbury Cottage.

▶ **DAY 1** Parking area to
Medbury Cottage

15.2 KM ◆ 5HR

It's worth arriving the night before to overnight in the lovely reed cabins, right on the edge of the Kariega River. We woke to birdsong and a bushbuck scuttled off as we staggered out for a morning swim to put us in the mood for the trail ahead. Once over the stream flowing from the dam we followed a narrow track through the for-

Reed cabins on the edge of the Kariega are available for hikers about to start the trail.

est. Up and down it went and the leader soon picked up a stick to avoid walking into one spiderweb after another. Then it was out onto open heathland – and almost at once I saw a bontebok, and what looked like another small antelope. In fact it was a young bontebok, its pale colouring quite unlike that of its parent. A couple of large hares fled as we approached and soon after we spotted a couple of mountain reedbuck – we hadn't expected to see much game on the trail so this was a wonderful surprise. After a couple of kilometres it was back down into the woods, a mystical place, with fascinating lichens and ancient trees. We followed a narrow track jumping over the streambed several times until we climbed again and emerged at a viewpoint overlooking steep cliffs. Our map indicated there were interesting succulents on the rocks of the next section, so we spent some time poking around and 'ooohing' and 'aaahing' at our finds. We stopped to swim in a big pond on which magnificent

blue lilies were floating, then traversed the base of some cliffs before detouring on a little loop through the fairyland.

We climbed again to another viewpoint, enjoying the mixture of aloes and other typical Eastern Cape vegetation along with equally typical bushveld, then followed the high ground to some old stone kraals before heading back to the river. The next pond was even more resplendent with lilies, their

The trail is a favourite of twitchers – sightings typically include malachite kingfisher.

The trail follows the river for much of the way and the water lilies lie in soft contrast to the thornveld …

heads turned in unison to the sun, so we rested for lunch, enjoying the sight of busy weavers, colourful kingfishers and wood-

… while the views from the highpoints are superb.

peckers. The forest canopy was a welcome respite from the heat of the day and the path was springy underfoot from all the dead vegetation. A thoughtfully placed sign near a bench advised 'Rest a while! Steep climb ahead' but we pushed on – thankfully, it was a very short albeit rather steep section until we joined the Old Settler Road.

Soon we were in a field inhabited by a big herd of beautiful Jersey cows – an incongruous sight after such a long time in the bush. The last few kilometres of the day's walk led first along the plateau, then down through magnificent stands of aloes. From here we could see right across the valley, past the farmhouses, the pastures and to the dam near what was obviously our overnight cottage. The trail continued its downward trajectory to the Old Bay Road, which led high above the farm buildings to a final river crossing over a footbridge and through the final stand of trees before Medbury Cottage was in our sights. What

The trail runs through a working dairy and citrus farm so you're often walking through grazing land.

a perfect hikers' abode. The old house has been lovingly restored by Sally and Neil Moss and old photographs on the walls depict the place as it was in the olden days.

Many of the artefacts of those days are still around – an old reaper binder, harrow and baler sit outside, and you can still draw water from the original well. There are hot showers and the cottage is spacious, with four bedrooms, a cosy living room with fireplace, and a lovely old barn-style dining room and braai area, and the fresh lick of paint and some lovely touches like pot plants and branches serving as hangers made us feel right at home. The setting sun turned the landscape golden as we sat

Top Tip

Stop frequently to swim and enjoy the riverine environment. Apply tick repellent frequently.

outside to enjoy the peace. Storks came in to roost in an old dead gum tree – quite an eerie skeletal structure.

► DAY 2 Medbury Cottage to parking area

15.3KM • 5–6HR

Colourful starlings greeted us as we emerged in the morning, their wings glinting blue in the sun. Day 2 started with a bit of an adventure. Soon after bidding Medbury farewell, we startled a bushbuck which bounded off apace. After that we crossed a wobbly suspension bridge built to access stock stranded on the other side of the river when the dam was full. It was a wonderful stretch of water and as we waited for each person to cross we enjoyed the antics of reed cormorants and darters preening themselves and diving for fish.

The trail runs parallel with the dirt road for a while before rejoining the Old Bay

Road, the first road to link Port Elizabeth to Grahamstown and constructed by Andrew Geddes Bain in 1844. In those days there would have been a motel and blacksmith every 7 miles along this road – serving the needs of the ox- or horse-drawn wagons. Once over the dam wall (where you can still see the buttresses of the old bridge and the water well of the old motel that was once located there) we headed off into the bush, through the deep donga of the buffalo wallow and up through forested slopes alive with birds. For the rest of the day the trail winds around the hillsides, sometimes in the open, but often in the shade of the canopy. It was a slow, pleasant walk and we caught glimpses of vervet monkeys and grysbok as well as yellowbilled kites and African crowned eagles soaring above. The forest was alive with birds and we felt refreshed and exhilarated by the time we reached our cars.

In a nutshell · Mosslands Two River Trail

BOOKINGS Sally Moss 046-622-8956, 082-473-5122, sallymoss@intekom.co.za

START/FINISH Hikers' parking area near the first night's cabins

TRANSFERS The trail is just off the main road between Port Elizabeth and Grahamstown, but getting there on public transport is difficult. If you're flying to PE, it's much easier to hire a car for a couple of days.

HIGHLIGHTS Valley bushveld vegetation; butterflies and indigenous birds and game; blue lilies; swimming in the rivers.

LONGEST DAY 15.3km

SHORTEST DAY 15.2km

GROUP SIZE Minimum 1, maximum 12.

UP TO IT? This is a moderate trail for nature lovers who want a scenic wander rather than an endurance event. Although the terrain is undulating there's not too much uphill and a fair amount of shade.

DON'T FORGET! A stick to use as a spider wand; binos and a bird book; crockery (pans, kettle and braai grid are provided). Sleeping bags, head torch, warm and fully waterproof clothing (including a backpack cover) and personal gear.

LOOK IT UP A printed map of the trail is sent out with bookings.

LOGISTICS Unguided, self-catered hike staying in well-equipped huts. Bags driven around.

WHEN TO GO The trail can be walked year round but April–June are the coolest and probably the best months for hiking.

BEFORE AND AFTER There's plenty of accommodation to suit all budgets in nearby Grahamstown.

Survival Notes

- Drinking water available at least once daily.

Other Slacker Trails

What follows are short descriptions of other trails I researched for this book. Some were in my original line-up as individual chapters, but as the book evolved I decided they did not merit a major feature because, for one reason or other, they didn't quite fit the mould. In some, you're based in 1 place rather than having the option to follow an A–B route, overnighting along the way; on others you have to carry your bag for a large part of the way. And, of these, the following are my pick of the bunch …

The ones that almost got away ...

Having decided which of the slackpacking trails to include, and which deserved at least a mention, I stumbled across further criteria I felt needed at least some consideration. There are, for example, special interest trails such as wine walks that are decent walks on which you cover a fair distance, but on which wine tasting and/or sit-down lunches are almost as important as the hiking; trails that have only recently come online or that are scheduled to be launching soon, and others which more-or-less duplicate trails already featured. That makes them no less worthy of inclusion, of course, so I hope to feature them in full in a future edition: the curse of guidebooks is that they seem to go out of date just as you finish one.

The wine walks lead through vineyards, orchards and buchu plantations surrounded by towering peaks.

33. Wellington Wine Walks

Western Cape

The 3- or 4-day, guided and fully catered trail won a 'Best of Wine Tourism' award in 2008 from the Great Wine Capitals Global Network. Centred around the beautiful Wellington valley in the Boland winelands, it's just an hour's drive out of Cape Town. The trail takes hikers through the indigenous fynbos, vineyards, orchards, buchu fields and olive groves of the fertile valley, with wine, olive and buchu tastings along the way. Overnight accommodation is in guesthouses on historic Huguenot farms, each of which offers traditional Cape cuisine in a superb setting. The Wellington bowl experiences extreme heat during the summer months, so wine walks operate only from March through to November. If you enjoy a good hike with comfortable accommodation, fine wines and good food along the way, this one's for you.

In a nutshell · Wellington Wine Walks

BOOKINGS Wellington Wine Walk, 083-313-8383, info@winewalk.co.za, www.winewalk.co.za.
HIGHLIGHTS The fynbos and natural scenery; wine and buchu tastings; knowledgeable guides.
STYLE Fully catered, guided hike staying in luxury guesthouse accommodation. Bags driven around.
UP TO IT? This is an easy trail that is suitable for hikers of all ages and fitness levels.
COST RRRR.

34. Walks for Wine

Western Cape

There are few things more appealing than walking through the glorious fynbos covered slopes and vineyards of the Cape Floristic Region. So I have a feeling this new trail, on the granitic hills in the Helderberg basin, on the Sir Lowry's Pass side of Somerset West, is going to be a roaring success. The guided walks follow biodiversity corridors, with proceeds from the hikes going towards restoring and preserving what has been identified as a 'critical irreplaceable biodiversity area'.

The 2-day, guided, slackpacking trail can be tailor-made to the interests and abilities of the group but generally starts with a 10 km circular route from the very comfortable overnight accommodation at Ongegund on Myrtle Grove farm. It takes hikers through the Onderkloof, Waterkloof and Mount Rozier farms and wineries for tastings. From there it's up through the fynbos to the Schaapenberg beacon, from where there are magnificent panoramic views of the Boland mountains, valleys and False Bay.

On day 2 day hikers head east through Journey's End farm and the historic Ravensberg estate, then follow the Sir Lowry's Pass

The granite outcrop of the Schaapenberg results in unusual fynbos species and far-reaching views from the low hills.

river through the Wedderwill Nature and Game Reserve where eland, bontebok, zebra, springbok and wildebeest are often sighted. A gentle climb follows, up through the fynbos to the Wedderwill winery and Da Capo vineyards for tastings, a distance of about 13 km. Hikers have the choice of picnic lunches on the way or dining at the excellent Waterkloof or Capelands restaurants. Wine lovers and gourmands, this is your trail.

In a nutshell · Walks for Wine

BOOKINGS Di Marais, 021-858-1532, 082-462-3624, or Cape Town Tourism 021-840-1400, info@walksforwine.co.za, www.walksforwine.co.za.

HIGHLIGHTS Superb guiding; outstanding views of the Cape Folded Mountains and the coast; beautiful fynbos and wild flowers; wine tastings.

STYLE Guided hike staying in luxury guesthouse accommodation on a B&B basis. Bags driven around.

UP TO IT? The distances are short and you can go at whatever pace is comfortable so the trail is suitable for hikers of all ages and abilities.

COST RRR.

Cradock Peak is the toughest of the hikes offered in this suite of trails – but just look at the rewards.

35. Garden Route Forest and Mountain Walks

Western Cape

If you want to stay in the heart of the Garden Route and indulge in a series of day walks, Knysna Forest Tours will tailor-make an itinerary. Their most popular option is a combo of 4 day walks in the Knysna Forest, Robberg Peninsula, up Cradock or George peaks, and from Nature's Valley to Salt River. They also offer a slackpacking option on the otherwise strenuous, self-catered and self-guided Swartberg Trail. The attractions vary but all are incredibly scenic: in the forest the indigenous trees, fungi and birds; along Robberg the outstanding cliffs, caves, sea birds, seals and sightings of dolphins and whales; the Nature's Valley trail has a bit of everything – wonderful fynbos, indigenous forest, birds and other wildlife, as well as great swimming and spectacular views; on the peaks it's mountain fynbos and incredible, often mist-covered, jagged peaks and standing at 1 579 m looking out over the Garden Route that appeals.

In a nutshell · Garden Route Forest and Mountain Walks

BOOKINGS Tony Cook 082-783-8392, 044-382-0260, arcent@mweb.co.za, www.knysnaforesttours.co.za.
HIGHLIGHTS If you opt for the 'classic' 4 trails outlined here, then you're in for a treat – a smorgasbord of outstanding mountain views; fynbos; coastal scenery; birdlife and marine mammals.
STYLE Guided day hikes with a choice of budget to luxury accommodation on catered or self-catered basis. Bags are driven around.
UP TO IT? The trails range in the degree of fitness required – the forest walks are easy to moderate, the long Nature's Valley walk is moderately difficult, while those up the peaks are strenuous.
COST RRRR.

Another hard day in Africa. Chilling out at Dennehof Country House in Prince Albert.

36. Swartberg Slackpacking Trail

Western Cape

This 3-day, 4-night, fully catered and guided trial takes hikers through the magnificent Swartberg mountains which divide the Little from the Great Karoo. Don't go confusing it with CapeNature's tough Swartberg Hiking Trail, however: this is very much a leisurely, luxury alternative. It starts with a short hike and an overnight stay in the Swartberg Private Nature Reserve, where you're likely to see eland, zebra, kudu, impala, red hartebeest and loads of baboons. The following morning you jump in a vehicle that whisks you effortlessly up to Ou Tol hut close to the top of the Swartberg Pass. From there, according to your fitness, you can choose 1 or both of circular trails: a 7 km easy walk or a 9 km more challenging hike to the top of Platberg – both afford incredible mountain views of this rugged range.

After a cosy night in the basic hikers' hut (for which you need to bring your own sleeping bag – make it a warm one) you hike down the mountain on the Valskerm Val (Parachute Fall) trail to Malvadraai, a 9.4 km walk through the gorge on which you'll enjoy the fynbos, wild flowers, large numbers of sunbirds and sugarbirds and the spectacular scenery.

Your final night is spent at Dennehof Country House in the quaint Karoo town of Prince Albert. You'll be spoilt rotten and treated to a delicious meal of Karoo lamb washed down with good wine, and the following morning you'll be transferred back over the Swartberg Pass to Knysna.

In a nutshell · Swartberg Slackpacking Trail

BOOKINGS Tony Cook 082-783-8392, 044-382-0260, arcent@mweb.co.za, www.knysnaforesttours.co.za.
HIGHLIGHTS The outstanding views; the diverse vegetation of the Swartberg; the birdlife; outstanding hospitality at Dennehof Country House.

STYLE Fully catered, guided staying in luxury guesthouses except on night 2 when the accommodation is rustic. Bags are driven round.
UP TO IT? This is a fairly strenuous trail but there are shorter and longer options.
COST RRRR.

The endless vistas of the Kouga Mountains on day 7 are really only the beginning of this epic trail.

37. The Eden to Addo – Great Corridor Hike

Western & Eastern Cape

The Eden to Addo – Great Corridor Hike traverses 400 km of some of the country's less-explored wilderness areas, spanning both the Western and Eastern Cape provinces. The highlight has to be the remark-

Crossing the Baviaanskloof River and side-stepping buffalo and black rhino on day 11.

able vistas of the Baviaanskloof, where there is ample opportunity to really get off the beaten track and deep into the mountains. Game-viewing opportunities include everything from giant tortoises to buffalo, rhino, leopard and antelope. What this trail attempts to do is create a walkable route from the Knysna Forest, where we still have the last free-roaming and unfenced elephant in South Africa, to the elephants in the Addo Elephant National Park.

The trail is really an annual fund-raising event for the Eden to Addo conservation-corridor initiative, with all profits going directly to protect the unique biodiversity of the region. In addition to being a luxury, fully catered hike, there is the fact that by participating you are also contributing to conservation. Be aware, however, that though the organisers have done all they can to make the hike available to people of different fitness levels and age groups, this hike is an endurance experience. Some of the days are very long and will test your strength, but the walking is mostly moder-

Typical camp scene on the Eden to Addo where tents are set up and excellent camp meals are served.

For the record …

The Eden to Addo – Great Corridor Hike is the longest hike of its kind in the country. But it's not only its length that sets it apart (though you will traverse close to 400 km of unique landscape), this hike is more like an event, a full immersion. Think of it as a combination of a conservation education, a wilderness safari experience and an epic physical challenge. Consider the following statistics – they might give you some idea of what makes this hike so appealing:

- Distance: 400 km
- Hiking days: 18–20
- Hike takes place only once a year
- Rest days: 2 half-days
- Crosses 7 mountain ranges, rivers, private lands and lots of fences
- Covers 5 distinct biomes
- Links the Garden Route National Park, the Baviaanskloof and Addo Elephant National Park.

ate. Nevertheless, there is something about doing a long-distance hike like this that allows you to get to know your body and your mind in a new way. Towards the end of the hike many people simply want to continue walking despite the blisters and the aching muscles, while for others it's a profound life-changing experience.

In a nutshell · The Eden to Addo – Great Corridor Hike

BOOKINGS Hike co-ordinator: Galeo Saintz 082-888-8181, hike@edentoaddo.co.za, www.edentoaddo.co.za.

HIGHLIGHTS Experiencing the transition between 5 distinct biomes; crossing numerous mountains and the expansive wilderness of the Baviaanskloof.

STYLE Guided, fully catered hike with safari-style tented camps. Bags driven around.

UP TO IT? This is a hike for the more adventurous hiker, for those with a thirst for the unusual and the epic. It requires endurance and a commitment to supporting private conservation initiatives. And you need to be physically and mentally strong. Although there are no technical or severely exposed sections, the days are long and varied, with a number of unpredictable river crossings.

COST RRRRR.

The Elephant Gorge Trail follows a historic wagon route to a luxurious base camp on a well-stocked game reserve – something you don't naturally expect to find on the Garden Route.

38. Elephant Gorge Trail

Western Cape

The Buffalo Hills Game Reserve just outside Plettenberg Bay offers guided trails up the scenic Elephant Gorge, as well as a mountain-biking alternative. The trails follow a historic wagon route through the indigenous forest and along fynbos-covered slopes of the Tsitsikamma hills, returning along the river where rock pools provide plenty of swimming opportunities and great bird sightings. Accommodation in the gorge is in luxury log cabins and hikers have the option of night walks from the cabins, staying additional nights in the main lodge and enjoying walking safaris and game drives in the reserve.

In a nutshell · Elephant Gorge Trail

BOOKINGS Buffalo Hills Game Reserve & Lodges 044-535-9739, buffalohills@mweb.co.za, www.buffalohills.co.za.
HIGHLIGHTS Game and bird sightings; indigenous flora; great food and accommodation.

STYLE Fully catered, guided hike staying in luxury cabins. Bags driven around.
UP TO IT? The trail is suitable for people of moderate fitness and is perfect for family groups. Limited arrangements can be made for people with special needs.
COST RRRR.

Endless views over the Nuweveld mountains and plains of the Karoo are the hiker's reward.

39. Karoo Erdvark Trail

Western Cape

The Karoo Erdvark Trail is a cloverleaf network of trails of differing lengths and difficulty. It's located on a working sheep farm in the Nuweveld Mountains of the 'high' Karoo, 80 km northwest of Beaufort West. The views of the flat-topped mountains and wide open plains are incredible and the trail options are designed to give hikers of all abilities a chance to appreciate the tranquillity of this remote, spectacular wilderness.

There are peaks such as Tafelkop for the fit hiker to bag, and opportunities for those seeking a more leisurely escape to take easy strolls in the shaded kloofs, where there are small perennial pools, listen to the twittering birds and enjoy the starry night skies. Hikers are accommodated in a well-equipped Karoo farmhouse (there's also a large farm shed available for larger groups or for those on a budget) and a typical Karoo lamb spit braai can be provided on request for larger groups who are keen to partake in the legendary Karoo hospitality.

In a nutshell · Karoo Erdvark Trail

BOOKINGS Flip and Marge Vivier 023-412-1669, pmvivier@telkomsa.net, www.rooiheuwel.com.
HIGHLIGHTS The starkly beautiful scenery and vistas of the Karoo; shaded kloofs; excellent overnight accommodation at Boplaas.
STYLE Self-guided, self-catered

cloverleaf trail network overnighting in comfortable farmhouse.
UP TO IT? Trails range from easy, short hikes to the challenging ascent of Tafelkop so this is a good trail for groups of different abilities and interests and for families.
COST R.

The folded rocks of Tierkloof in the Gamkaberg Reserve contain rock-art sites and fossilised shells.

40. Gamka Reserve to Bonniedale Wilderness Hike

Western Cape

This 7-day fully guided and catered wilderness hike in the Klein Karoo leads from the Gamka Reserve to Bonniedale farm. Hikers are rewarded with spectacular views of the Swartberg and Outeniqua mountain ranges and over the far-reaching plains of the intervening Little Karoo rain-shadow valleys. The trail also offers a fascinating insight into life in this arid region – the way in which the plants, animals and people have adapted to the harsh but beautiful landscape. This is much more than just a hike; it's a journey of self-discovery and renewal facilitated by your host and guide, Elsa Davids.

In a nutshell · Gamka Reserve to Bonniedale Wilderness Hike

BOOKINGS Elsa Davids 072-877-7798, riverwoman@telkomsa.net, www.trails.co.za/hikes/wcape/karoo.
HIGHLIGHTS The wide open spaces of the Karoo and the sense of wilderness; interacting with the local communities; Elsa's storytelling.
STYLE Guided, catered hike utilising a variety of accommodation options. Bags driven round.
UP TO IT? This is a hike for someone looking for an uplifting experience, an immersion in the spirit of the Karoo, rather than a strenuous hike. Shorter trails are also offered.
COST RRR.

The trail crosses the Wolf River several times; this crossing is at around the 4.5 km mark.

41. Wolf River Trail

Eastern Cape

The community-run Wolf River Trail gives hikers the opportunity to interact with the Xhosa host community, and enjoy the best of the famous but challenging Amatola Trail – without having to lug a heavy pack.

The 2-day trail is centred around the base camp, a Xhosa homestead on the edge of the forest in the picturesque Upper Zingcuka area, roughly halfway between Hogsback and Keiskammahoek. Trails lead along the river and through the Wolf River Forest to lovely waterfalls and rock pools and links up with the route taken on day 5 of the Amatola Trail – generally considered the most beautiful day on this classic, but tough, hike. It includes some of the finest mature Afro-montane forest in the country.

In a nutshell · Wolf River Trail

BOOKINGS 043-642-1747, info@
speirstours.co.za, www.speirstours.co.za
HIGHLIGHTS The indigenous forests,
mountain streams and rock pools.
STYLE Fully catered, guided hike staying
in Xhosa-style rondavels.
UP TO IT? The distance you hike each
day is up to you so the trail is suitable
for all sorts.
COST RRR.

Hikers on the Wild Coast will be blown away by the views from the rugged cliffs.

42. Cebe to Cintsa B&B Trail

Eastern Cape

This 4-day, 5-night trail follows a very similar route to the Wild Coast Meander and Amble trails (see pages 129 and 137) starting at Cebe Cottages (just north of Wavecrest Hotel) and ending at the pretty resort village of Cintsa close to East London. Hikers stay in either chalets or local B&Bs, with all meals provided.

You have the option of carrying your own bags, or organising porters. A range of optional extra activities, such as canoeing and nature/culture tours, can be integrated into the trail.

In a nutshell · Cebe to Cintsa B&B Trail

BOOKINGS SA Adventure Trails 033-343-1217, reservations@trails.co.za, www.wildcoastwalk.co.za/cbhikes.
HIGHLIGHTS Spectacular scenery; empty beaches.
STYLE Catered, self-guided hike, with the option of porterage.
UP TO IT? This trail is suitable for fit hikers who are looking for comfortable rather than luxury accommodation. All meals are provided at the guesthouses.
COST RRR.

Interacting with the locals is as much a highlight as the geological features of the trail.

43. Coffee Bay to Mbashe Trail

Eastern Cape

This 3- to 4-day backpacking trail starts at Coffee Bay and ends at Mbashe River mouth to the south. It leads past one of the country's most stunning coastal features, the island rock tunnel of Hole in the Wall, and utilises very affordable, and funky, backpackers and small guest lodge accommodation. The Mbashe Trail can also be hiked as an extension to SA Adventure Trails' variant of the 6-day Ports St Johns to Coffee Bay hike (see page 147).

In a nutshell · Coffee Bay to Mbashe Trail

BOOKINGS SA Adventure Trails 033-343-1217, reservations@trails.co.za www.wildcoastwalk.co.za/cbhikes.
HIGHLIGHTS Wonderful coastal scenery and beaches; fun backpacker accommodation.
STYLE Guided hike staying in backpackers and one hotel on a B&B basis. Porters can be arranged.

UP TO IT? This is a trail for intermediate to fit hikers. It can be hiked as one long, 18 km day from Hole in the Wall to Bulungula, or in 2 days (of 9 km each) staying at a fishers' lodge at Mpame on the second night. The steep coastal dunes on some sections will test most people's fitness levels.
COST RRR.

Waterfall Bluff is one of the most impressive sites along the breathtaking Wild Coast.

44. Wild Coast Pondo Walk

Eastern Cape

The Wild Coast Pondo Walk is actually a series of 4 separate day hikes centred around the wonderful Wild Coast resort of Mbotyi River Lodge a way north of Port St Johns. It's the most dramatic section of the Transkei coast, and the guided hikes to the spectacular Waterfall Bluff, Ilityyelentaka (Rock of the Bird) and Magwa Falls and through towering indigenous forest showcase the natural beauty and diversity of the area. And if that isn't enough, at the end of the day you're spoilt at Mbotyi hotel, where you can sit out on the deck of your wooden chalet and enjoy the view at your leisure. If you're there during June/July you might be treated to the spectacle of the sardine run – this is one of the best spots along the coast to watch the incredible marine migratory event.

In a nutshell · Wild Coast Pondo Walk

BOOKINGS Wild Coast Holiday Reservations 043-743-6181, meross@ iafrica.com, www.wildcoastholidays. co.za.
HIGHLIGHTS Dramatic coastal landforms and waterfalls; superb overnight accommodation and food.

STYLE Luxury, catered, guided day hikes, staying in one resort.
UP TO IT? The individual day hikes range from moderate to fairly strenuous, but the longer, harder ones are definitely worth sweating over!
COST RRR.

The Swissland Cheese Saunter is exactly as the name suggests, a leisurely amble through Midland pastures.

45. Swissland Cheese Saunter

KwaZulu-Natal

This Swissland Cheese Saunter is a 3-day, self-guided, 44 km hike in the Lidgetton Valley of the KwaZulu-Natal Midlands. The trail leads through the Lidgetton Conservancy following the Lion River through pine plantations, farmland and open pastures to Swissland Cheese, a farm which specialises in producing goats'-milk cheeses, where after a delicious lunch – which includes said cheeses – you continue hiking through forest to Lythwood Lodge, the overnight accommodation.

On day 2 you continue to Blesberg Farm enjoying similar scenery and spoils, returning to Pleasant Places via the Dargle Valley on day 3.

The trail is open year round and each season has its attractions but autumn, when all the trees are clothed in their reds, browns, yellows and vibrant colours, is a special time of year, particularly for artists and photographers. There are also 1- and 2-day trail options.

In a nutshell · Swissland Cheese Saunter

BOOKINGS Pleasant Places Country Guest House 033-234-4396, pleasantplaces@pleasantplaces.co.za, www.pleasantplaces.co.za.
HIGHLIGHTS The green hills of KwaZulu-Natal, indigenous forests, abundant bird life, luxury accommodation and wonderful hospitality.

STYLE Fully catered, guided hike staying in luxury guesthouse accommodation. Bags driven around.
UP TO IT? This is a leisurely, straightforward trail that is suitable for hikers of all ages and fitness levels.
COST RRR.

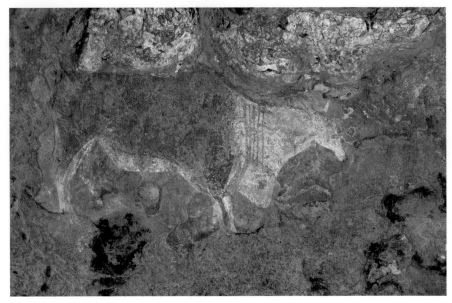

Many of the sandstone caves on the trail contain exquisite and irreplaceable San rock art.

46. Cannibal Trail

Free State

The Cannibal Trail is an easy, well-marked 2-day trail on a beautiful farm in the Rooi-berg and Witteberg highlands, near Clarens in the eastern Free State. This is a rustic, self-guided, self-catering trail and most hikers carry their own packs. However, there is an option of having bags transported around. The scenery is spectacular, with stunning mountain views, river and forest walks and there is rock art in many of the caves. The first night is spent in a restored cow barn with bunk beds and mattresses for 17 hikers, hot showers, electricity, and enclosed kitch-enette/braai area with a fridge, gas stove, cast-iron pots and a kettle, while on night 2 hikers sleep in an overhang cave (where there is rock art) equipped with mattresses, flush toilets, a cold shower, wood, a braai grid, pot and kettle.

In a nutshell · Cannibal Trail

BOOKINGS Annali Bossert 058-256-1595, annali.bossert@gmail.com.
HIGHLIGHTS Beautiful mountain scenery; rock art; forest and river walks and the swimiming hole
STYLE Self-guided, self-catered trail

staying in rustic accommodation. Bags driven around for a small fee.
UP TO IT? The 16 km circular trail is suitable for hikers of all ages and experience.
COST R.

---

47. Queen Rose Trail

Mpumalanga

This 2-day, 2-night is, according to people who about these things, one of the – if not the – best inland weekend trails in the country. It follows the high mountainous ground near Barberton, starting in plantation but soon descending steeply through aloe-pocked grasslands, then more steeply into the Montrose River gorge, with Alvin's Falls and a big pool at the bottom of the descent. The remainder of day 1 is spent following the river, walking through dense riverine forest, with many stream crossings. There are some magnificent and rare forest trees in this valley, some of which are numbered, so you really should carry a tree guide. Makesh hut, at the halfway mark, is an old house with all the mod-cons (including microwave).

On day 2 you follow the Queens River for the first half of the walk, starting in forest and crossing Matumi Island, with lots of superb swimming holes along the way. A large pool and *foefie* slide marks the halfway point. From there it's a steep climb up to the hut, part of it on a steep gravel road and partly in forest, where there are several swing bridges. The hike ends where it started, at Queen's View hut, an old forestry college. Although short, this day is quite tough and, with the heat and humidity of the valley, it can be rather tiring.

Bliksem, Bucket and human hiking companion enjoy the view of the Queens River valley, in a wooded gorge below Cupid Falls some 5 km from the end of the trail.

In a nutshell · Queen Rose Trail

BOOKINGS Marie Kotze 083-545-0900 (telephone only).
HIGHLIGHTS The forested river gorges; endless pools; river crossings; suspension bridges; the amazing views; walking among the oldest sedimentary rocks on earth, the Barberton greenstones.
STYLE Self-guided and self-catered.

Bags driven around for a small extra fee.
UP TO IT? Although the days are short – 13 and 8 km, heat, humidity, frequent rain and steep landscape make it tougher than you'd expect. Drinking water is plentiful, but you still need to take it slowly.
COST R.

Lush vegetation and tumbling waterfalls are just some of the attractions of this Mpumalanga escarpment trail.

48. Num Num Trail

Mpumalanga

This 5-day, roughly 50 km trail, named after the forest num-num tree (*Carissa wyliei*), takes hikers along the spectacular rim of the escarpment from the peak of the Skurweberg to the base of the Brides Leap Falls on the Mpumalanga escarpment. The route, through a private nature conservancy, offers hikers the chance to enjoy Highveld grassland plains game such as the black wildebeest, blesbok and the rare oribi as well as an extraordinary range of other fauna, flora, geology dating back to when the earth was still a young planet, and ancient human ruins. It's very much a self-guiding path rather than just a marked trail, with more than 100 different indigenous species of trees marked along the route. The comfortable overnight accommodation, set in spectacular environments, consists of a variety of buildings complete with showers and kitchens, sleeping a maximum 20 hikers.

In a nutshell · Num Num Trail

BOOKINGS Christia Newbery 079-877-6909, newbery@vodamail.co.za.
HIGHLIGHTS The interpretive nature of the trail; outstanding views from the escarpment; plains game, birds and wild flowers.

STYLE Self-guided and self-catered. Bags driven around for a small extra fee.
UP TO IT? This is a fairly easy trail covering approximately 10 km a day for 5 days.
COST R.

Index

SUNBIRD
PUBLISHERS

First published in 2007
Second edition in 2010

Sunbird Publishers (Pty) Ltd
(A division of Jonathan Ball Publishers (Pty) Ltd)
PO Box 6836
Roggebaai 8012
Cape Town, South Africa

www.sunbirdpublishers.co.za

Registration number: 1984/003543/07

Cartographer James Berrangé
Designer & typesetter Lauren Rycroft
Editor David Bristow
Indexer and Proofreader Sean Fraser
Publisher Ceri Prenter

Printed and bound by Tien Wah Press (Pte) Ltd, Singapore

ISBN 978-1-920289-14-0

FRONT COVER: Hikers on the Amphitheatre Heritage Hike, Shaen Adey.